The education of multilingual learners requires both a depth of knowledge among leaders to ensure that systems are established and resourced to provide equitable opportunities for students and equitable access for families. *Transforming Schools for Multilingual Learners: A Comprehensive Guide for Educators* provides both the research foundation and the practical application for schools, through the requisite asset-based lens. This framework can assist schools in planning school improvement plans and in their equity, diversity, and inclusion goals. In the end, schools can be places where all are welcomed, all are celebrated, and all can achieve.

—Kellie Jones, **Director of Bilingual Education, Brockton Public Schools**

Transforming Schools for Multilingual Learners: A Comprehensive Guide for Educators is a must-have resource for school leaders, as well as in-service teachers and preservice teachers, to better understand how to create policies, practices, and programs for multilingual learners to thrive. In this second edition, Debbie Zacarian provides the latest, detailed information for all educators to better understand the needs of multilingual learners and what to do to support their success. This book should be a staple in everyone's professional library.

—Maria G. Dove, Professor, **Molloy University, School of Education and Human Services**

As a nation, we have undergone and continue to experience changes in school policies, practices, and programs for multilingual learners. Through myriad real-life vignettes and exemplars, in this updated edition we come to witness how effective language programs can meet the requirements for federal compliance while slowly evolving on the local level to be more inclusive of the voices of educators, students, and families. Debbie Zacarian adeptly captures this transformation as she juxtaposes the increasingly important roles of educators as collaborators and advocates for multilingual learners in program planning, delivery, and evaluation against a backdrop of a less-than-adequate workforce that is not well informed in understanding the social, cultural, and linguistic assets of these students.

—Margo Gottlieb, **WIDA Co-founder and Lead Developer, Wisconsin Center for Education Research, University of Wisconsin-Madison**

The second edition of *Transforming Schools for Multilingual Learners: A Comprehensive Guide for Educators* definitely joins the short list of books that all teachers and schools who serve English language learners should be reading!

—Larry Ferlazzo, **High School Teacher, *Education Week* Teacher Advice Columnist, Author**

This newly revised edition of *Transforming Schools for Multilingual Learners: A Comprehensive Guide for Educators* is a must-have for schools on the journey of creating equitable learning opportunities for all students. In these times of racial injustices, the COVID-19 pandemic, natural disasters, and a slew of global and regional crises, it is critically important that all educators hear Debbie Zacarian's argument and act on her carefully created recommendations for supporting multilingual learners.

—Andrea Honigsfeld, **Professor and Author, Molloy University**

Under the guidance of well-informed and dedicated district leadership, multilinguals can thrive. Debbie Zacarian's second edition addresses the most recent topics in our field while anchored firmly on decades of sound research around what works for multilingual students. The first edition lit the way for many, and this second edition promises to illuminate the path for school leaders committed to the march for educational equity for multilingual students.

—Tan Huynh, **Language Specialist, Author, Blogger, Podcaster**

Debbie's second edition brings to the forefront of school reform the importance of assets-based approaches to strengthen the success of multilingual learners. School teams will definitely welcome the ideas, rubrics, and strategies for creating effective policies, practices, and structures for transforming schools.

—Margarita Espino Calderón, **Professor Emerita, Johns Hopkins University**

Debbie Zacarian's heartfelt and strategic guide is a must-read for leaders designing and refining programs for MLs!

—Tonya Ward Singer, **Author of *EL Excellence Every Day* and Founder of Courageous Literacy LLC**

Transforming Schools
for Multilingual Learners

Second Edition

This book is dedicated to educators who are transforming schools to support the strengths, talents, and contributions of multilingual learners.

Transforming Schools for Multilingual Learners

A Comprehensive Guide for Educators

Second Edition

Debbie Zacarian

Foreword by Katie Toppel

FOR INFORMATION:

Corwin

A SAGE Company

2455 Teller Road

Thousand Oaks, California 91320

(800) 233-9936

www.corwin.com

SAGE Publications Ltd.

1 Oliver's Yard

55 City Road

London EC1Y 1SP

United Kingdom

SAGE Publications India Pvt. Ltd.

B 1/I 1 Mohan Cooperative Industrial Area

Mathura Road, New Delhi 110 044

India

SAGE Publications Asia-Pacific Pte. Ltd.

18 Cross Street #10-10/11/12

China Square Central

Singapore 048423

President: Mike Soules

Vice President and
Editorial Director: Monica Eckman

Program Director
and Publisher: Dan Alpert

Senior Content Development
Editor: Lucas Schleicher

Content Development Editor: Mia Rodriguez

Editorial Assistant: Natalie Delpino

Editorial Intern: Ricardo Ramirez

Production Editor: Tori Mirsadjadi

Copy Editor: Sarah J. Duffy

Typesetter: C&M Digitals (P) Ltd.

Proofreader: Barbara Coster

Indexer: Integra

Cover Designer: Gail Buschman

Marketing Manager: Melissa Duclos

Printed in Canada

ISBN 978-1-0718-8460-7

This book is printed on acid-free paper.

23 24 25 26 27 10 9 8 7 6 5 4 3 2 1

Contents

Visit the companion website at
resources.corwin.com/transformingschoolsformultilinguallearners
for downloadable resources.

Foreword

In 2016, I co-founded a virtual book chat with Tan Huynh on Twitter to connect and learn from other educators who teach multilingual learners. Since then, I have led educators from across the globe in over 30 book studies focused on improving practice and instruction for multilingual learners. Educators from a variety of time zones, backgrounds, and educational contexts connect virtually with shared interest in enhancing our professional learning around meeting the needs of multilingual learners. Learning with and from this network has dramatically shifted my practice, and I owe a debt of gratitude to all the researchers, authors, and educators in the field who humbly and openly share their expertise. Debbie Zacarian is a prime example of someone who continuously shares important information to support educators with varying levels of expertise about working with culturally and linguistically diverse students. She has participated in several book studies as a featured author and generously engages with audiences as an advocate for inclusive and asset-based practices.

Although many educators are dedicated to effectively teaching and supporting multilingual learners, we know that teachers alone cannot bear the responsibility of knowing and providing what that entails. In particular, the sole responsibility cannot fall to language teachers alone—the success of such learners warrants a communal response. In the opening pages of *Transforming Schools for Multilingual Learners: A Comprehensive Guide for Educators*, Dr. Zacarian affirms the need for a collective effort among a larger network of stakeholders to share responsibility and collectively shape policies and decisions that impact the school experiences of multilingual learners. Shared ownership requires that we collectively learn and increase our awareness so that educators in a variety of roles can make informed decisions in the best interest of multilingual learners. Dr. Zacarian's guide provides foundational information about multilingual learners that is valuable to anyone who works in and on behalf of school systems.

Whether you are a teacher, coach, building or district-level leader, university faculty, or you serve students in another capacity, the information in this book will equip you with tremendous insight and tools to strategically inform and improve language education programming.

As I read, I came across sections that made me reflect on my journey across my life cycle as an educator. When I got my first job teaching in a bilingual Head Start program for migrant children, I quickly realized that my teacher program had not sufficiently prepared me to teach the students in my classroom. I truly don't remember learning much, if anything, about how to support students learning English, and I certainly did not have extensive, or even adequate, knowledge about language acquisition, instructional strategies, or working with diverse families. I appreciate Dr. Zacarian's advocacy for professional learning that aligns with the needs of educators, much in the way that we tailor our instruction to the unique needs of the students we serve. I am excited thinking about this book being in the hands of instructional coaches, administrators, and other influencers who can be instrumental changemakers in support of educating multilingual learners. I am equally excited for this book to be in the hands of educators and others so we may be empowered to better advocate for what we and our students need.

When I became a language specialist, a colleague introduced me to the concept of coteaching, and we took an interest in establishing more collaboration between classroom teachers and language specialists to better align content and language instruction. We gathered informative resources on collaboration and coteaching, which we used to advocate for program change. I wish this book had been among those resources because of its comprehensive approach.

Dr. Zacarian emphasizes how important it is to critically reflect on the factors that influence program success and for whom. She provides insight on the differences within populations of students who qualify for language support as well as the educators who teach them. She wholly addresses how these differences require thoughtful consideration when selecting programming and planning instruction for multilingual learners. She helps us see that English learners are not a homogenous group, providing us with essential tools for learning about the various multilingual learners in our contexts and making informed decisions given the multitude of language program options.

Something else I loved in this book is the phrase *constellation of caregivers* in reference to the various adults who make up students' families and extended support systems. It brings to mind the idea that constellations are all beautifully unique, which is true for students and their circumstances. Part of our work is becoming familiar with each constellation so that we see its uniqueness among the others but also to understand the collective beauty that exists in the larger expanse of sky.

I hope this book influences your knowledge, intentions, decisions, and actions so that your multilingual learners can shine brightly.

Katie Toppel

English Language Development Specialist

Co-author of *DIY PD: A Guide to Self-Directed Learning for Educators of Multilingual Learners* and *Making Content Comprehensible for Multilingual Learners* (6th ed.)

Acknowledgments

This book was written with the support of many people. Dr. Cristina Sánchez López reviewed and contributed to the chapter on identifying and working with multilingual learners with learning differences and disabilities. Kristina Robinson reviewed and contributed to the chapter on family engagement. Becky Corr, Montserrat V. Diazotello, Dr. Jennifer Love, Jessica Panfil, Joe Ristuccia, and Carol Salva provided outstanding examples that make the principles and strategies for transforming schools come alive. Rose Aldubaily, Lydia Breiseth, Gloria Cho, Kellie Jones, Jo Napolitano, and Natalie Pohl took time to support this edition. All show us why we should be full of hope for the success of multilingual learners.

Dan Alpert greatly supported the genesis and manuscript from start to completion. Lucas Schleicher, Mia Rodriguez, Natalie Delpino, Tori Mirsadjadi, Sarah Duffy, Barbara Coster, and Gail Buschman deftly supported the editing and production process.

No book could ever be written without the loving support, patience, and understanding of family. Thank you, Matt, Katie, and Jackie. You inspire me every day.

About the Author

Dr. Debbie Zacarian, founder of Zacarian Consulting, provides professional development, strategic planning, and technical assistance for K–16 educators of culturally and linguistically diverse populations. She has served as an expert consultant for school districts, universities, associations, and organizations including the Massachusetts Parent Information Resource Center and Federation for Children with Special Needs.

Debbie has worked with numerous state and local education agencies as well as community and technical colleges and universities, and she has written the language assistance programming policies for many rural, suburban, and urban districts. Debbie served on the faculty of University of Massachusetts-Amherst, where she co-wrote and was the co-principal investigator of a National Professional Development grant initiative supporting the professional preparation of educators of multilingual learners. Debbie also designed and taught courses for pre- and in-service administrators and teachers on culturally responsive teaching and supervision practices, multilingual development, and ethnographic research. In addition, she served as a program director at the Collaborative for Educational Services, where she provided professional development for thousands of educators of multilingual students, mentored many community-technical and university faculty on responsive practices with culturally and linguistically diverse populations, and partnered with Fitchburg State University in co-writing and enacting a National Professional Development initiative that supported STEM education. Debbie also directed the Amherst Public Schools bilingual and English learner programming, for which she and the district received state and national honors.

The author of more than 100 publications, her most recent professional books include *Beyond Crises: Overcoming Linguistic and Cultural Inequities in Communities, Schools, and Classrooms; Responsive Schooling for Culturally and Linguistically Diverse Students; Teaching to Empower: Taking Action to Foster Student Agency, Self-Confidence, and Collaboration;* and *Teaching to Strengths: Supporting Students Living With Trauma, Violence, and Chronic Stress.*

Introduction

The first edition of this book was written as a comprehensive resource of the most up-to-date research and evidence-based strategies to create successful programming for the rapidly changing population of multilingual learners (MLs). It was also written as a user-friendly guide for educators to put pedagogy into practice. Highly received by leading scholars and practitioners across the country, it became the go-to book nationally and required reading for many pre- and in-service administrators, teacher-leaders, coaches, and other stakeholders.

A good deal has transpired since the first edition was published, including

- changes to federal laws and regulations;

- increased understanding about the urgency to use strengths-based and culturally and linguistically sustaining pedagogies and practices;

- deeper understanding about the epic number of children experiencing adverse childhood experiences, including children fleeing crises in their home countries, children who are undocumented, children of undocumented families, and unaccompanied minors who live in constant fear of deportation;

- the global COVID-19 pandemic, racial injustices, and natural disasters; and

- increased awareness about the importance of supporting and enhancing student, family, school, and community partnerships.

As a result of these changes, most educators and stakeholders at the school, district, and state levels are seeking support in building, strengthening, and sustaining successful programming for MLs. It has been my honor to work with many state and local educators across the country during these unprecedented times and to see the creativity, flexibility, and downright genius that so many have engaged to transform practice.

What's New in the Second Edition?

This second edition adds to the practice by looking closely at the lessons learned during the past decade and the changes that are likely to occur in the future. The change in the title to *Transforming Schools for Multilingual Learners: A Comprehensive Guide for Educators* reflects a renewed spirit of inclusion and solidarity by reflecting the strengths that all MLs, their families, educators, and local, school, and classroom communities possess and bring to creating successful programming for MLs. This edition also acknowledges the move away from using a deficit-based approach where MLs and their families are seen as having missed something (such as English) to acknowledging and infusing the assets they bring to all that we do. In this spirit, a range of terms and associated acronyms have been used interchangeably, including English learners (ELs); English language learners (ELLs); heritage language learners; long-term English learners (LTELs); students in dual language, two-way, and immersion programs; and students with limited or interrupted formal education (SLIFE). However, the strengths-based term *multilingual learner* is used throughout the book to describe this broad range of students. It encompasses those who have learned or are learning two or more languages and cultures.

The new edition also reflects the trends of leadership in our ever-changing society, from the singular person sitting atop the mantle of power to a collective of people who work together. While leaders have a prominent role in shaping and supervising state policy implementation at the district, school, and classroom levels, they also are charged with creating a school and classroom culture and climate that fully support MLs to succeed. One of the largest lessons we learned during the COVID-19 crises is that we cannot do this work alone. It becomes much more possible when we work in close collaboration and partnership with others. Working groups composed of multilingual, multicultural family liaisons, teachers, coaches, counselors, and others are foundational for creating and sustaining successful language assistance programs. As such, the term *educators* is used throughout this book to reflect the agency that we all exercise, as leaders, advocates, policy makers, and truly inspirers of educating MLs. The book also moves from the term *parents/guardians* to *families* to reflect the ever-changing constellation of caregivers in our society, from the traditional two-parent home to two parents, single parents, foster parents, grandparents, custodial parents, aunts, uncles, brothers, sisters, unrelated people, and extrafamilial people who care for a child. The new edition also includes various voices from the field to illustrate the ideals of creating language assistance programming that works.

Transforming Schools for Multilingual Learners: A Comprehensive Guide for Educators focuses on the ways in which school leaders—including superintendents, principals, curriculum supervisors, coaches, mentors, teachers, teacher educators, and other stakeholders—can create effective school policies, practices, and structures for MLs in their contexts. The goal of this second edition is to help educators who are just beginning to work with MLs as well as those who are veterans build a school environment where MLs can flourish. Each chapter opens with a scenario and focuses on a key element of language assistance programming.

Chapter 1: Starting With Our Students and Ourselves describes this ever-expanding population of students, their educational programming, and their teachers. It presents an analysis of what the demographics tell us and a rationale for developing programming for MLs that is targeted to the needs of individual districts.

Chapter 2: Integrating the Regulations and Principles presents the major historical events that led to the current laws and regulations governing the education of MLs, key principles of second language acquisition, and a description of the various types of program models for teaching MLs.

Chapter 3: Selecting Effective Program Models discusses the processes and protocols for identifying MLs, selecting a program model, staffing the model, and evaluating its effectiveness. It includes forms and protocols associated with the various processes involved in the identification, program selection, and ongoing evaluation tasks and procedures.

Chapter 4: Designing, Implementing, and Strengthening the English Language Development Component details the organizational structures, such as time allocation and staffing considerations, and practices that should be included to effectively implement this critical component into all that educators do.

Chapter 5: Addressing the Core Content Component of a Language Education Program. As schools build, strengthen, and maintain programs for MLs, it is important to define what constitutes a high-quality core content lesson and learning environment. This chapter provides eight guiding principles for providing such lessons for language and content learning and a checklist for teachers, peers, supervisors, and others to use in assessing the overall success of content planning and delivery.

Chapter 6: Emphasizing the Importance of Family Engagement acknowledges that establishing relationships with families is an important objective for educators at all levels. Many educators are not familiar with the various cultural norms of MLs and their families, and many families of MLs are not familiar with school practices in the United States. This chapter provides a strengths-based framework for creating, enacting, and sustaining strong family–school partnerships.

Chapter 7: Identifying and Working With Multilingual Learners With Learning Differences and Learning Disabilities describes U.S. special education trends, the application of a Multi-Tiered Systems of Support, and the factors that should be considered to use this framework effectively with MLs. It presents a team approach for evaluating and improving the learning environment and outcomes for MLs and a protocol for engaging in this process.

Chapter 8: Putting It All Together: Making Data-Driven Decisions to Strengthen the Success of Language Assistance Programs discusses the application of strengths-based assessment and evaluation of language assistance programming by exploring the following questions: What role can educators play in enacting language education instruction policies and programming that are evidence based, properly resourced, and proven to work? What are key considerations for enacting strengths-based policies and practices that empower MLs and their families? What rubrics and monitoring charts should we consider for examining the effectiveness of our language assistance programming in relation to MLs? This chapter also offers a rationale for selecting and using a collaborative process for understanding MLs' academic performance and needs. Included in this chapter are protocols for examining the effectiveness of the classroom as well as school–parent engagement and community building.

CHAPTER 1

Starting With Our Students and Ourselves

Manuel moved to the United States from El Salvador when he was 13 years old. In El Salvador, he had worked on his uncle's bus as the ticket taker and money exchanger. He is a very sweet, polite Spanish speaker who came to the United States without any formal schooling or prior exposure to English. His family moved to Centerville, a small town, to work in a relative's restaurant, where they hoped they could earn a living wage. Although Manuel had no prior schooling, Mr. Pronowitz, the principal at Centerville Middle School, decided to place Manuel in the eighth grade so that he could be with his same-age peers.

Ernesto moved from Mexico to the same town as Manuel. His father, an engineer, had been transferred to work in a city near Centerville. Before moving, Ernesto had completed seventh grade in a private school where he had received an excellent education. He loved mathematics and had won an award for "most promising mathematician." When his parents enrolled him in Centerville Middle School, his father tried to convey Ernesto's prior schooling experiences to Mr. Pronowitz. But because Ernesto's father's English was limited and Ernesto and his mother could not speak any English at all, Mr. Pronowitz could not understand much about Ernesto's strengths, achievements, and needs. He assigned him to the same grade as Manuel.

A few days after Manuel and Ernesto began school, they were given a standardized test to determine their fluency in English. Both scored at the beginning level. With this testing information, Mr. Pronowitz assigned them to the English as a second language (ESL) class that met for one 45-minute class period a day. He also placed them in the same remedial classes for the rest of their school day. He assumed that Manuel and Ernesto would feel more comfortable with each other because they were the school's only Spanish-speaking multilingual learners (MLs). He also thought that placing them in remedial classes would be less demanding for them because they were both beginning learners of English, unlike the other MLs in the school. Overall, Mr. Pronowitz thought that these placements were academically appropriate and sensitive to the boys' needs.

When Manuel and Ernesto began speaking to each other, Ernesto quickly realized that Manuel had never been to school. Ernesto felt that his classes, especially math, were much easier than he was used to. He assumed that being a Spanish-speaking ML in the United States must mean that he was not a smart or good student. He felt isolated and divorced from everything that was familiar to him. Within a few weeks, he began to feel very depressed. By the end of the first term, Ernesto had decided to stop attending school. His parents quickly moved him to a parochial school, assuming that it would be a much better place for their son than Centerville Middle School was. When Mr. Pronowitz was made aware of Ernesto's absences, he called Ernesto's home. He was unable to communicate with Ernesto or his parents. While he thought about Ernesto occasionally, he never knew why he missed so much school. When Ernesto stopped attending altogether, Mr. Pronowitz assumed that he had moved to another town.

Manuel also felt entirely lost. He could not understand any of his classes. They were moving much too quickly for him. He was constantly exhausted from trying to learn. At least Ernesto could help him understand a little about what was happening. But when Ernesto was absent, which had become a frequent occurrence, Manuel's day was hopelessly confusing. He began thinking about quitting school. After a month of struggling, he decided to meet with Mr. Pronowitz. He was failing all his classes and desperately wanted to do well. He asked his uncle if he would come to translate for him at the meeting. When they met, Mr. Pronowitz decided that Manuel should be referred for a special education evaluation to see if he had a learning disability. With Manuel's parents' approval (they trusted the school and didn't believe it was their place to do anything more than listen and heed the principal's advice), the referral process began. The assessors assumed that Manuel's poor progress was due to a disability as opposed to what it really was: lack of prior formal education and academic skills, even in his first language.

Sergi, a Ukrainian American multilingual learner who was born in the United States and had attended Centerville Middle School for 3 years, then moved to New York City, where he enrolled in the ninth grade. He was one of the city's 140,000 MLs (New York City Department of Education, 2020–21), and when his English proficiency was tested, Sergi was found to be at the fourth of five English proficiency levels for MLs (New York City Department of Education, 2022). The school decided that he did not need to be enrolled in the language education program as he appeared to be able to learn in the same classes as his English-fluent classmates. Within the first few weeks, Sergi was unable to keep up with his peers. He had trouble grasping some of the vocabulary and course assignments and tasks. He pored over his homework and stayed up well after midnight each night. He also attempted to go for after-school help but worried that he would be fired from the after-school job that his family depended on. As a result, Sergi began failing many of his courses and thinking that school was not for him. By the end of the ninth grade, Sergi was like 28% of the city's MLs—a dropout (New York State Education Department, 2019).

These scenarios are not unusual among MLs in the United States. Many are failing, being referred to special education programs, and dropping out of school. When we measure achievement by the tests that each state administers to its students, as required by federal regulations (U.S. Department of Justice & U.S. Department of Education [USDOE], 2015) or the graduation rates of MLs in the United States (USDOE, n.d.-c), the achievement gap between the nation's MLs and the overall student population is significant and growing. Data from the U.S. Department of Education (n.d.-a) show that close to 80% of eighth-grade English-fluent students scored at the basic or above level in reading, whereas only 32% of MLs performed at these levels. Additionally, 84% of students graduated from high school in 4 years as opposed to 67% of MLs (USDOE, n.d.-c). The difference in graduation rates between the two groups exposes a grave consequence to consider—especially because we know the economic and employment benefits of possessing at least a high school diploma.

In March 2020, the COVID-19 pandemic struck the nation. One month into the crisis, Dr. Anthony Fauci, advisor to the White House, stated that the pandemic "shines a very bright light on some of the real weaknesses and foibles in our society" (C-SPAN, 2020). His words affirm the data that have been presented thus far about the growing ML population, and there are additional data that are as important for us to consider as we make our way forward. Shortly after the pandemic began, over 1.1 million students—2% of the total student population and five times more than what was anticipated—dropped out of school. It may take years for enrollment to return, if at all, to its prepandemic level (Lennon & Stanton, 2021). After a year of the COVID-19 crises, absenteeism surged among the nation's MLs (Lehrer-Small, 2021) and was in sharp contrast to prepandemic findings that MLs were 15% more likely to attend school than never-MLs (USDOE, n.d.-b). Further, the U.S. Government Accountability Office (2022), in its "nationally representative report of elementary and secondary public school teachers" (p. v), found that during the 2020–21 school year (the height of the pandemic), many MLs lacked access to school meals and school supports and lacked appropriate workspace to learn remotely. The cascade of obstacles that so many MLs and their families faced led many of us to see just how impactful the pandemic was for the most vulnerable of our students.

All of the data that have been presented about MLs thus far speaks not only to the need to think of more responsive ways of designing more effective language assistance programming, but also to the ways in which we must transform our practices for MLs to succeed in school and in their lives. This book focuses on creating, implementing, and sustaining effective language assistance programs for MLs. It is intended for school- and district-level leaders, teachers, leaders, advocates, and others who are charged with administering and supervising the curriculum, instructional programming, teachers and support staff, family and community outreach and engagement, and all related activities regarding the successful education of MLs.

The following questions are intended to help us in this reexamination process:

- Who are MLs?
- Typically, who are the educators of MLs?
- How does what we are doing complement our district's and school's mission and vision?

Who are MLs?

MLs represent a large and growing population in U.S. schools. Between 2000 and 2017, the number of MLs in the United States increased by more than 1 million, from 8% to close to 10% of the total student population (Mitchell, 2020; USDOE, Office of English Language Acquisition, 2020). During the same time, the total number of students flatlined (National Center for Education Statistics [NCES], 2019, 2021). Urban schools, which were once dominated by monolingual speakers of English, have quickly become much more linguistically diverse. Simultaneously, suburban districts that had never had MLs are "rapidly becoming more culturally, economically, linguistically, and racially diverse, yet these diverse groups are likely to live in neighborhoods where they are isolated from whites regardless of income" (Edwards et al., 2017, p. 109–110. Rural areas of the United States are also experiencing significant growth in MLs (REL Central, 2019).

Almost half of the nation's students lived in poverty before the COVID-19 pandemic (Southern Education Foundation, 2020), and the number of MLs living in poverty is disproportionately higher than those who speak English only (Century Foundation, 2021). Further, MLs are much more likely to attend socioeconomically segregated schools with fewer resources (Quintero & Hansen, 2021).

One of the most profound factors among all the nation's students is the epic number of them who are exposed to adverse childhood experiences. Almost half of U.S. children and youth have experienced or are experiencing trauma, violence, and/or chronic stress in the form of abuse, neglect, or household challenges such as a family member who is seriously ill or has died, is incarcerated, abuses drugs, and more (Bethell et al., 2017; Child and Adolescent Health Measurement Initiative, 2013). In addition to this startling statistic about the prevalence of adverse childhood experiences, many MLs and their families have also had major disruptions in their lives. Millions of MLs have experienced the following:

- ✓ living in war or conflict zones;
- ✓ being persecuted in their home countries; being displaced;
- ✓ the long, arduous, and extremely dangerous trip to perceived safety in the United States;
- ✓ being separated from families; being inhumanely treated in detention centers; and
- ✓ living in constant fear of being deported and/or becoming homeless.

(Zacarian et al., 2021, p. 47)

As a result, they have not had the continuous systematic acculturation experiences of schooling. Further, when many enroll in U.S. schools, it may be their first exposure to literacy and content learning (Calderón, 2007).

What constitutes a family is also evolving in our contemporary society to include children being raised by two parents, a single parent, foster parents, grandparents, blended parents, extended family, and/or with extrafamilial supports (Zacarian & Silverstone, 2015). It also includes MLs who have come to the United States as a whole family unit and those who have been separated from their families, as well as undocumented children or citizen children of undocumented families (Menjívar & Cervantes, 2016), many of whom are living with unrelated people and in extreme isolation (Yoshikawa, 2011).

To say the least, MLs are not a monolithic group. In addition to all the factors that have already been presented, MLs in the United States represent 400 languages (USDOE, n.d.-d). While 75% are Spanish speakers and 2% each Arabic, Chinese, and Vietnamese speakers, the diversity of languages is important to consider as we build language assistance programming for all MLs. Equally important is the reality that some schools have MLs from a wide range of language groups, while others have students from just one, and adjacent districts may have MLs who speak different languages than their neighbors. Further, there may be speakers of one language in one school and speakers of another language in another school in the same district. The sheer diversity of MLs' home languages is important for us to consider.

The primary language that a student speaks is but one descriptor. Even students who speak Spanish, for example, have distinct cultures and represent many countries. Some hail from countries in Central and South America, others are from Caribbean nations, and many others were born in the United States. They also speak different dialects. Similar diversity is the reality for students from any language group.

Additionally, some of the nation's MLs have had rich literacy and prior schooling experiences (Zacarian, 2013; Zacarian & Soto, 2020). Typically, these students' families have had strong literacy experiences and their child-rearing practices are oriented to developing the language and cognitive skills that their children will need in school. It is typical in these homes to observe families reading a variety of texts and for their children to observe these literacy behaviors as part of their development. As such, their home life includes everyday practices such as observing a family member reading the newspaper, recipes, books, and other written materials that demonstrate literacy as a cultural way of being and acting. Thus, one segment of MLs enters school with the type of school-matched language and thinking skills that are used in school regardless of what language(s) they speak. However, this does not negate the fact that they need responsive cultural supports to become members of their school and classroom communities and language supports to become proficient in English and able to perform at grade level in core academic subjects in English (Zacarian & Soto, 2020; Zacarian et al., 2021).

Conversely, there is also a large group of MLs who have not yet had the opportunity to be exposed to the repeated and continuous school-matched language and literacy experiences that are used in school. While they must receive the same types of culturally responsive practices that support them to feel safe, a sense of belonging, valued, and competent, as do all MLs, they must also engage in learning and using the type of vocabulary, language functions, and context knowledge that is used in school settings (Zacarian & Soto, 2020). This is not to say that such students do not possess communicative skills or that they are not academically inclined! Indeed, they possess a repertoire of language practices that they routinely use, as we all do, to communicate, think, and much more. An essential condition, which is discussed in later chapters of this book, is that educators designing, implementing, and sustaining effective ML language assistance programming must take time to understand, affirm, and acknowledge the various experiences of such students and draw from this knowledge to support them in learning successfully in school settings (Solorza & Garcia, 2020).

Each of these factors is important to consider when building and sustaining effective language assistance programs for MLs. While many of us are most concerned with the speed at which students learn English and are often impatient with the process, the variation among MLs in the United States must not be ignored, as it will greatly help us in creating, implementing, and sustaining programs that work.

In sum, MLs in the United States come from a wide range of personal, linguistic, cultural, educational, and socioeconomic backgrounds. They also continue to grow significantly as an important segment of the nation's students. However, overall, they are performing at a much lower rate than their English-fluent peers and have been dramatically impacted by the COVID-19 pandemic.

To advocate for the best language assistance program and support students' success, district- and school-based administrators, teachers, specialists, and others need to understand their ML populations very well, from personal, social, cultural, and linguistic perspectives. They also need to understand that MLs come from diverse backgrounds, including the epic number that have experienced one or more adversities and have varying degrees of school readiness. Simultaneously, we must acknowledge and affirm the wealth of personal, social, cultural, and linguistic assets and experiences that all MLs and their families possess and support these in all we do to create effective programming on behalf of this growing population.

Are there commonalities among the ways in which we organize programming for MLs?

If you were to visit classrooms in the United States that have MLs, you might notice many different features. In some, you would hear the student's native language being spoken. In others, you would hear only English because even using another language informally is discouraged. You might also observe students having little to no support to learn English in some schools, while in others you would observe MLs in multigrade classrooms spending the school day with other MLs. You might travel only a few miles to another school and see students spending half of their school day learning in one language and half in another. There are literally hundreds of programming models for MLs to learn English as they learn academic content (Goldenberg & Coleman, 2010; Soltero, 2004). While many believe that the name of a program, such as *transitional bilingual education*, defines how it is practiced, the reality is that any program model can be enacted differently in one district than it is in the next, adding up to the hundreds of types of language assistance programming offered (Lessow-Hurley, 2008). We will look more closely at these in the next chapter.

School leaders have to sift through each of these types to try to identify the one that they believe will work most effectively in their context. They also must consider how prepared their school's or district's teachers are to work with MLs.

Typically, who are the educators of MLs?

In the early 1990s, most of the nation's teachers were white, middle-class, monolingual English speakers (Zeichner & Hoeft, 1996), and the situation has not changed dramatically since then (NCES, 2018). Further, the percentage of teachers and administrators formally trained in ESL or bilingual education has not kept pace with the growth in the nation's ML population (National Academies of Sciences, Engineering, and Medicine, 2017). Teacher preparation programs are overwhelmingly dominated by faculty who are white (NCES, 2020). Additionally, in an empirical review of 101 studies that were conducted between 1980 and 2002 to investigate teacher preparation to work with students from diverse populations, Hollins and Guzman (2005) found that most students enrolled in teacher preparation programs were more comfortable and preferred working with students and parents from backgrounds similar to their own. Further, many educators who work in poor urban and rural areas were fast-tracked into teaching without the depth of training required to effectively teach MLs (National Academies of Sciences, Engineering, and Medicine, 2017).

Because many educators have no experience working with students unlike themselves—including students who live in poverty, students who have experienced adversities, and older students who have had limited exposure to literacy, or none at all, and no prior formal schooling—they have no experiential framework to draw from. Further, many report feeling inadequate in working with this growing population (Heineke & Vera, 2022; Samson & Lesaux, 2015). All these factors pose complex challenges for educators to truly create effective programs for MLs (Arias & Markos, 2016; Lindholm-Leary, 2015). Research in this critical area demonstrates the disparities between the significant number of MLs and the less-than-adequate workforce prepared to teach them (National Academies of Sciences, Engineering, and Medicine, 2017).

We must pay far more attention to the federal laws and regulations governing the preparation of educators and resources required on behalf of the growing population of MLs in the United States. The U.S. Department of Justice and the U.S. Department of Education (2015) stated:

> School districts have an obligation to provide the personnel and resources necessary to effectively implement their chosen EL [English learner] programs. This obligation includes having highly qualified teachers to provide language assistance services, trained administrators who can evaluate these teachers, and adequate and appropriate materials for the EL programs. At a minimum, every school district is responsible for ensuring that there is an adequate number of teachers to instruct EL students and that these teachers have mastered the skills necessary to effectively teach in the district's program for EL students. (p. 14)

While Title II of the federal Every Student Succeeds Act (ESSA) changed the previously used term "highly qualified" to the term "effective" (National Academies of Sciences, Engineering, and Medicine, 2017, p. 436), the sheer number of teachers that need to be trained across the country is staggering. In 2013–14, the 10 states with the highest percentage of MLs needed about 82,000 "effectively" prepared teachers in the succeeding 5 years. When we consider the growth that has occurred in the ML population across the country, it is likely that most of the nation's teachers need training on how to work successfully with MLs. Just as we don't want MLs to sink or swim in the educational system, we all want educators who are prepared to meet the needs of our ever-growing, ever-changing MLs.

What about teachers who have had training?

Some schools do have general education teachers who are trained to teach MLs. Many are members of the same language-minority groups as their students and have a solid understanding about their students' language, culture, and prior schooling as well as the developmental process of learning a new language and are prepared to teach this diverse population.

It is critical to support such educators to feel and be empowered as leaders in their schools and valued as assets for teaching MLs. In a study of a large group of teachers who participated in a longitudinal study that led to what is known as the *sheltered instruction observation protocol* (Echevarria et al., 2008), researchers from the Center for Applied Linguistics and the Center for Research on Equity and Diversity spent 5 years observing classroom teachers at schools in which MLs were performing well. At the heart of this research and the findings associated with it is a strong belief in working as collaborative partners on behalf of the success of MLs. In writing about moving beyond crises, such as the COVID-19 pandemic and other crises that students experience, Zacarian et al. (2021) demonstrate the critical importance of partnerships among students, families, and educators in creating successful programming for MLs and overcoming longstanding inequities that have persisted for linguistically and culturally diverse students.

We need to understand ways to transform our schools so that students, families, and educators have a voice in the programming that we implement. MLs can succeed in the learning process and become active members of their school community when we work together and are copowered to do so. Educators and other stakeholders have an enormous, if not the most essential, role in the educational programming for the nation's MLs. We are the primary architects and supervisors of the instructional programming that is provided.

How does what we are doing complement our district's and school's mission and vision?

Many, if not most, schools have a mission statement. Mission statements typically mean that educators have examined their school and its core purpose to define and make available to the community their school's or district's goals and how they will be measured. Mission statements might be considered the symbolic heart of the school, as they describe the best of an organization's core values and beliefs for building a school culture and climate. In mission statements, school leaders often encapsulate what they believe to be important for learners and the school community.

The same type of process is needed for creating a language assistance program for MLs. Doing so takes time, collaboration, and a belief that the program must complement the mission of the school while also addressing the complex needs of language-minority students. Selecting a one-size-fits-all model does not work for the widely diverse population of MLs.

To create optimal language education assistance programming, whether for large or small numbers of MLs, requires that we think of learners as individuals, members of the school community, and members of the town or city community as well. To lead our schools, we must collaborate with our students, their families, teachers, and other stakeholders.

In Chapter 2, we begin to look more closely at developing a rationale for a district's or school's program model for its MLs.

References

Arias, M. B., & Markos, A. M. (2016). *Characteristics of the workforce who are educating and supporting children who are English language learners.* Unpublished manuscript.

Bethell, C. D., Davis, M. B., Gombojav, N., Stumbo, S., & Powers, K. (2017, October). *A national and across-state profile on adverse childhood experiences among children and possibilities to heal and thrive.* Johns Hopkins University, Bloomberg School of Public Health. https://www.greatcircle.org/images/pdfs/aces-brief-101717.pdf

Calderón, M. (2007). *Teaching reading to English language learners, grades 6–12.* Corwin.

Century Foundation. (2021, December). *A new federal equity agenda for dual language learners and English learners.* https://tcf.org/content/report/new-federal-equity-agenda-dual-language-learners-english-learners/?session=1&agreed=1

Child and Adolescent Health Measurement Initiative. (2013). *Overview of adverse child and family experiences among US children.* https://www.childhealthdata.org/docs/drc/aces-data-brief_version-1-0.pdf

C-SPAN. (2020, April 9). *User clip: Fauci: Coronavirus "is shining a bright light" on health disparities.* https://www.c-span.org/video/?c4867412/user-clip-fauci-coronavirus-is-shining-bright-light-health-disparities

Echevarria, J., Vogt, M. J., & Short, D. J. (2008). *Making content comprehensible for English learners: The SIOP model* (3rd ed.). Allyn & Bacon.

Edwards, P. A., Domke, L., & White, K. (2017). Closing the parent gap in changing school districts. In S. B. Wepnew & D. W. Gomez (Eds.), *Challenges facing suburban schools: Promising responses to changing student populations* (pp. 109–123). Rowman & Littlefield.

Goldenberg, C., & Coleman, R. (2010). *Promoting academic achievement among English learners: A guide to the research.* Corwin.

Heineke, A. J., & Vera, E. M. (2022). Beyond language and academics: Investigating teachers' preparation to promote the social-emotional well-being of emergent bilingual learners. *Journal of Teacher Education, 73*(2), 145–158. https://doi.org/10.1177/00224871211027573

Hollins, E., & Guzman, M. T. (2005). Research on preparing teachers for diverse populations. In M. Cochran Smith & K. Zeichner (Eds.), *Studying teacher education: The report of the AERA panel on research and teacher education* (pp. 477–548). Lawrence Erlbaum.

Lehrer-Small, A. (2021, September 30). *Exclusive 74 data: Absenteeism surged among English learners during pandemic.* https://www.the74million.org/article/exclusive-data-absenteeism-surged-among-english-learners-during-pandemic/

Lennon, C., & Stanton, A. (2021, October 18). *Rising HS dropout rates and declining community college enrollment are twin COVID crises. How to fix the broken education pipeline.* https://www.the74million.org/article/lennon-stanton-rising-hs-dropout-rates-declining-community-college-enrollment-are-twin-covid-crises-how-to-fix-the-broken-education-pipeline/

Lessow-Hurley, J. (2008). *Foundations of dual language instruction* (5th ed.). Allyn & Bacon.

Lindholm-Leary, K. J. (2015). *Fostering school success for English learners K–12: Language and academic development of dual language learners during the school years.* Unpublished manuscript.

Menjivar, C., & Cervantes, A. G. (2016, November). The effects of parental undocumented status on families and children. *CYF News.* https://www.apa.org/pi/families/resources/newletter/index

Mitchell, C. (2020, February 18). The nation's English-learner population has surged: 3 things to know. *Education Week.* https://www.edweek.org/leadership/the-nations-english-learner-population-has-surged-3-things-to-know/2020/02

National Academies of Sciences, Engineering, and Medicine. (2017). Building the workforce to educate English learners. In *Promoting the educational success of children and youth learning English: Promising futures* (pp. 432–455). National Academies Press. https://doi.org/10.17226/24677

National Center for Education Statistics. (2018, May). *Characteristics of public school teachers.* https://nces.ed.gov/programs/coe/indicator/clr

National Center for Education Statistics. (2019). Chapter 1. In *Digest of education statistics.* https://nces.ed.gov/programs/digest/d19/ch_1.asp

National Center for Education Statistics. (2020). Characteristics of postsecondary faculty. In *Condition of education.* https://nces.ed.gov/programs/coe/pdf/coe_csc.pdf

National Center for Education Statistics. (2021). *Fast facts: Enrollment trends.* https://nces.ed.gov/fastfacts/display.asp?id=65

New York City Department of Education. (2020–21). *ELL demographics at a glance.* https://infohub.nyced.org/docs/default-source/default-document-library/sy-2020-21-ell-demographics-at-a-glance.pdf

New York City Department of Education. (2022). *Tests for English learners.* https://www.schools.nyc.gov/learning/testing/tests-for-english-language-learners

New York State Education Department, Office of Bilingual Education and World Languages. (2019). *Multilingual learner/English language learner graduation rate improvement and dropout prevention planning tool.* http://www.nysed.gov/common/nysed/files/programs/bilingual-ed/ellmll-grad-and-dropout-toolkit_4_12_19_final.pdf

Quintero, D., & Hansen, M. (2021, January 14). *As we tackle school segregation, don't forget about English learner students.* Brookings Institution. https://www.brookings.edu/blog/brown-center-chalkboard/2021/01/14/as-we-tackle-school-segregation-dont-forget-about-english-learner-students

REL Central. (2019, May 19). *The growth of English learners in rural areas.* https://ies.ed.gov/ncee/edlabs/regions/central/pdf/slides_webinar-english-language-learners.pdf

Samson, J. F., & Lesaux, N. K. (2015). Disadvantaged language minority students and their teachers: A national picture. *Teachers College Record, 117*(2), 1–26. https://doi.org/10.1177/016146811511700205

Solorza, O., & Garcia, C. R. (2020). Academic language and the minoritization of U.S. bilingual Latinx students. *Language and Education, 35*(6), 505–521. https://doi.org/10.1080/09500782.2020.1825476

Soltero, S. (2004). *Dual language: Teaching and learning in two languages.* Pearson.

Southern Education Foundation. (2020). *New majority series.* https://www.southerneducation.org/what-we-do/research/newmajorityreportseries/

U.S. Department of Education. (n.d.-a). *Academic performance and outcomes for English learners.* https://www2.ed.gov/datastory/el-outcomes/index.html

U.S. Department of Education. (n.d.-b). *Chronic absenteeism in the nation's schools.* https://www2.ed.gov/datastory/chronicabsenteeism.html

U.S. Department of Education. (n.d.-c). *Graduation rates.* https://www2.ed.gov/datastory/el-outcomes/index.html#two

U.S. Department of Education. (n.d.-d). *Our nation's English learners: What are their characteristics?* https://www2.ed.gov/datastory/el-characteristics/index.html

U.S. Department of Education, Office of English Language Acquisition. (2020, February). *English learners: Demographic trends.* https://ncela.ed.gov/files/fast_facts/19-0193_Del4.4_ELDemographicTrends_021220_508.pdf

U.S. Department of Justice & U.S. Department of Education. (2015, January 7). *Dear colleague.* https://www2.ed.gov/about/offices/list/ocr/letters/colleague-el-201501.pdf

U.S. Government Accountability Office. (2022, May). *Pandemic learning: Teachers reported many obstacles for high-poverty students and English Learners as well as some mitigating factors.* https://www.gao.gov/assets/gao-22-105815.pdf

Yoshikawa, H. (2011). *Immigrants raising citizens: Undocumented parents and their young children*. Russell Sage Foundation.

Zacarian, D. (2013). *Mastering academic language: A framework for supporting student achievement*. Corwin.

Zacarian, D., Calderón, M. E., & Gottlieb, M. (2021). *Beyond crises: Overcoming linguistical and cultural inequities in communities, schools, and classrooms*. Corwin.

Zacarian, D., & Silverstone, M. A. (2015). *In it together: How student, family, and community partnerships advance engagement and achievement in diverse classrooms*. Corwin.

Zacarian, D., & Soto, I. (2020). *Responsive schooling for culturally and linguistically diverse students*. Norton Professional Books.

Zeichner, K., & Hoeft, K. (1996). Teacher socialization for cultural diversity. In J. Sikula, T. Buttery, & E. Guyton (Eds.), *Handbook on research on teacher education* (2nd ed., pp. 525–547). Macmillan.

CHAPTER 2

Integrating the Regulations and Principles

When Olivier moved from Cape Verde to Massachusetts, his mother enrolled him in a neighborhood school with the help of a relative who could speak English. The school's guidance counselor welcomed Olivier and his family and provided him with a class schedule. The schedule did not include anything to address his lack of English. Rather, it was the same one that his English-fluent peers received. It was felt that Olivier should be treated like everyone else. By the end of the first week, both Olivier and his teachers were very frustrated. The teachers weren't sure how to teach him because they couldn't communicate with him, and he was totally lost. What should or could the school have done?

Actually, it is required by federal law that schools identify their multilingual learners (MLs; U.S. Department of Justice & U.S. Department of Education, 2015). Additional regulations require that when MLs are identified, they must be placed in programming that is known to be sound, properly resourced, and proven to be effective and that adjustments must be made when it isn't (U.S. Department of Justice & U.S. Department of Education, 2015). The history behind these regulations provides important information for all educators to institute programming for MLs. In this chapter, we examine three important questions; these form an essential backdrop against which to answer the specific question about Olivier's school:

- What key historical events led to the laws and regulations governing the education of MLs?

- What are the key principles of second language acquisition?

- What are the various models for language assistance programming?

What key historical events led to the laws and regulations governing the education of MLs?

The regulations governing the education of MLs are an outcome of major historical events. Some of these involved judicial decisions made by the U.S. Supreme Court, and others were formed in the court of public opinion. The civil rights movement of the 1960s led to many actions involving the rights of MLs (Reese, 2005). Prior to the 1960s, the right to an equal education was interpreted to mean that all students, regardless of their proficiency in English, were treated equally when they attended the same classrooms as their peers, or classrooms like their peers', and when instruction was delivered using the same books and curriculum. This practice was challenged during the civil rights movement when the country began to look more carefully at some of its discriminatory practices, including the education of its MLs (Reese, 2005).

In 1964, the Civil Rights Act was enacted. It states that any institution that receives federal funding cannot deny access to anyone to any program or activity based on their race, color, or national origin (U.S. Department of Justice, Office of Civil Rights, n.d.). Then, in 1968, the Elementary and Secondary Education Act was amended to include the Bilingual Education Act. This was the first federal statute that addressed the learning needs of MLs (Baker, 2006; Osorio-O'Dea, 2001). Some believe that it was the result of a political movement intended to attract the Latino vote, while others claim that it was a genuine attempt to remedy the high failure rates among the nation's MLs (Crawford, 1996). Regardless, it marked the first time that the rights of MLs were brought into focus. Unfortunately, it did not lead to many changes as it failed to include specific regulations other than the general notion that schools could use innovative programming in the native language to teach English to the nation's students (Crawford, 1996; Reese, 2005). However, it did pave the way for schools to implement programming that allowed students to learn in their native language while they were learning English.

Many federal regulations about MLs are a result of lawsuits filed in local courts across the country and appealed all the way to the Supreme Court. Table 2.1 highlights six of the major Supreme Court cases. The ones that are shaded are the most seminal. In *Lau v. Nichols,* for example, the Supreme Court ruled that schools must provide programming to help students overcome barriers to learning English. The definition of such students includes those who are not able to perform ordinary classwork in English.

Each of the rulings in Table 2.1 should provide important safeguards for students so that they can receive a quality education. In sum, they require schools to identify MLs, provide research-based programming that is known to be sound, use adequate resources (including personnel and materials), evaluate the effectiveness of the programming, and make necessary changes using sound research-based models that are known to be effective to ensure that students learn English and content successfully.

Table 2.1 U.S. Supreme Court Cases Related to Multilingual Learners

YEAR	CASE NAME	DESCRIPTION	RULING
1973	*Keyes v. Denver School District*	The first de facto segregation case was heard in the United States; it argued that particular groups of students (Latinos and Blacks) were largely separated from their peers.	Districts must desegregate their students (Horn & Kurlaender, 2006).
1974	*Lau v. Nichols*	Lau argued that the district was not providing an adequate education to its MLs because they could not sufficiently comprehend English.	Districts must take the steps needed to provide MLs with an instructional program in which they can perform ordinary classwork in English. One year later (1975), the U.S. secretary of education issued the Lau Remedies, providing districts with guidelines for identifying and working with MLs (Crawford, 1996).
1974	*Serna v. Portales*	Latino plaintiffs claimed that their school district had ignored the English language and learning needs of their children. They believed that their children's rights to equal protection and equal educational opportunity were being denied.	Districts must do the following when there are a substantial number of MLs from the same language group: 1. expand bilingual bicultural instruction, 2. measure student achievement, and 3. recruit and employ bilingual personnel (Crawford, 1996).
1975	*Aspira v. Board of Education of the City of New York*	This case argued that students who spoke little English were forced to attend schools in which instruction was offered primarily in English and that the results of this practice were inadequate programming, higher rates of underachievement and dropping out, and a much lower rate of economic opportunity compared with English-fluent peers.	Districts must provide intensive instruction for students to learn English and can provide bilingual education in content areas when it is needed and reinforces students' use of their primary language. Students must not be isolated or separated from their peers.
1978	*Cintron v. Brentwood Union Free School District*	This case argued that children were being segregated and isolated from their English-fluent peers.	Districts must provide methods for identifying and assessing MLs and transferring them into general education English classrooms using a method that does not segregate students (Dunklee & Shoop, 2006; Mid-Atlantic Equity Consortium, 1995).
1978	*Castañeda v. Pickard*	The district was segregating children based on their race and ethnicity and had failed to implement a successful bilingual education program in which children would learn English.	Districts must establish a three-pronged test for ensuring that their educational program for MLs is consistent with a student's right to an education. It established that programming should be 1. based on sound educational research, 2. implemented with adequate commitment and resources, and 3. evaluated for its effectiveness, after a period of time, and that alternative research-based programming be sought if found not to be effective.

However, as seen in Chapter 1, many of the issues that led to these court cases have not been remedied. Some believe that persisting disparities are a result of continued prejudice and discrimination toward the nation's language-minority population (Cummins, 2000, 2018). Without question, politics has continued to strongly affect language policies. Four states (California, Arizona, Colorado, and Massachusetts) ran ballot initiatives to restrict or eliminate bilingual education. Proponents of these initiatives argued that bilingual education was a failure and a reflection of the wrong language policies (Mendoza & Ayala, 1999; Montero & Chavez, 2001; Tamayo et al., 2001; Unz & Tuchman, 1997). They also claimed that it was too expensive and promoted an English-only ideology coupled with an unfounded belief that English could be learned in a year (Crawford, 1996; R. D. Gonzalez, 2000). Arizona, California, and Massachusetts voted for ballot initiatives to repeal bilingual education entirely. Years after the resulting policies went into effect, research was conducted to assess their outcome. Were students doing any better? The results did not show the significant improvements that the proponents had promised, and the achievement gap between MLs and their English-fluent peers continued (American Institutes for Research & WestEd, 2002; Burdick-Will & Gomez, 2006; Uriarte & Karp, 2009). Later, these laws were repealed as a direct result of these outcomes (National Academies of Sciences, Engineering, and Medicine, 2017). As we saw in Chapter 1, MLs across the nation—whether the states they live in have or have not passed or repealed bilingual education laws—continue to perform much more poorly than their English-fluent peers.

In 2001, while these anti-bilingual education initiatives were occurring, President George W. Bush signed the No Child Left Behind Act (NCLB) into law with the intent of improving student achievement (U.S. Department of Education, 2002). The new law replaced the Elementary and Secondary Education Act, including the Bilingual Education Act; set new standards for the ways in which schools used federal funds; and set achievement standards for schools and students. It included four principles:

1. stronger accountability for results;

2. greater flexibility among the nation's states, school districts, and schools in the use of federal funds;

3. more choices for parents from disadvantaged backgrounds; and

4. an emphasis on teaching methods that have been proven to work (U.S. Department of Education, 2002).

New standards were also set to improve the achievement gaps between MLs and fluent speakers of English because "a congressionally mandated study found that these students (i.e., MLs) receive lower grades, are judged by their teachers to have lower academic abilities, and score below their classmates on standardized tests of reading and math" (U.S. Department of Education, 2002, p. 91). Under NCLB, federally funded schools with MLs were to focus on using what had been found to be successful practices for teaching MLs.

To do this, it required

- teachers to be certified as English language proficient and proficient in the languages in which a program model is taught,

- using curriculum that is scientifically based and proven to be effective,

- states to have flexibility in choosing the teaching method for teaching MLs, and

- that 95% of the Title III funds used at the local level be used to teach MLs.

NCLB also placed a heavy emphasis on student performance:

- It established annual achievement objectives for MLs based on a set of standards and benchmarks for raising the English proficiency levels of MLs.

- It required annual assessments of students in English language arts and reading.

- It required states to ensure that their districts and schools were making measurable annual achievement objectives.

Additionally, NCLB required school districts to inform parents about the programming that was specifically targeted for teaching their children English, and it gave parents the right to choose among different program models, if more than one was available, as well as the right to remove their children from a program.

A little over a decade after NCLB was passed, two initiatives were launched at the beginning and end of 2015 (see Figure 2.1). The first was directly intended to remedy longstanding inequities for MLs and the second added new accountability standards.

Figure 2.1   Dates of the Dear Colleague letter and Every Student Succeeds Act

Image source: iStock.com/ineskoleva

1. January 7, 2015: The U.S. Department of Justice and the U.S. Department of Education jointly wrote a letter, known as the *Dear Colleague* letter, to all state education agencies, districts, and schools about educating the nation's MLs.

2. December 10, 2015: The Every Student Succeeds Act was signed into law.

Dear Colleague Letter From the U.S. Department of Justice and U.S. Department of Education

On January 7, 2015, the U.S. Department of Justice's Civil Rights Division and U.S. Department of Education's Office for Civil Rights sent a letter to every state education agency (SEA) and public and public charter school district in the nation (U.S. Department of Justice & U.S. Department of Education, 2015). This *Dear Colleague* letter (U.S. Department of Justice & U.S. Department of Education, 2015) reinforced the laws and regulations that had been implemented as part of the *Lau v. Nichols* U.S. Supreme Court case and the Elementary and Secondary Education Act to ensure that schools were "meeting the legal obligations" that ensured that all MLs "can participate meaningfully and equally in education programs and services" (p. 2) and that their parents are meaningfully informed about their child's education.

What was the impetus for this letter? Investigations by the Departments of Justice and Education found that many districts nationwide were out of compliance and not following the laws. The letter, a first of its kind, provided guidance about the steps that SEAs and districts must take to adhere to the laws and regulations

1. governing the identification and education of MLs, and

2. ensuring that all families of MLs are given

   a. equal and meaningful access to the same school-related information as their English-fluent peers and

   b. information about their child's specific language education programming to support them in becoming proficient in English.

The document also provided specific guidance about families who decline language assistance programming for their children (also known as *opt out*). It did so because the two agencies found that a significant number of educators were "steering families away from language programs or providing incorrect or inadequate information to parents about the EL [English learner] program, particular services within the program, or their child's EL status" letter (U.S. Department of Justice & U.S. Department of Education, 2015, p. 30)

Ayanna Cooper (2021), author and former U.S. Department of State advocate for culturally and linguistically diverse learners, shared some of the common reasons that families decline services, which affirm the findings of the *Dear Colleague* letter:

- A staff member or another parent provides inaccurate information about the program models

- Scheduling conflicts with other classes

- Concern about the amount of quality work being assigned or missed if their child(ren) were to be pulled out for a segment of English language support

- A staff member explains to parents that certain classes (e.g., bilingual education) are full, encouraging opting out

- Concerns about programs offered are not fully explained or addressed

- Confusion between English language support and special education services

- Low confidence in the quality of the program models offered

- Disagreement with school officials that their child(ren) needs language support

- Disagreement with the philosophy of the program model being offered

- A decision to opt out for one school year is not revisited, and parents/guardians are not offered a chance to change their decision in subsequent school years

- Belief that once they decline services, they cannot request participation in the future (pp. 47–48)

The *Dear Colleague* letter clarifies what is required under federal law. Most notably, when parents decline language education programming or specific services for their children, schools and districts are obligated to support the English language and other academic needs of their opt-out EL students under the civil rights laws. The *Dear Colleague* letter also specifies that such students' progress must be monitored and that language education program services must be offered and reoffered when needed:

> To ensure these needs of opt-out EL students are being met, school districts must periodically monitor the progress of students who have opted out of EL programs or certain EL services. If an EL student who opted out of the school district's EL programs or services does not demonstrate appropriate growth in English proficiency, or struggles in one or more subjects due to language barriers, the school district's affirmative steps include informing the EL student's parents of his or her lack of progress and offering the parents further opportunities to enroll the student in the EL program or at least certain EL services at any time. (U.S. Department of Justice & U.S. Department of Education, 2015, p. 31)

The *Dear Colleague* letter is a foundational document for the nation's educators to use. It is the blueprint of what to do to build effective programming for MLs by following the federal laws, and key elements of the letter are referenced throughout this book.

Every Student Succeeds Act

On December 10, 2015, President Barak Obama signed into law the Every Student Succeeds Act (ESSA), reinforcing the nation's "longstanding commitment to equal opportunity for all students" and the accountability standards for all the nation's students to "ensure success for students and schools" (U.S. Department of Education, n.d.). ESSA requires SEAs to "monitor LEAs [local education agencies] to ensure that they are providing ELs meaningful access to grade level core content instruction and remedying any academic deficits in a timely manner" (U.S. Department of Education, 2016, p. 1). It also requires every school and district to engage in the following accountability standards:

- Monitor the progress of all ELs in achieving English language proficiency (ELP) and in acquiring content knowledge.

- Establish rigorous monitoring systems that include benchmarks for expected growth and take appropriate steps to assist students who are not adequately progressing toward those goals.

- Document that an EL has demonstrated English proficiency using a valid and reliable ELP assessment that tests all four language domains.

- Students exiting from EL status must be monitored for at least two years, to ensure that (1) they have not been prematurely exited; (2) any academic deficits incurred as a result of participating in the EL program have been remedied; and (3) they are meaningfully participating in the standard program of instruction comparable to their never-EL peers.

- Report on the number and percentage of former ELs meeting state academic standards for four years. (U.S. Department of Education, 2016, pp. 1–2)

The *Dear Colleague* letter (January 2015) and ESSA (December 2015) reinforce what we must do to ensure that MLs do not face obstacles and barriers to learning. Public schools can face lawsuits; tremendous expenses, including the termination of financial assistance; and arduous scrutiny for successive years for denying MLs equal access to an education and/or denying their parents equal and meaningful access to the same information that other parents receive and specific information about their child's language programming (U.S. Department of Education Office of Civil Rights, n.d.; U.S. Department of Justice & U.S. Department of Education, 2015). An example of a lawsuit related to equal access to an education can be found in Jo Napolitano's (2021) book *The School I Deserve: Six Young Refugees and Their Fight for Equality in America.*

Educators involved in designing, enacting, and supervising language assistance programming need to know and steadfastly follow the federal laws regarding the education of MLs. Whether we are in Alaska or Florida or any state in the nation, these provide us with a broad set of guidelines for creating and maintaining effective programming. Returning to the example presented in the opening of this chapter, had Olivier's school principal adhered to these guidelines, he would have taken steps to provide Olivier with sound programming and the needed resources. He would also have instituted a process by which the program could be examined to ensure that it was working or change it as needed.

Another important step for understanding how to put the regulations into practice is to understand some of the key principles of second language acquisition, including the major research studies that have focused on MLs. They provide important information about the various program models for leading, transforming, and strengthening schools with MLs.

What are the key principles of second language acquisition?

Jim Cummins has contributed greatly to what we understand the principles of second language acquisition to be. To communicate effectively in social situations, Cummins and Swain (1986) state that we must have the *basic interpersonal communication skills* (BICS) to interact with others. He claims that this takes a much shorter time (1 to 3 years to attain native-speaker proficiency) than it does to learn the language we use to express the higher-order thinking skills that we need for academic learning. A very common example of the impact of academic versus social language is a student who can speak in English easily with peers on the school bus but cannot perform grade-level academic tasks in English in the classroom. Teachers, administrators, and other educators and specialists may well wonder whether such a student is lazy in class or has some learning disability when in reality that student is merely working their way through a very predictable process and timetable of second language learning.

Using language socially is different than using it for academic purposes.

Using language with peers on the playground, at lunch, on the school bus, or in play after school is quite different than using language in academic contexts. One reason is that social situations are often supported by a context, physical cues such as facial gestures and body movements, and the environment in which they are taking place. Consider an ML playing jump rope at recess. She can participate actively in the event by observing and imitating her peers. Because her friends' language use is so contextual, the words they use during this play event are clear and relatively simple, and their sentence structures are probably simple as well. The event facilitates the student's ability to communicate while playing and to quickly take ownership of some of the language.

In contrast, the language used in an academic setting is more implicit and abstract, more complex, and less reliant on context and interpersonal cues. For example, let's say that the kids playing jump rope have returned to class from recess and are engaged in a science lesson about mammals. While there are some pictures, there is a lot of reading as well as lists of attributes. Language use quickly moves from the social event at recess to a context in which there are far fewer contextual cues. Students are required to use complex and specialized language and language structures to listen, speak, read, write, and learn. Certain background knowledge about mammals is also needed.

Cummins refers to academic language development as *cognitive academic language proficiency* (CALP; Cummins & Swain, 1986). Academic success requires the development of communicative skills (listening, speaking, reading, and writing) in the content area (e.g., math, science, social studies) along with the much-needed "content knowledge, use of higher-order thinking skills, and mastery of basic academic skills" (Goldenberg & Coleman, 2010, p. 83). Research shows that building these CALP skills takes time-intensive instruction, and it is a developmental process (August & Shanahan, 2006, 2008; Collier & Thomas, 1989, 2002; Cummins, 1981; Goldenberg & Coleman, 2010; National Academies of Science, Engineering, and Medicine, 2017). While the terms *BICS* and *CALP* have been replaced with "informal less demanding conversational language and the more formal generally more demanding academic language necessary for school success" (Goldenberg & Coleman, 2010, p. 62), the two are not mutually exclusive, nor is it really one versus the other. Both are critical.

Using Strengths-Based Principles

Our ever-changing MLs bring many strengths and assets to our schools including, to say the least, their linguistic and cultural understandings and ways of being and acting. One of the biggest tasks for every school leader, teacher, specialist, and others involved in education is to do our very best to integrate MLs' many assets into our schools and classrooms so that they experience four essential conditions: safety, a sense of belonging, acknowledgment, and competence. Research points to the urgent need for us to move away from a deficit-based view of MLs toward a fully integrated assets- or strengths-based approach. Let's look more closely at the principles of a strengths-based pedagogy.

All too often we or our colleagues worry that our multilingual multicultural students don't know English, have been in the language assistance program in our schools forever, or have not been to school. We also lament that their families are too poor or too busy to help, don't speak English and can't help, or that their life is too chaotic to help us. Does this sound familiar to you? These deficit-based perceptions often lead us to feel that our students cannot possibly be successful, and our professional situations sometimes feel so impossible that they lead to burnout. This was especially true during the COVID-19 pandemic when we made the gigantic shift from in-person to remote schooling or were doing a hybrid of both and as we worried about our own health, the health of our families, and more.

Rather than feel like Sisyphus trying to roll that impossibly huge rock up a hill, we have great reasons to think anew. For years, the fields of psychology, psychiatry, and social work looked at what was wrong, like the pieces of broken glass depicted in Figure 2.2.

Figure 2.2   Broken Glass Metaphor

Source: Annie Wilkinson

We then took these perceived pieces of broken glass to treat the problem by trying to find remedies for it. The field of education drew heavily from this framework. Focusing on what was wrong, like educators lamenting that a child doesn't speak English, their families are working so much that they cannot help, or their families are too poor to help, led to us having a deficit-based view of culturally and linguistically diverse students and to negative outcomes (Zacarian et al., 2017, 2021).

Chapter 1 began with the following example:

> Manuel moved to the United States from El Salvador when he was
> 13 years old. In El Salvador, he had worked on his uncle's bus as the ticket
> taker and money exchanger. He is a very sweet, polite Spanish speaker who
> came to the United States without any formal schooling or prior exposure
> to English.

Take a moment to consider Manuel and the deficit-based lens we are discussing. What might you share with someone about him? Here are some typical responses that educators share:

> He doesn't speak English.
>
> He's never been to school.

That type of deficit-based dialogue leads to more dialogue about what Manuel can't do instead of what he can do. Imagine what many educators might share to continue this deficit-based dialogue, knowing that they too have a student with no prior formal schooling before coming to the United States as an adolescent.

However, when we shift our patterns of thinking to what is right, what is strong, and what is a strength, we can successfully support MLs in seeing their many assets and competencies by integrating these into our instructional practice so that students have a much better chance to be successful in school and in their lives. The same holds true for us working together. When we see our strengths and assets, we have a much better chance of being successful in our work and more.

A helpful way to consider this is to picture a mosaic (such as the one in Figure 2.3) being assembled and view each piece as one strength that a person possesses.

Figure 2.3   Mosaic Metaphor

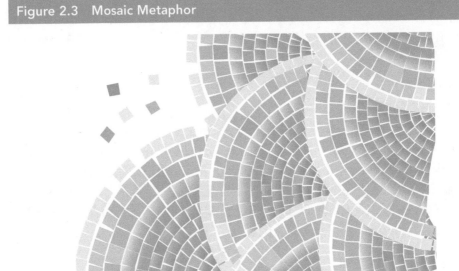

Source: Annie Wilkinson

Research points to the urgent need for us to focus on students' strengths as this approach has been shown to have the best outcomes (Seligman et al., 2006). To do this means that we must look for students' existing strengths, acknowledge these, help students see these in themselves, and build school- and classroom-wide practices and connections that integrate these into what we do.

So let's go back to Manuel. Consider the following list of strengths that he already possesses:

- He speaks Spanish.
- He has depth of cultural experience.
- He has lived in more than one place and experienced some differences to share.
- He has depth of math experience as a money exchanger.
- He is polite.

Now, let's say he comes to your mathematics class and you see that he is trying to make himself understood. We might also add to the list by sharing how brave he is to attempt to engage in the mathematics lesson and use a new language.

One of the key principles of multilingualism is looking at human behavior through the lens of the assets and qualities that empower people. Psychologist Abraham Maslow (1987, 1999), a pioneer in the field of positive psychology, used the term *self-actualization* to describe what is possible when we look at human behavior through the lens of strengths, capacities, and qualities. One of the most exciting and even inspiring aspects of being an educator is seeing students as capable and competent learners. N. Gonzalez et al. (2005), renowned for their seminal research about the knowledge and assets that all families possess, coined the term *funds of knowledge* to highlight their research on populations living in the regions along the U.S.-Mexico border. While many of these families had limited prior schooling, the researchers found that they possessed incredible skills, talents, and attributes in child-rearing, farming, and more and that these greatly supported their children's development. They also found that when educators value and honor the strengths of all families, it can have a positive outcome for students.

Renowned research scholar Dweck (2006) greatly supports the principles put forth by Maslow et al. (1987, 1999). Her research findings demonstrate the positives that can be achieved when we focus on the many strengths of individuals and communities and support students in seeing these in themselves and others. She points to the differences between having fixed perceptions of ourselves and others versus ones that are flexible and capable of growing and expanding. Known for using the terms *fixed mindset* versus *growth mindset* to describe the distinctions between the two perceptions, her research affirms a strengths-based approach. Additionally, Dweck et al. (2014) contributed greatly to our understanding of students, particularly MLs, who have experienced one or more adverse childhood experiences and live in communities with few resources. Can these students experience success? Resoundingly, yes!

Though the diverse personal, social, linguistic, cultural, schooling, and life experiences of MLs represent an eclectic mix, each possesses great assets. These include MLs who

- are newcomers and came to the United States during the past 6 months,

- have had limited or interrupted formal education,

- have been learning English for 7 years or more and are known as *long-term MLs,*

- have learning differences or disabilities,

- are in the process of learning English,

- are fully bilingual,

- have experienced one or more adverse childhood experiences.

The point in presenting the critical urgency of using an assets-based approach to create, implement, and sustain programming is twofold: It acknowledges the varied literacy learning journeys of each of these distinct groups, and it pays attention to identifying the personal, social, cultural, linguistic, academic, and life experience assets that each ML brings so that we may support them, ourselves, and others in having a growth mindset.

Joel Ristuccia is the lead clinical faculty for the Lesley University Institute for Trauma Sensitivity, in Cambridge, Massachusetts, which focuses on supporting children impacted by traumatic experiences. He discusses the importance of community/belonging:

Research shows that the prevalence of adverse experience among our students is almost universal (studies show upwards of 80%; Philadelphia ACE Project, 2021).[1] Our ML students have the added experience of leaving their home countries and coming to live in a foreign place with a different culture and language, whether under duress or by choice. One of the most significant resiliency factors we can provide for anyone with adverse experience is belonging/meaningful connection to community, and for school-aged children, school is one of their most important communities. How can we support our students' sense of belonging to our school/classroom communities?

An assets or strengths-based approach is central to our students' (including MLs) sense of belonging to their school/classroom communities. Leveraging students' islands of competence to contribute to the classroom/school community combined with efforts to help the students feel valued and important in the school community are two complementary areas of support that can enhance our students' sense of connection and belonging. Various strategies that schools have used to achieve this include the following:

1. Student interest survey: new students complete a survey of their interests and strengths on their first day in school. This supports developing connections with others in the school who share the interests, as well as identifying the student's islands of competence (see sample Resource 3.4 in Chapter 3).

2. Bi-multilingual student ambassadors to welcome and mentor new students from their first day in school.

3. School supplies backpacks, with books, materials, and other important items for school success.

4. Identification of linguistically/culturally competent resources in the community to support the school, family, and student as needed. (Ristuccia, personal communication, April 21, 2022)

---

[1] The research was initially presented by Felitti et al. (1998).

How long does it take to learn a second language?

All educators must have a good understanding of the time and the conditions that are needed to learn a second language well enough to be able to perform ordinary classwork in that language. All MLs must be given sufficient time to develop the social-emotional as well as academic language and literacy skills that are needed to be successful in school. Programming for MLs must be created, delivered, and maintained with this purpose in mind.

Two major government-funded reviews of research (August & Shanahan, 2006; Genesee et al., 2006) provide comprehensive findings about the education of language-minority students (Goldenberg & Coleman, 2010). These reviews found that it takes 1 to 3 years to become conversationally fluent and 4 to 6 years or more to achieve a level 4 on a five-point scale of proficiency in English. Further, such progress may not be directly related to how fluent a student is in social conversational situations (Goldenberg & Coleman, 2010). For example, a student's capacity to engage in a social conversation about the previous night's school basketball game is not an indicator of their capacity to engage successfully in an academic context. Developing academic proficiency in English is a long process; no stage is the same in terms of the length of time that it takes to move from one to another. Indeed, Goldenberg and Coleman (2010) found that "progress was slower between level 3 and advanced levels 4 and 5" (p. 69). One of the most important factors regarding the length of time that it takes is students' prior consistent and routine exposure to academic language and literacy.

Collier and Thomas (1989) have examined the length of time that it takes for MLs to become "proficient in English," a phrase that, under federal law, means that they are able to perform ordinary classwork in English. They conducted a longitudinal 10-year study of 2,000 students in a large urban school district whose families were fairly affluent, literate, and oriented to supporting literacy practices at home. The researchers' goal was to find out how long it took for beginning learners of English from this community to reach native-like performance in English at the 50th percentile on norm-referenced tests (i.e., the ability to perform ordinary classwork in English).

For their study, Collier and Thomas (1989) selected MLs whose academic achievement scores in their native language were at or above grade level. These high-achieving groups of students were selected as the researchers believed that they would learn English the fastest and that the results would provide key information about learners at the high end of the spectrum. They also selected students who had the same program model for learning English: instruction in English as a second language (ESL) on a pull-out basis. No support in the native language was provided, and students did not receive content support in ESL.

The students were first given 2 years to learn English. At the end of the second year, norm-referenced tests were administered, and these tests were subsequently readministered yearly in English language arts, reading, mathematics, science, and social studies. Collier and Thomas (1989) found that the group that achieved proficiency the fastest were those who had entered school between ages 8 and 11. This age group reached the 50th percentile in reading within 5 to 7 years. They also found that this group achieved the 50th percentile in mathematics in 2 to 3 years and reading in 5 or more years. Students who arrived when they were younger than

8 or older than 11 took as long as 7 to 10 years to achieve proficiency in English. Collier and Thomas also looked at other studies, particularly those conducted with students who continued to learn in their primary language while they were learning English. In these studies, students in bilingual programs achieved academic proficiency in English more quickly, in 4 to 7 years. It is important to note that this study included only students from fairly affluent high-literacy homes and no others, such as students with limited or interrupted prior schooling. More recent research, including Hart and Risley (1995), August and Shanahan (2006, 2008), and Genesee et al. (2006), points to the importance of time as well as the type of instruction that must be provided for students, especially those with limited or interrupted prior schooling. However, one of the most important factors to consider is the first language(s) students use to communicate. After all, it is one of the greatest assets!

Does first language learning affect second language learning?

Collier and Thomas's (1989) findings, as well as those of August and Shanahan (2006), Genesee et al. (2006), and a report from the National Academies of Science, Engineering, and Medicine (2017) summarizing research on promoting the educational success of MLs, tell us a lot about second language learning, at least from the perspective of students with strong first language and literacy backgrounds. First, students who have developed grade-level or above-grade-level abilities in language arts, reading, science, social studies, and mathematics in their native language appear to learn English more quickly than do younger learners, those under the age of 8, who have not yet developed literacy skills in their primary language. Second, older MLs (over the age of 11) usually need much longer to learn English than their time in public schools may allow. Third, continuing to teach students content and language arts in their native language while they are learning English appears to be a much more effective and faster way for students of all ages to learn English for academic purposes.

However, many students do not possess school-matched, age-appropriate language skills in their strongest language. They often present a dilemma for educators in determining whether these students should be taught in their home language or English. As we will see in the succeeding chapters about academic content and language learning, these students must receive an educational program that, besides addressing language proficiency per se, is wholly focused on the following:

- instruction that strongly integrates the whole of students' backgrounds and experiences

- systematic development of social-emotional and academic language skills

Many program models fail because they are not focused on these two critical elements.

We learn language through receiving input that is meaningful, and we become literate through the same process (Krashen, 1985). By the time young children enter school, they have already had 3 to 5 years of language learning experiences. While they have the cultural, linguistic, and cognitive skills that enable them to be meaningful participants in their home communities, students come with a range of preliteracy exposure and experiences. To provide effective programming, we must account for all MLs, and really all students from diverse literacy backgrounds.

Perhaps we think that an English-only model is the best way to go. Not so! Collier and Thomas (2020) provide the strongest research base about the efficacy of learning through two languages and closing the opportunity gaps that have persisted. They reported on 20 years of research they "conducted in 23 large and small school districts from 15 different states, representing all regions of the U.S. in urban, suburban, and rural contexts" (Collier & Thomas, 2004, p. 1). They found that all students, including MLs and English-fluent learners from a broad swath of socioeconomic, linguistic, and cultural backgrounds, did "astoundingly" well when they were instructed in a two-way model that supported them to learn in their home language and a target language. Indeed, all benefited tremendously from dual-language programming, and the opportunity gaps closed at a much faster rate and more comprehensively than for students exposed to only one language of instruction. Because many parents want their child to be fluent in more than one language, dual-language programs, also referred to as bilingual education, bilingual programming, and two-way, are taking hold across the country. Let's look at all the models of instruction, beginning with bilingual programming.

What are the various models for language assistance programming?

In the United States, there are program models (1) that promote bilingualism and biliteracy, (2) that promote a gradual reduction of bilingualism as a means for learning English with monolingualism as its goal, and (3) in which the language of instruction is entirely in English. In most of these models, English language development (often referred to as ESL) is a component of the model. In some models, ESL classes are considered the sole means by which students learn English. In some, students are offered bilingual programming. How do we select the model that makes the most sense for our district? Research about which models have been found to be the most successful can help guide us in this process.

Collier and Thomas (2002) conducted a study between 1996 and 2001 in which they looked at the standardized test outcomes of over 200,000 students. The students were from the northeastern, northwestern, southeastern, and south-central United States and were enrolled in eight different program types. For the purpose of understanding the various models, the following are provided:

- a short case example of a beginning learner of English

- a description of the program model in which the student enrolled

- Collier and Thomas's findings about the model type

Programs That Promote Bilingualism and Biliteracy

When Ying was 5 years old, she moved from Beijing to Ocean City, on the west coast of the United States. She was given some language assessments that indicated that she was a beginning-level ML. The school principal told Ying and her family that she would have the opportunity to continue learning her native Mandarin while she learned English and that the school's goal was for her to become bilingual and biliterate in English and Mandarin. The dual-language program would include an ESL class and classes in Mandarin in language arts, mathematics, science, and social studies. The principal explained that about 90% of Ying's school day would include learning in Mandarin, and the remaining 10% would be in English. He stated that this would shift to 50% in each language by the time Ying reached third grade. He also explained that fluent English speakers were enrolled in the dual-language program as well. They spent 90% of their day learning in English and 10% learning in Mandarin, and the program model had the same goal of moving them to the 50/50 Mandarin/English model by third grade. Ying's family was excited that their daughter would continue to develop her skills in Mandarin while she learned English.

Several models are based on the belief that bilingualism and biliteracy are important and preferred goals. In some of these models, MLs maintain and continue to develop their primary languages while learning English (Collier & Thomas, 2002, 2004; Soltero, 2004). These are generally referred to as *bilingual maintenance* programs. In others, such as the program that Ying enrolled in, MLs and fluent speakers of English maintain and continue to develop their primary languages while learning a second language. These are generally referred to as *bilingual immersion* programs to reflect the participation of both English-fluent and EL populations. Bilingual immersion models draw on the belief that students learn best when they interact socially and academically in both languages and that language learning should be provided to participating students for at least 4 to 6 years. These models require a long-term commitment from parents, students, school personnel, and other stakeholders as well as a stable population of students to ensure the models' capacity to work (Howard & Christian, 2002).

In bilingual maintenance and immersion models, beginning learners of a target or second language spend most of their school day learning in their primary language and small amounts learning in the second language. As students increase their capacity to learn in the second language, classes are increased in this language. Often, these programs begin by introducing language arts classes in the second language, with content classes introduced as students develop increased skills in this language. A 90/10 model is an example of this: Students initially spend 90% of the school day learning in their primary language and 10% learning in the second language.

Bilingual immersion programs may begin for students in all grades. The idea is that students will continue to develop in their primary language and academically while learning a target language. Some bilingual immersion models are introduced for children in prekindergarten through second grade as a 90/10 model and then gradually move to a 50/50 model, some begin and continue as a 50/50 model, and some districts use different percentage increments for each language. As a result, there is wide variation among bilingual immersion programs (Goldenberg & Coleman, 2010;

Soltero, 2004). Optimal bilingual immersion programs have a solid balance of MLs and fluent speakers of English. The Center for Applied Linguistics (n.d.) and the Center for Research on Education, Diversity and Excellence (Howard & Christian, 2002) recommend that the total population of MLs be equal to the total population of English-fluent students, or at least represent one-third to two-thirds. Ensuring that these proportions are consistent throughout the grades is critical for bilingual immersion programming.

Generally, in bilingual maintenance and immersion models, language arts are continuously taught in the primary and target languages. Table 2.2 lists the various names for these bilingual biliterate models, and Table 2.3 shows more detail on a sample model.

Table 2.2   Programs That Promote Bilingualism and Biliteracy

PROGRAM TYPE	ALSO KNOWN AS	GOAL	CHARACTERISTICS
Maintenance bilingual education	Developmental Enrichment Heritage language	To develop bilingualism and biliteracy	All participants are MLs.
Bilingual immersion	Dual language Two way Double immersion Two-way immersion	To develop bilingualism and biliteracy	Participants consist of both MLs and fluent English speakers.

Table 2.3   Sample of a Bilingual Biliterate Program Model

YEAR 1	YEAR 2	YEAR 3	YEAR 4
Language arts in primary language	Language arts in primary language	Language arts in primary language	Language arts in primary language
Math in primary language	Math in target language	Math in target language	Math in target language
Science in primary language	Science in primary language	Science in target language	Science in target language
Technology in primary language	Technology in primary language	Technology in primary language	Technology in primary language
Social studies in primary language	Social studies in primary language	Social studies in primary language	Social studies in primary language
Language arts in target language	Language arts in target language	Language arts in target language	Language arts in target language

Shaded cells show the transition from primary to target language.

Collier and Thomas (2002) found that students who participated in a bilingual biliterate model had the best outcome among all the program models that they studied (see Table 2.4).

Table 2.4 English Achievement Findings From Standardized Tests of Reading for Students in Bilingual Biliterate Programs	
PROGRAM TYPE	**FINDINGS**
90/10 two-way bilingual immersion: primary language is provided 90% of the time in Grades PreK–2 and gradually reduced to 50%	Students performed above grade level by Grade 5 and outperformed comparison groups.
50/50 two-way bilingual immersion	58% of students met or exceeded state standards in English reading by the end of Grades 3 and 5.
50/50 one-way developmental bilingual education: one group is being educated in two languages	Students reached the 72nd percentile after 4 years of bilingual schooling and continued to be above grade level in Grade 7.
90/10 one-way developmental bilingual education: primary language is provided 90% of the time and gradually decreases to 50% by Grade 5 and continues in secondary school	Students reached the 34th percentile by the end of Grade 5.

Source: Collier and Thomas (2002).

Programs That Promote Transitional Bilingual Education

When Juan was 5 years old, he moved from Puerto Rico to a city on the east coast of the United States. His new school provided MLs with a program for gradually transitioning from Spanish to English. Juan would spend his kindergarten year receiving ESL instruction in lieu of English language arts, and his math, science, and social studies instruction would be in Spanish. Art, music, and physical education instruction would occur in English with his grade-level English-fluent classmates. In first grade, he would transition from receiving math in Spanish to receiving it in English in the general first-grade classroom. In second grade, the same transition would occur with science and social studies. In third grade, he would move fully out of the transitional bilingual education program to the general education classroom, where he would be taught solely in English.

Transitional bilingual education models like this promote a gradual reduction of the primary language as students learn English. The major goal is for students to build their capacity to learn solely in English. Typically, students begin by learning most subjects in their primary language and receiving ESL instruction. Initially, transitional programs may look like maintenance programs. However, over time students are gradually transitioned to an all-English environment.

There are two types of transitional models (see Table 2.5). In an *early-exit* program, students move from learning in the primary language to learning in English when they have demonstrated the capacity to do ordinary classwork in English. In a *late-exit* program, students continue to learn in the primary language for a few more years after they have demonstrated proficiency in English. Most programs in the United States are early-exit programs (Soltero, 2004) and do not yield the same successes as late-exit programs. Table 2.6 shows more detail on a sample transitional program.

Table 2.5   Programs That Promote Transitional Bilingual Education

PROGRAM TYPE	GOAL	CHARACTERISTICS
Early exit	To develop the ability to learn solely in English in general education classrooms conducted entirely in English	MLs receive instruction in their primary language and English. Students transition from learning in the primary language as their ability to learn in English increases.
Late exit	To develop the ability to learn solely in English in general education classrooms that are conducted entirely in English with a continuation of the native language for a few years after English proficiency is demonstrated	MLs receive instruction in their primary language and English. Students transition from learning in their primary language a few years after they demonstrate proficiency in English.

Table 2.6   Sample of a Transitional Bilingual Education Program Model

YEAR 1	YEAR 2	YEAR 3	YEAR 4
Language arts in primary language	Language arts in primary language	Language arts in primary language	Language arts taught in general English-instructed classroom
Math in primary language	Math taught in general English-instructed classroom	Math taught in general English-instructed classroom	Math taught in general English-instructed classroom
Science/technology in primary language	Science/technology in primary language	Science/technology taught in general English-instructed classroom	Science/technology taught in general English-instructed classroom
Social studies in primary language	Social studies in primary language	Social studies in primary language	Social studies taught in general English-instructed classroom
English as a second language	English as a second language	English as a second language	English language arts taught in general English-instructed classroom

Shaded cells show the transition from primary to target language.

Collier and Thomas's (2002) study also included outcomes for students who participated in transitional bilingual educational programming. Table 2.7 describes their finding that students who participated in late-exit programs had better outcomes than students in early-exit programs.

Table 2.7	English Achievement Findings From Standardized Tests of Reading for Students in Transitional Bilingual Education Programs	
PROGRAM TYPE	**FINDINGS**
90/10 transitional bilingual education: 90% of instruction in Grades PreK–2 is in primary language, and this decreases until Grade 5, when all instruction is in English in the general education classroom	Students reached the 32nd percentile by the end of Grade 5.
50/50 transitional bilingual education: instruction is 50% in both primary and target languages for 3–4 years, followed by English immersion in the general education classroom	Students achieved the 47th percentile by Grade 11.

Source: Collier and Thomas (2002).

Programs That Use English to Teach English

Example 1

When Lily was 5 years old, she moved from Poland to a small town in the midwestern United States. She had never been exposed to English, and language testing found her to be a beginning learner. In her new school, she left her kindergarten classroom to meet with her ESL teacher, who gave her instruction for 90 minutes a day. The rest of the day, Lily remained with her English-fluent classmates in the classroom. Her kindergarten teacher had never worked with an EL and received no specialized help to do so.

Example 2

When Fernanda moved from Cape Verde to Massachusetts at the age of 5, she had never been taught in English. She was placed in a kindergarten classroom with a teacher who had been trained to teach English and content to MLs. Twice a week, Fernanda left class for 30 minutes to work with an ESL teacher.

Example 3

When Petro moved from Ukraine to New York at the age of 5, he too had never been exposed to English. He was placed in a kindergarten classroom with a teacher who had been trained to teach MLs. He also was provided with a bilingual Ukrainian/English-speaking aide who helped him understand his classes and become acquainted with his new school and classmates. Every day for an hour, Petro's ESL teacher came into his class and provided him and the other MLs with instruction in English.

Generally, programs that use only English with MLs include ESL classes. They can also, but do not always, include content classes that are specifically designed and delivered for students to learn English as they learn content. This is commonly called *sheltered English immersion* and/or *content-based ESL* (Echevarria et al., 2017; Soltero, 2004). These programs also can, but do not always, include bilingual support or clarification in the native language, whereby instruction is delivered in English and explained in the primary language as needed. This model is often used when there are speakers of many different languages and not enough of any one language to implement bilingual programming. Table 2.8 lists the various names for this model, and Tables 2.9 and 2.10 show more detail on sample models.

Table 2.8   Programs That Use English to Teach English

PROGRAM TYPE	ALSO KNOWN AS	GOAL	CHARACTERISTICS
Structured English immersion	Pull out Push in Content-based ESL ESL pull out ESL	To develop the ability to learn solely in English in general education classrooms conducted entirely in English	MLs are taught entirely in English with little to no support in their native language.

Table 2.9   Sample of a Structured English Immersion Model That Includes Content Classes

YEAR 1	YEAR 2	YEAR 3	YEAR 4
English as a second language	English as a second language	English as a second language	English language arts in general classroom
Math taught using structured format	Math taught using structured format	Math taught in general classroom	Math taught in general classroom
Science/technology taught using structured format	Science/technology taught using structured format	Science/technology taught in general classroom	Science/technology taught in general classroom
Social studies taught using structured format	Social studies taught using structured format	Social studies taught using structured format	Social studies taught in general classroom

Shaded cells show the transition from primary to target language.

Table 2.10   Sample of a Structured English Immersion/ESL Pull-Out Model

YEAR 1	YEAR 2	YEAR 3	YEAR 4
English as a second language	English as a second language	English as a second language	English taught in general classroom
Math taught in English in general classroom	Math taught in English in general classroom	Math taught in English in general classroom	Math taught in English in general classroom
Science/technology taught in English in general classroom	Science/technology taught in English in general classroom	Science/technology taught in English in general classroom	Science/technology taught in English in general classroom
Social studies taught in English in general classroom	Social studies taught in English in general classroom	Social studies taught in English in general classroom	Social studies taught in English in general classroom

Shaded cells show the transition from primary to target language.

In Table 2.11, you can see the results of Collier and Thomas's (2002) study regarding MLs who participated in program models that used English to teach English. Generally, students did not fare well in this model.

Table 2.11   English Achievement Findings From Standardized Tests of Reading for Students in Programs That Use English to Teach English

PROGRAM TYPE	FINDINGS
ESL content classes provided for 2–3 years, followed by immersion in general education classes	Average score on tests was at the 23rd percentile by high school.

Source: Collier and Thomas (2002).

Researchers from the Center for Applied Linguistics and the Center for Research on Education, Diversity and Excellence worked closely with teachers to secure a better-articulated model of sheltering instruction. Through years of research and collaboration with teachers, they developed the Sheltered Instruction Observation Protocol (SIOP; Echevarria et al., 2017), which includes eight elements for planning and delivering instruction and providing clarification in the native language. While the SIOP model is not intended for beginning learners of English, when it has been employed by teachers who are trained to use it, student performance has been found to increase dramatically. The researchers claim that the model works well with students from a variety of prior schooling experiences and in a variety of classroom situations, including those composed solely of MLs as well as those with MLs and fluent speakers of English. Because of this work, it may be that the conclusions we draw about the efficacy of various program models from Collier and Thomas's (2002) study need to be refined.

What happens when students are provided with no support to learn English?

When Alberto moved to New York from Colombia, his parents refused to let him participate in the bilingual program in his new school. They believed that he would be better off in the general kindergarten classroom with his English-fluent peers.

As Figure 2.12 shows, Collier and Thomas's (2002) study also looked at the educational outcomes of students like Alberto, whose parents refused to have their children participate in any programming for MLs. Sadly, this group did the poorest among all the groups.

Table 2.12	English Achievement Findings From Standardized Tests of Reading for Students With No Specialized Language Programming
PROGRAM TYPE	**FINDINGS**
No specialized language programming for MLs	Students performed significantly less well in math by Grade 5 than peers in bilingual programs and had the highest dropout rate among all groups. Those remaining in school scored at the 25th percentile on standardized reading tests during their high school years.

Source: Collier and Thomas (2002).

Programs That Are Targeted for Students With Limited Prior Schooling

As mentioned earlier in this chapter, some MLs have not had consistent education. It is essential that these students' learning needs be intentionally addressed as they learn English. Students with limited or interrupted formal education have experienced significant educational disruptions in their home country due to war, civil crisis, natural disaster, or severe economic deprivation. Many schools have implemented programming specifically designed for MLs with interrupted or limited formal education. In addition, several resources are available to support educators in meeting the needs of this population (Calderón & Minaya-Rowe, 2010; Calderón & Montenegro, 2021; Custudio & O'Loughlin, 2017; Decapua et al., 2020). Table 2.13 describes this type of programming, and Table 2.14 shows more detail on a sample model. The following characteristics are commonly found in programs that are targeted for these students (Calderón & Montenegro, 2021; Echevarria et al., 2017; Freeman & Freeman, 2002; Short & Boyson, 2003; Soltero, 2004, 2016):

- is separate from what is offered to the general student population

- specifically addresses the particular gaps and social-emotional, language, and learning needs of students

- includes courses in English language, literacy development, and U.S. cultural practices

- uses curriculum materials targeted to students' English proficiency levels

- adapts instruction often using theme-based units of study

- allocates the appropriate number of personnel resources needed to address students' needs

- contains an outreach component to families to build connections between the school, family, and student

- is taught in English or the primary language of students

Table 2.13   Programs for Students With Limited Prior Schooling

PROGRAM TYPE	ALSO KNOWN AS	GOAL	CHARACTERISTICS
Programs for students with limited prior schooling	Newcomer programs	To learn English and catch up with peers in order to be able to handle grade-level content	Instruction may be in the primary language or English, and the population typically includes secondary school–age students. Programming is separate from the general education classroom. Personnel resources are allocated to provide instruction in English and content.

Table 2.14   Sample of Programs for Students With Limited Prior Schooling

YEAR 1	YEAR 2	YEAR 3
English as a second language	English as a second language	English as a second language
Math taught at student's academic level*	Math taught at student's academic level*	Math taught at student's academic level*
Science/technology taught at student's academic level*	Science/technology taught at student's academic level*	Science/technology taught at student's academic level*
Social studies taught at student's academic level*	Social studies taught at student's academic level*	Social studies taught at student's academic level*

*May be taught in English, the primary language, and/or English with clarification support in the primary language.

What does the research tell us?

Whether students are enrolled in bilingual maintenance or sheltered English models, these models are more effective when they incorporate students' native language (Collier & Thomas, 2020; Francis et al., 2006; Goldenberg & Coleman, 2010; Slavin & Cheung, 2005). At the same time, selecting a program model depends on a number of variables. It is important to consider the following when designing a program for MLs:

- its context within a specific school and/or district

- the needs of the students and the resources available for implementation

- the number of students involved

- the languages and grades that students represent

- students that have had limited or interrupted formal education

- students' prior school experiences

Regardless of which program is chosen, there can be no doubt that the quality and overall effectiveness of programming depends on the structures that leaders, teachers, specialists, and others create to support implementation. In the next chapter, we will discuss the steps for selecting the program model(s) for your school.

References

American Institutes for Research & WestEd. (2002). *Effects of the implementation of Proposition 227 on the education of English learners, K–12: Year 2 report.* http://www.wested.org/online_pubs/year2finalrpt.pdf

August, D., & Shanahan, T. (2006). *Literacy in second language learners: Report of the National Literacy Panel on Language Minority Children and Youth.* Lawrence Erlbaum.

August, D., & Shanahan, T. (2008). *Developing reading and writing in second language learners: Lessons from a report of the National Literacy Panel on Language Minority Children and Youth.* Routledge.

Baker, C. (2006). *Foundations of bilingual education and bilingualism* (4th ed.). Multilingual Matters.

Burdick-Will, J., & Gomez, C. (2006). *Assimilation versus multiculturalism: Bilingual education and the Latino challenge.* Lawrence Erlbaum.

Calderón, M. E., & Minaya-Rowe, L. (2010). *Preventing long-term MLs: Transforming schools to meet core standards.* Corwin.

Calderón, M., & Montenegro, H. (2021). *Empowering long-term Els with social-emotional learning, language, and literacy.* Valázquez Press.

Center for Applied Linguistics. (n.d.). Two-way immersion education: The basics. https://www.cal.org/twi/toolkit/PI/Basics_Eng.pdf

Collier, V., & Thomas, W. (1989). How quickly can immigrants become proficient in school English? *Journal of Educational Issues of Language Minority Students, 5,* 26–38.

Collier, V., & Thomas, W. (2002). *A national study of school effectiveness for language minority students' long-term academic achievement.* Center for Research on Education, Diversity and Excellence. http://eric.ed.gov/ERICWebPortal/contentdelivery/servlet/ERICServlet?accno=ED436087

Collier, V., & Thomas, W. (2004, Winter). *The astounding effectiveness of dual language education for all*. https://www.berkeleyschools.net/wp-content/uploads/2011/10/TWIAstounding_Effectiveness_Dual_Language_Ed.pdf?864d7e

Collier, V., & Thomas, W. (2020). *Why dual language works for everyone PK–12*. https://www.gocabe.org/wp-content/uploads/2020/02/CABE-ME-MAG2020WEB.pdf

Cooper, A. (2021). *And justice for ELs: A leader's guide to creating and sustaining equitable schools*. Corwin Press.

Crawford, J. (1996). *Bilingual education: History, politics, theory, and practice*. Bilingual Education Services.

Cummins, J. (1981). Age on arrival and immigrant second language learning in Canada: A reassessment. *Applied Linguistics, 2*, 132–149.

Cummins, J. (2000). *Language, power, and pedagogy: Bilingual children in the crossfire*. Multilingual Matters.

Cummins, J. (2018). Foreword. In O. García & J. A. Kleifgen (Eds.), *Educating emergent bilinguals: Policies, programs, and practices for English learners* (2nd ed., pp ix–x). Teachers College Press.

Cummins, J., & Swain, M. (1986). *Bilingualism in education*. Longman.

Custudio, B. K., & O'Loughlin, J. B. (2017). *Students with interrupted formal education: Bridging where they are and what they need*. Corwin.

Decapua, A., Marshall, H. W., & Tang, F. (2020). *Meeting the needs of SLIFE: A guide for educators* (2nd ed.). University of Michigan Press.

Dunklee, D. R., & Shoop, R. J. (2006). *The principal's quick reference guide to school law: Reducing liability, litigation, and other potential legal tangles*. Corwin.

Dweck, C. (2006). *Mindset: The new psychology of success*. Ballantine Books.

Dweck, C., Walton, G. M., & Cohen, G. L. (2014). *Academic tenacity: Mindsets and skills that promote long-term learning*. https://ed.stanford.edu/sites/default/files/manual/dweck-walton-cohen-2014.pdf

Echevarria, J., Vogt, M., & Short, D. (2017). *Making content comprehensible for English learners: The SIOP model* (5th ed.). Pearson.

Felitti, V. J., Anda, R. F., Nordenberg, D., Williamson, D. F., Spitz, A. M., Edwards, V., Koss, M. P., & Marks, J. S. (1998). *Relationship of childhood abuse and household dysfunction to many of the leading causes of death in adults: The Adverse Childhood Experiences (ACE) Study*. http://erikwblack.pbworks.com/w/file/fetch/104348885/AllFilesIPLH2.2016.pdf

Francis, D., Lesaux, M., & August, D. (2006). Language of instruction. In D. August & T. Shanahan (Eds.), *Developing literacy in second-language learners: Report of the National Literacy Panel on Language-Minority Children and Youth* (pp. 365–413). Lawrence Erlbaum.

Freeman, Y. S., & Freeman, D. E. (with Mercuri, S.). (2002). *Closing the achievement gap: How to reach limited-formal schooling and long-term English learners*. Heinemann.

Genesee, F., Lindholm-Leary, K., Saunders, W., & Christian, D. (2006). *Educating English language learners*. Cambridge University Press.

Goldenberg, C., & Coleman, R. (2010). *Promoting academic achievement among English learners: A guide to the research*. Corwin.

Gonzalez, N., Moll, L. C., & Amanti, C. (Eds.). (2005). *Funds of knowledge: Theorizing practices in households, communities, and classrooms*. Lawrence Erlbaum.

Gonzalez, R. D. (2000). *Critical perspectives of the English only movement* (Vol. 1). Lawrence Erlbaum.

Hart, B., & Risley, T. R. (1995). *Meaningful differences in everyday experiences of young American children.* Paul H. Brookes.

Horn, C. L., & Kurlaender, M. (2006). *The end of Keyes: Resegregation trends and achievement in Denver Public Schools.* Civil Rights Project at Harvard University.

Howard, E. R., & Christian, D. (2002). *Two-way immersion 101: Designing and implementing a two-way immersion program at the elementary level.* Center for Research on Education, Diversity and Excellence. https://www.cal.org/twi/pdfs/two-way-immersion-101.pdf

Krashen, S. (1985). *The input hypothesis: Issues and implications.* Laredo.

Maslow, A. H. (1987). *Motivation and personality* (3rd ed.). Pearson Education.

Maslow, A. H. (1999). *Toward a psychology of being* (3rd ed.). John Wiley & Sons.

Mendoza, M., & Ayala, H. (1999). *English language education for children in public schools.* http://www.onenation.org/aztext.html

Mid-Atlantic Equity Consortium. (1995). *Legal responsibilities of education agencies serving language minority students.* Author.

Montero, R., & Chavez, J. (2001). *Be it enacted by the people of the state of Colorado.* http://www.onenation.org/cotext.html

Napolitano, J. (2021). *The school I deserve: Six young refugees and their fight for equality in America.* Beacon Press.

National Academies of Sciences, Engineering, and Medicine. (2017). *Promoting the educational success of children and youth learning English: Promising futures.* National Academies Press. https://doi.org/10.17226/24677

Osorio-O'Dea, P. (2001). *Bilingual education: An overview.* http://www.policyalmanac.org/education/archive/bilingual.pdf

Philadelphia ACE Project. (2021). *Philadelphia ACE Survey.* https://www.philadelphiaaces.org/philadelphia-ace-survey

Reese, J. (2005). *America's public schools: From the common school to "No Child Left Behind."* Johns Hopkins University Press.

Short, D. J., & Boyson, B. A. (2003). *Establishing an effective newcomer program.* Center for Applied Linguistics.

Slavin, R., & Cheung, A. (2005). A synthesis of research on language of reading instruction for English language learners. *Review of Educational Research, 75,* 247–281.

Seligman, M. E. P., Rashid, T., & Parks, A. C. (2006). Positive psychotherapy. *American Psychologist, 61*(8), 774–788.

Soltero, S. W. (2004). *Dual language: Teaching and learning in two languages.* Pearson.

Soltero, S. W. (2016). *Dual language education: Program design and implementation.* Heinemann.

Tamayo, L., Porter, R., & Rossell, C. (2001). *An initiative petition for a law: An act relative to the teaching of English in public schools.* http://www.onenation.org/matext.html

Unz, R., & Tuchman, G. M. (1997). *English language education for children in public schools.* http://www.onenation.org/fulltext.html

Uriarte, M., & Karp, F. (2009). *English language learners in Massachusetts: Trends in enrolments and outcomes.* Mauricio Gaston Institute for Latino Development and Public Policy. http://www.gaston.umb.edu/UserFiles/09ELLsinMA%20brief.pdf

U.S. Department of Education. (2002). *No Child Left Behind: A desktop reference.* http://www2.ed.gov/admins/lead/account/nclbreference/reference.pdf

U.S. Department of Education. (2016, November). *Tools and resources for monitoring and exiting English learners from EL programs and services.* https://www2.ed.gov/about/offices/list/oela/english-learner-toolkit/chap8.pdf

U.S. Department of Education (n.d.). *Every Student Succeeds Act (ESSA)*. https://www
.ed.gov/essa?src=rn

U.S. Department of Justice, Office of Civil Rights. (n.d.). *Title VI of the Civil Rights Act of
1964*. https://www.justice.gov/crt/fcs/TitleVI

U.S. Department of Justice & U.S. Department of Education. (2015, January 7). *Dear
colleague*. https://www2.ed.gov/about/offices/list/ocr/letters/colleague-el-201501.pdf

Zacarian, D., Alvarez-Ortiz, L., & Haynes, J. (2017). *Teaching to strengths: Supporting
students living with trauma, violence, and chronic stress*. ASCD.

Zacarian, D., Calderón, & Gottlieb, M. (2021). *Beyond crises: Overcoming linguistic and
cultural inequities in communities, schools, and classrooms*. Corwin.

CHAPTER 3

Selecting Effective Program Models

When elementary school principal Mr. Paxton began working at Main Street School in a small city, he learned that a significant number of multilingual families had moved into a newly opened apartment complex and that their children would be attending his school. Assuming that the children would be multilingual learners (MLs), he began to consider the various **language assistance program** model options that would work best for the students and his school. What steps should Mr. Paxton take as he makes this important decision?

In this chapter we discuss the various steps that should be involved in selecting appropriate program models. As with the earlier chapters in the book, we use an asset-based approach that draws from the strengths and assets of our students, families, and ourselves.

Identifying MLs

Initially, the most important step is identifying the MLs in each school. This information is needed to determine the program model or models that are best suited. The following questions are intended to help in the process:

1. What steps are needed for effectively identifying MLs?

2. What additional information should be included about the students to select, plan, and deliver the most effective model?

One might think that, because the dominant population in most U.S. schools is monolingual speakers of English, a home language survey seems like a nice but unnecessary or even impractical idea. A school may decide that it can figure out on its own which families should be given the survey. But how would a school know? Would it be when a parent speaks with an accent? This may lead to unintended discriminatory practices, and a school may miss many potential MLs if this process is done by guesswork alone. Therefore, a home language survey should be given to every new enrollee. The sample survey provided in Resource 3.1 includes a series of questions about a child's language use with family members and others as well as a few questions about prior schooling.

A *home language survey* is by far the most common tool to determine who might or might not be an ML. It is intended for use in determining who should be assessed. The purpose is not to decide who is and is not an ML. This document should be furnished to families at enrollment, one for each enrollee, as a means of initially determining the students who use a language other than English. For example, Mr. Paxton will include this as part of the enrollment forms that families will complete.

If the answer to any question on the home language survey indicates that a child uses a language other than English (e.g., when speaking with friends or a grandparent), the child must be assessed to determine whether they are an ML. As we learned in Chapter 2, according to federal regulation, MLs must be identified. The home language survey is a crucial first step in this process.

However, this survey should not be the only means of identifying MLs. Some parents may indicate that their children use only English when that is, in fact, not the case. This may occur for a variety of reasons, including the fear that their children will not be allowed to attend school or will not be treated like other children. When a school suspects that a student may be an ML, the student must be assessed.

Screening New Students to Identify MLs

The federal definition of an ML is a student who is not yet able to do ordinary class-work in English. The capacity to do ordinary classwork requires English proficiency in all four areas: listening, speaking, reading, and writing. The purpose of identification assessments is threefold:

- identifying a student's need for services
- establishing an ML's English proficiency level
- determining the number of MLs in a district and their English language and learning needs

There are reliable, commercially available screening tests that are designed specifically for identifying MLs. The following are commonly used English language proficiency tests:

- IDEA Proficiency Test (IPT)
- Language Assessment Scales (LAS)
- WIDA Screener

Educators should refer to the specific regulations of their state education agency (SEA) for information about what initial screening assessments they are required to use to identify MLs. For example, the Massachusetts Department of Elementary and Secondary Education (2022) states that districts must use the following:

> To screen students in grades 1–12, districts must use WIDA screening assessments, including *WIDA Screener online* and paper forms. To screen students in kindergarten, districts must use *K W-APT, K WIDA MODEL or K WIDA Screener* for initial identification. For students in pre-kindergarten districts must use *Pre-IPT, pre-LAS or pre-LAS Observational Tool.* (p. 7)

Assessment in the Primary Language

It is very helpful, when possible, to test students in both their primary language and English, especially for the purposes of planning and implementing bilingual programming. Doing so provides key information about a student's ability to listen, speak, read, and write in both languages.

Educators should check with their SEAs to determine if conducting identification testing in a language other than or in addition to English is in compliance with state requirements.

When Identification Testing Should Be Done

Potential MLs should be tested as soon as possible. State regulations may require schools to complete identification testing within a certain period after enrollment. A good rule of thumb is to assess a student within their first 5 days at school. There are two very good reasons for completing identification testing quickly:

1. It allows a school to determine programming needs as soon as possible.

2. It enables students who have been identified as MLs to receive appropriate programming as soon as possible.

Allocating Staff and Time for Testing

Educators should consult with their SEA to determine whether those who identify MLs must be properly licensed (also known as credentialed) to do so. Generally, credentialed practitioners and/or teachers trained to administer identification testing should be the ones to do it. In the absence of this, leaders/supervisors of ML programming must make every effort to assign and train staff to do this task according to their SEA's regulations. They must also ensure that there is enough staff to complete the testing that needs to be done in a timely manner. Further, whoever is assigned to do it must be proficient in the language that is being tested.

It is helpful for districts to keep a record of the time that it takes to conduct their identification testing and to use these calculations from year to year to estimate the time needed for it. Most testing is administered individually and may take anywhere from just a couple of minutes (e.g., for MLs with no prior exposure to English) to an hour or more; the more proficiency a student has in the language being tested, and the older the student, the longer the assessment will probably take. The time needed to complete this task is important to factor into one's planning. School administrators, ML identification evaluators, scheduling staff, and others involved in the ML screening process, especially those in districts with large numbers of MLs, should also calculate the anticipated number of enrollees per year and the hours needed for identification testing so that this activity can be completed successfully, efficiently, and in the shortest time possible.

It is also important that the testing be done in a comfortable, quiet location to ensure the most accurate results. This may mean having staff travel to the school in which the student is enrolled or training staff in each school to provide the testing. Districts that have central registration centers should allocate appropriate space for identification testing to occur.

Documenting Language Proficiency Test Findings

It is important to document test findings and use the data. Resource 3.2 is a sample document for summarizing test findings as well as tracking student growth. This and the home language survey provide key information about the MLs who have been identified.

Including a Family and/or Student Interview When an ML Is Identified

As essential as they are, neither the home language survey nor ML testing provides information about a student's prior schooling; personal, social, cultural, and life experiences; needs; dreams; interests; and other relevant information. When a student is identified as an ML, it is important to gather such information in order to design and implement successful programming. This is particularly true for students with limited or interrupted formal education. An interview with the family and/or their child is an important next step. Resource 3.3, a sample parent/student interview, is intended to support districts in this activity. Families and students should be provided with bilingual staff/translators as needed to conduct the interview or provide the needed interpreting support for the interview.

It is also important to note that the first interaction with families sets the tone for the future and that as much as the meeting is to gather information, it is also to support families in building partnerships with you on behalf of their child's education. Anticipate that meetings held with the support of translators will take longer than meetings with students and families who are fluent in English.

Analyzing Home Language Survey, Testing, and Interview Findings

The initial analysis of home language survey, ML assessment, and interview data guides school leaders, teachers, specialists, and all involved in selecting the most appropriate ML program model(s) for their school or district. Programming should be understood as an inclusive way for a school's MLs to be active learners in and members of their school community. The more information that is gathered, the better the chances that the program model will be successful.

Determining commonalities and differences in the data is crucial for selecting the most appropriate program model. For example: Do many of the district's MLs speak the same primary language? Are they in the same grades, separated among all the grades, or scattered throughout the district? Are there commonalities in their language proficiency levels? Resource 3.5 was created to help districts sort through and collate the findings of the assessment/enrollment process and select program models. Each category has been separated by grade as well as by the following:

- home language

- country of origin

- English proficiency level

- interrupted or limited prior schooling

- receiving free or reduced-price lunch

- receiving Title 1 services

Program model options will become clearer through the analysis process. For example, a district may find that it has many speakers of the same language and that a dual-language program model is therefore an optimal choice.

Creating a Work Group to Develop or Revise Program Models

It is very helpful to form committees or work groups to design programming for MLs. The U.S. Department of Education (2020) suggests that these be as inclusive and comprehensive as possible: "administrators, teachers . . . , educational assistants, school counselors, and other staff who work with the district's ELL student population . . . [as well as] parents, students, or community representatives who work with the same students in other settings" (para. 3). It also states that committees should take steps to evaluate success and to make changes when needed. It calls for those who facilitate or lead work groups to continuously do so

- with a sense of collaborative curiosity, openness, and flexibility to various perspectives;

- by promoting and nurturing the mission of selecting and analyzing the efficacy of their language assistance model choices.

Let's look at the steps that Mr. Paxton took to form a working committee.

Case example: By analyzing data about actual students, Mr. Paxton learned that 34 MLs would be enrolling in his school, 23 of whom spoke Mandarin. Some of their families had moved to the city to work in local Chinese restaurants and others to work in one of the city's agricultural companies. Through the family interviews that were conducted, Mr. Paxton learned that some of the MLs had attended school in their home countries and engaged in literacy learning activities that were similar to the activities conducted in his school and some had had interruptions to their education. In addition, there were two Egyptian speakers of Arabic, five Puerto Rican speakers of Spanish, and four Brazilian speakers of Portuguese with various prior school experiences.

Mr. Paxton invited parent and community representatives from each of the language groups to join a work group that would advise him in selecting a program model for the children. Bilingual staff and translators were also included to ensure that parents and school personnel could communicate well and that parents would feel welcome and comfortable. Initially, some of the parents did not want their children to participate in any specialized program. They assumed that their children would learn English more quickly if they remained in the general English-instructed classroom. The work group meetings provided time for the parents to learn about the value of ML programs, and various research-based models for those programs, while school personnel learned much about the families and their communities. Their interactions reflected the preponderance of research about the tremendous benefits of culturally and linguistically diverse work groups (Güver & Motschnig, 2017). Indeed, their collaborative dialogue laid the foundation for a very important relationship built on mutual respect and trust between the school and the family communities, which had many long-term benefits aside from the specific task of discussing program models.

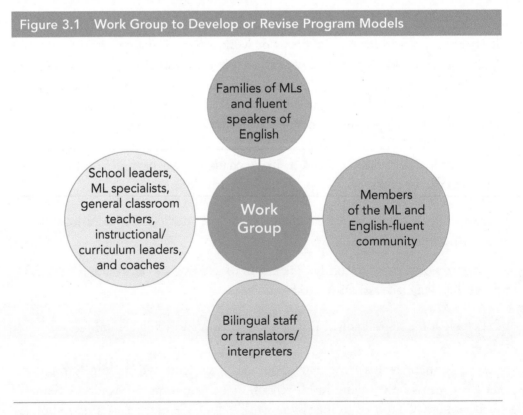

Figure 3.1   Work Group to Develop or Revise Program Models

The work group in Mr. Paxton's school recommended a program of *dual language* education for its Mandarin speakers and a *structured English immersion model* with clarification in the native language for the other language groups. Parent participation helped in many ways

- to secure the multilingual staff and tutors needed, and

- to be more intentional in creating inclusive programming that supported MLs in being more active and participatory.

Like Mr. Paxton chose to do, the U.S. Department of Education (2020) suggests that districts organize work groups for developing ML programming and that they include the following groups:

- school leaders and teachers, including teachers of MLs and general classroom teachers;

- parents;

- students; and

- community representatives of MLs.

A comprehensive plan is more likely to occur with support from these stakeholders. It is far more likely that it will be inclusive, supportive, and meaningful if many members are involved in it. A work group can greatly help in assessing what is working and what needs strengthening. A work group can also help in identifying school, district, and community resources on behalf of MLs' overall success in and out of school and their parents in being our partners in their child's education. The case example highlights the importance of work groups in selecting a program model(s). Figure 3.2 illustrates three elements of what a work group should focus on:

- the academic and social-emotional development of students

- instructional practices that capitalize and expand on the rich cultures, languages, and positive identities of MLs

- carefully and strategically implementing and evaluating plans for MLs to possess full and high levels of proficiency in academic and social language and social-emotional development

Figure 3.2 Work Group Goals

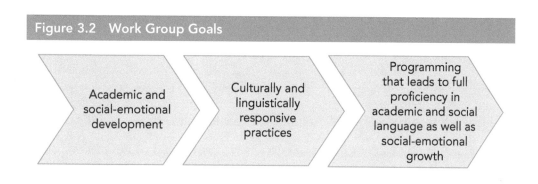

Gathering Information About Program Model Options Based on Sound Research

Whether a district is new to providing programming for MLs or expanding and/or revising its programming, it is important that it select a research-based model that is most likely to be successful in ensuring that MLs

- become proficient in English,

- learn subject matter at grade level,

- are integrated with English-fluent peers and members of the school community, and

- demonstrate high levels of proficiency in academic and social language and social-emotional development.

Educator, consultant, and renowned author Elisa MacDonald (2022) describes the importance of setting work group goals by considering the desired student outcomes and the pathways or strategies that the group will use to achieve these. The following are examples of the pathways that Mr. Paxton and the work group might enact:

- Identify MLs and get to know the students and families.

- Select an effective program model for MLs.

- Support implementation of the selected program model (e.g., securing the needed multilingual staff, instructional resources, space allocation, and professional development).

- Develop curriculum for English language and academic development for MLs.

- Adopt instructional practices that capitalize and expand on the rich cultures, languages, prior schooling, and positive identities of MLs.

- Carefully and strategically implement plans for MLs.

Resource 3.6 provides suggested readings that can greatly assist work groups in selecting and implementing program models.

In addition, the goals for MLs should be the same as for non-ML students; that is, the goals for all students should be inclusive of MLs.

Defining the Goals of the Work Group

The following questions are intended to support the work group:

1. How will the selected model promote the overall goals and vision of the district?

2. How will it address the English language development and content learning needs of all the MLs who have been identified?

3. What staffing, instructional, personnel, and professional development resources are needed to support this ML program model?

4. How will the model support, as seamlessly as possible, MLs in achieving full proficiency in academic and social language and social-emotional growth?

5. What methods will be used to determine the effectiveness of the model and any changes that are needed to strengthen its outcomes?

6. How will families be involved as partners? What does that involvement look like?

It is fundamental that the program provide MLs with meaningful access to the school district's educational programming. Each district has its own, individual circumstances as well as mission and vision for its students, and the program that is selected for its MLs should strongly relate to these. Figure 3.3 helps guide us in the program selection process.

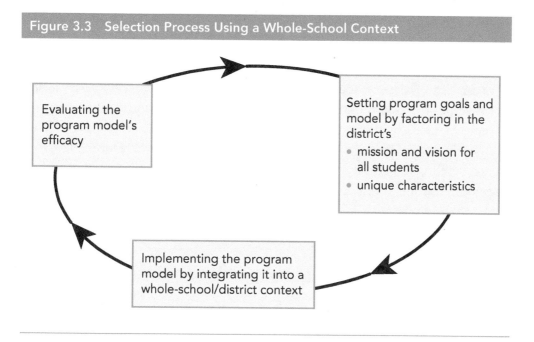

Figure 3.3   Selection Process Using a Whole-School Context

Selecting Program Models

School leaders must also determine the time frame in which the goals for its MLs will be reached and how success will be measured. In Chapter 2, we learned that MLs are not a monolithic group. A school needs to create and implement a differentiated program model while integrating it within the context of the whole school. To do this, educators must consider the school's mission and vision for all learners *and* integrate the programming for MLs seamlessly into the mission so that it affirms the goal of supporting students to feel safe, a sense of belonging, value, and competence.

One mistake to avoid is creating one set of program characteristics and expectations for all MLs. Doing so usually disadvantages students who don't yet possess school-matched literacy skills in their home language. In the case presented earlier, for example, Mr. Paxton learned that some of the Mandarin-speaking MLs in his school had prior literacy learning experiences that were similar to those in his school and some had had interruptions to their education. He ensured that newcomers from the latter group were given additional supports and time to learn English and subject matter. He also created a study group that met throughout the school year. Teachers read books on students with limited and interrupted schooling and explored different approaches that they tried with these students (see Resource 3.6 for resource suggestions on this topic).

Another mistake to avoid, one that is often made unintentionally, is segregating MLs. This may occur because programming is thought of as separate from, and not part of, a whole-school community. Indeed, whether it is done unintentionally or intentionally, segregation of linguistic-minority students is known to be a major problem in U.S. schools (Gándara, 2010) and should be avoided. Indeed, segregation has been identified as one of the most common reasons for noncompliance in adhering to federal laws (U.S. Department of Justice & U.S. Department of Education, 2015).

MLs can be in isolated schools or isolated within one school. In either case, it does not yield positive results in terms of MLs' academic performance and membership or status in their school community (Cohen & Lotan, 2014; Constantino de Cohen & Clewell, 2007; Dove & Honigsfeld, 2018, 2020; Zacarian & Dove, 2020). Mr. Paxton wisely considered the ways in which the MLs in his school would be actively engaged in learning communities with English-fluent peers.

Reexamining a School or District Mission, Vision, and Distinct Characteristics

An important step in selecting a program model is to reexamine a school's or district's core mission and vision to figure out optimal ways in which the ML program will complement and expand them. For example, a school district may have found that its core mission is to value diversity. While this mission may have been formed to honor students with learning differences and disabilities, the implementation of a program model for MLs can fit quite nicely with this mission. The same district may be in a rural farming community and thus designed and implemented its curriculum to connect with its environment. Some MLs and their families may not be familiar with this farming context and will need the opportunity to learn about it in a meaningful way. Similarly, a school within a district may be designated as the site for students with significant disabilities. If it is decided that the program model for MLs is to be implemented in this school, efforts should be made to help the two programs be part of the school community as a whole and not two separate programs within the school.

Integrating a Program Model in a Whole-School Context

As the various program models are examined, school leaders must take time to determine how the model will be integrated meaningfully in the school. This requires a real examination of and reflection about the everyday routines that occur and how these will interact seamlessly with the program model that is implemented. It also requires school leaders to become familiar with MLs and their families and take additional steps to reexamine various common school activities to ensure that they are understood meaningfully by the ML community. Let's look at two examples. As you read them, think about the steps that you would take to help MLs and their families be fully integrated and participatory in your particular context.

Case example 1: Mrs. Fields sent her students home with a permission slip for a field trip to the science museum. When Tren, a Vietnamese ML, heard the phrase *going on a field trip,* he was afraid that the school would be taking him away from his mother. Acting on his fears, he did not bring the note home to his mother. Because he did not have a permission slip, he had to be left behind—the only one of his classmates to not go on the trip.

Case example 2: During Mr. Paxton's second year as the principal of Main Street School, a religious group sponsored several Somali refugees to live in the community. When they enrolled the Somali children in his school, he conducted a family interview, with the help of a translator, and learned that the children had not had any prior formal schooling and dressed very differently and had different dietary customs than their U.S. peers. To help the families feel welcome and learn more about the community, Mr. Paxton and his school's ML work group decided to meet with them during the first month of school. To prepare for the meeting, he made plans to meet with community representatives who were familiar with the Somali families.

In addition to the findings that are gathered about the identified MLs, the following factors should be considered to better ensure that effective programming is implemented. School leaders should plan these with the work group, teachers of MLs, and other stakeholders to ensure that they are as successful as possible:

- the district's or school's familiarity and experience with as well as preparation to work with the MLs who have been identified,

- how MLs and their families will be meaningfully informed about the school's routine practices and activities,

- the professional development needs of the district to teach its MLs,

- curriculum development for teaching English as a second language (ESL) and academic content to MLs, and

- how MLs' families, the school, and the district will partner together to support students' success.

Let's examine the Manthala George, Jr. Global Studies School, one of the Brockton Public Schools in Brockton, Massachusetts. Spanning Kindergarten to Grade 5, it offers dual-language programs in French, Portuguese, and Spanish. A top priority of the district's superintendent, Michael P. Thomas, is to support the physical and social-emotional well-being of students and families. In kind, a primary goal of this school is to empower students "to take an active role in their own learning to reach their greatest potential for academic, social, emotional and physical growth" (George Global Studies School, n.d., para. 1). One of the empowerment activities the school engages in is involving graduates in its recruitment efforts, which is emblematic of Brockton's efforts to provide students with meaningful community service projects to further the goal of empowerment. Below is an example from Montserrat V. Diazbotello (personal communication, March 31, 2022), a high school student who had attended the George Global Studies School through her elementary school years.

Translated from Spanish to English, here is what Montserrat shared with families about the power of her experience in the Juntos Spanish-English two-way program at the George Global Studies School:

> Two-way is an amazing program that can help your children develop their social and academic skills in another language. Two-way allows your kids to read, write, speak another language as they move up throughout school. They can eventually enhance these skills at a higher level than most when they reach a higher age. In high school, I was placed in a heritage program, where the language is taught in a proficient way. It serves as a bridge to participate in higher or college level Spanish classes the following year. I can also get the Seal of Biliteracy in high school, which is an official stamp saying I can understand the language at a distinguished degree. Looking even further into the future, it can also open more job opportunities. While in the program, your kids will also form connections with other kids speaking the language. Two-way has made me closer to many of my classmates that have been in the two-way since kindergarten. It has grown more into a family than a class. I would deeply consider this program for any parent or guardian that wishes to add another language to your child's learning experience, present and future, as well as gaining new social experiences.

Regardless of the program model that is selected, it is important for school leaders, teachers, and others who work with MLs to learn as much as possible about the students and their families. In addition to the family survey (seen in Resource 3.3), newly identified MLs should be asked about their interests and strengths to assist educators in building an asset-based language assistance program. Resource 3.4 provides a sample student survey, which can be adapted to support your instructional program and MLs. In addition, routine practices such as open houses, field trips, parent conferences, and post-high school planning, including the college application process, are often taken for granted as known activities when in fact they are not familiar to many MLs and their families (Zacarian et al., 2021; Zacarian & Silverstone, 2015, 2020; Zacarian & Soto, 2020). Educators must learn as much as possible about their ML community in order to implement school–family partnership tasks and activities that complement its various linguistic and cultural representatives (Zacarian et al., 2021; Zacarian & Silverstone, 2015, 2020; Zacarian & Soto, 2020).

The Role of a Student's Primary Language

The primary languages of students should be a critical component of any program. When there are a significant number of MLs who represent the same primary language and who are in the same grade, a *bilingual biliteracy model* of bilingual immersion (e.g., dual language) has been shown to be highly effective for promoting language learning and value (Collier & Thomas, 2020). When implementing a bilingual immersion program, it is best to begin in an early grade, such as kindergarten, and to build programming by adding another grade level each successive year. The intent must be that English-fluent students and MLs will become bilingual biliterate and that both languages will be used for instruction from elementary grades through high school graduation.

A good alternative choice, when there aren't enough speakers of a language other than English in the grade levels associated with a bilingual immersion model, is a *maintenance bilingual education* or late-exit *transitional bilingual education* program because of the merits that have been found in maintaining a student's primary language while they are learning English. As we will examine in this book, each transition from one level of English proficiency to the next is a significant one for MLs in transitional models because it means that less language support will be provided. Late-exit transitional bilingual education programs give students much-needed time to fine-tune their understanding of English while becoming active members of their school community.

Many schools, however, do not have the population of MLs needed for these bilingual program models. In these cases, a sheltered immersion model with clarification support in the native language may be a good solution. This support may be provided by teachers, aides, and/or volunteers. No matter what model is used, whenever possible, the primary languages of students should be included.

Bilingual Programming Indicators

Several students who speak the same language other than English are needed for bilingual maintenance, immersion, and transitional bilingual education models. In some states, it is required that bilingual education be provided when a specific number of students speak the same language; districts should consult with their SEAs to ascertain this important information. For example, bilingual education programming is required in New York when there are more than 20 identified MLs whose primary language is the same and who are in the same grade and school (New York State Department of Education, 2015–16, p. 15). When it is determined that bilingual education programming is either required or desired, schools must decide which type of such programming will serve them best.

Bilingual Immersion Models

An immersion model may be an ideal choice in districts that value multilingualism. It provides a solid means for MLs and English-fluent students to develop bilingual skills, learn academic content successfully, and engage in positive social and academic cross-cultural and language experiences. As we learned in Chapter 2, this type of programming is optimally provided when there is a balance of students representing both language groups, and one-third to one-half of the total should be MLs. A long-term plan that begins in kindergarten is critical, as is considering the type of dual-language programming that will continue through students' school years so that they are fully bilingual at graduation and can earn a diploma that signifies students who are biliterate, commonly referred to as a *seal of biliteracy* (Davin & Heineke, 2018). In addition, school administrators, teachers, specialists, and all involved in creating and enacting bilingual language assistance programming must decide how much students will engage in the study of each language at the various grade levels. This decision is quite dependent on the following:

- the number of trained and appropriately licensed or prepared personnel to deliver instruction in English and the additional language;

- curriculum materials that are available in both languages;

- transition plans for secondary schooling to include programming for students to achieve biliteracy;

- family, community, and schoolwide support, including families of MLs and English-fluent speakers;

- school leaders' capacity to advocate for the program among staff, families, and the community and to integrate it into the school; and

- long-term commitment of at least 4 to 6 years for the model to be effective.

Dr. Jessica Panfil, principal at Claremont Immersion Elementary School, in Arlington, Virginia, discusses some of the productive challenges and rewards of building and sustaining successful dual-language programming.

Hiring teachers who are a match for the program is my biggest responsibility and best reward. When we interview candidates, we look for the teacher who not only has the educational background, teaching experience, and language skills to work at a dual-language school, but also who has the commitment to the mission of dual language—to create an equitable educational environment for culturally and linguistically diverse students. When we have evidence that a teacher believes in this mission and understands that they will be part of a team of educators who will work together to create a school in which all students' home language and culture are valued and honored, then we know we have found the right candidate for the position.

As a school, we work to sustain the work of teachers through team structures and processes that facilitate collaboration and community. Especially at a dual-language school, it is critical teachers have time during their busy workday to communicate with each other and share what is working with students, and what needs to be adjusted both in the classroom immediately, and also planning for future lessons. This ongoing collaboration and communication about students is an additional positive outcome of sharing students across teachers and languages. We build our community at the student and adult level, where diverse languages, cultures, perspectives, and ideas are valued and where we can focus as a team on each student's academic and social-emotional success in two languages. (Jessica Panfil, personal communication, April 4, 2022)

Bringing work groups composed of English-fluent and ML families together is critical in the formation and sustained continuation of a bilingual immersion program. Unlike other program models, it requires the continuous commitment among the two language populations for its existence. The program simply cannot exist without a balanced student population and committed teachers and families. Resource 3.6 provides bilingual immersion work groups and others with suggested readings about the theoretical underpinnings and practical applications of the model.

Staffing Considerations

There must be resources for implementing any program model. For example, a bilingual immersion model requires teachers who are fluent in both languages at each of the grade levels involved. In Chapter 1, we learned that many educators in the United States are not trained to work with MLs and that administrators and all involved in the education of MLs must take steps to ensure that they receive this training. An important component of the training is that staff know and understand the model that has been chosen and its purpose. This will help them make instructional decisions that are more intentionally targeted for the model's success. Districts should consult with local colleges and universities, their state department of education, and educational service agencies to create a professional development plan that is targeted for building and sustaining a trained workforce in the chosen program model. Some districts, for example, may recruit bilingual aides to become trained teachers to implement a program model. Ensuring that well-trained staff are in place should be a priority for any administrator and work group involved in the education of MLs.

Program Enactment

It is important to develop steps such as the following to enact a program model:

1. Gather as much information as possible about the program, including visiting schools that use it. Consult with experts about it.

2. Develop a mission statement about the program as well as an implementation timeline for it. It is also helpful to develop a detailed program description and to plan to share it with all the stakeholders who will be involved in it. This includes the school superintendent or designee, school principals, teachers, resource and special education staff, families, and others.

3. Draft letters to parents about the program. These should be simply and clearly written and intended for translation into all the languages that parents indicated that they use on the home language survey. The letters should include information about identifying their children as MLs, the program that is recommended, annually assessing student progress to learn English, and when a student is no longer classified as an ML and has moved to the classification of being a former ML (see Resource 3.7 for a sample parent letter). Also, see Chapter 6 for further information about working and partnering with families.

4. Develop a plan of action for ensuring that the English and academic learning needs of MLs are not ignored if families decline (i.e., opt out of) language assistance services/programming for their child. Include an analysis of students whose families declined services. A tool for this analysis can be found in Resource 3.5.

5. Develop planning meetings, and designate time to implement the model. This includes gathering the curricular materials, organizing classroom space, and meeting with families and other stakeholders about the program model launch.

6. Schedule time for the ML program staff to meet regularly with general classroom teachers, guidance counselors, and support staff to launch the program and assess it.

7. Develop a process whereby students demonstrating proficiency in English will be monitored for at least two consecutive years to ensure a successful transition out of English language education programming.

Program Evaluation

It is critical to evaluate the success of a program model. Interim evaluations should be used and include the following:

- annual assessments to measure MLs' English proficiency gains

- progress reports and report cards (Resource 3.8 is a sample for documenting MLs' English proficiency gains)

- local assessments of literacy

- statewide assessments of mathematics and reading

- monitoring reports of former MLs (see Resource 3.9); note that under the Every Student Succeeds Act, monitoring is required for a period of four consecutive years after a student has demonstrated proficiency in English (U.S. Department of Education, 2016).

The interim review should include an analysis of individuals as well as groups of students to determine the effectiveness of the program. The results of this analysis will help to assess the effectiveness of the program model and to make revisions where and as they are needed. Once a program model has been selected and implemented, an important next step is to create the instructional model that will be used for the English language development of MLs, commonly referred to as ESL instruction. Chapter 4 focuses on this component.

ML Programming Handbooks

Every school has handbooks that are used to provide information about school policies, attendance, student code of conduct, and the school calendar. These resources are intended to support families, students, and educators in understanding the routines and practices of the school or district *and* to support working and even partnering together. While they might be translated into the various languages of the school's MLs, that alone is not going to push the many positives, purposes, and goals of whatever ML programs are chosen. Having cowritten the policies of many rural, suburban, and urban districts across the nation, I can say without a doubt, these are a must! They serve the same purpose as do other school handbooks: to make the programming known to families, students, and ourselves as we work together on behalf of the success of our MLs. Here are some of the elements we have discussed in this chapter:

- vision and mission of the program

- identifying MLs in the school/district

- program model description, including family involvement

- work group description and recruitment efforts to support all ML families to be involved

- annual assessment of ML programming and the steps the work group will continuously take to strengthen programming

- rights of families about their child's language education programming/services and declining language education programming

- resources

RESOURCE 3.1

Home Language Survey

School Name

  Address

  Contact Information

Dear Parent/Guardian:

To help your child succeed in school, we ask that you please answer the following questions for each child attending [name of school]. Your answers will help us create the best possible educational program for your child.

Student's Name (Please Print): _____ Date: _____

School: _____ Grade: _____

HOME LANGUAGE QUESTIONS	ANSWERS
1. What language did your child first understand or speak?	
2. What language do you or others use most often when speaking with your child at home?	
3. What language does your child use most often when speaking at home?	
4. What language does your child use most often when speaking with other family members?	
5. What language does your child use most often when speaking with friends?	
6. What language(s) does your child read?	
7. What language(s) does your child write?	
8. At what age did your child start attending school?	
9. Has your child attended school every year since that age? If no, please explain.	Yes ☐ No ☐
10. Would you prefer oral and written communication from the school in English or in your home language?	English ☐ Home language ☐: Name of language: _____

Signature of Parent/Guardian: _____ Date: _____

Please return the completed form to the school office.

 Available for download at **resources.corwin.com/transformingschoolsformultilinguallearners**

RESOURCE 3.2

Identification, Annual, and Transition Assessment

Findings and Recommendations

[Name of District]

Student Name: _____ Gender: M F Grade: _____ Date Tested: _____

Student Assessed By: _____ Position: _____

Assessment Type:

New Student ☐

Annual ☐ _____ # Years in Program [Name of program model type]

Exit/Transfer From Program ☐

Summary of Listening and Speaking (Include name of the assessment, scores, and summary of findings)

Summary of Reading and Writing (Include name of the assessment, scores, and summary of findings)

Placement Recommendations:

Does not need language education services ☐

Needs language education programming ☐

Reclassify as former ML ☐

ESL level for identified ML (check box that applies)

1 ☐

2 ☐

3 ☐

4 ☐

5 ☐

6 ☐

Clarification in native language needed: No ☐ Yes ☐ Language needed: _____

Description of levels for identified MLs drawn from the state education agency in our state:

RESOURCE 3.3

Interview of Family and/or Newly Identified ML

Newly identified MLs and/or their families should be interviewed to assist in building an effective instructional program. The following questions are intended for this purpose. The interview may be conducted with parents/ guardians, parents/guardians and their child, or the student. The person conducting the interview should complete this form.

Date of Interview: _____

Student Name: _____ Grade: _____

Interviewer: _____ Position: _____

Who was interviewed: (family ☐, family with student ☐, or student ☐)

Interpreter (if applicable) _____ Tel: _____

1. What makes [name of child] special (things that set the child apart from others, qualities that the child possesses, things the child values)?

2. What are some things you enjoy about [name of child]?

3. What talents and skills would you like me to know about [name of child]?

4. What are things you enjoy doing as a family?

5. We want to be a welcoming place for you and your child(ren). What would make the experience of coming to our school more enjoyable?

6. We see parents as our partners. Is there any way you would like to help me make your child's experience a great one?

7. What special talents or interests would you consider sharing with the students in [name of child's] class or with students' families?

8. What are your hopes and dreams for [name of child's] education?

9. What activities does your child enjoy doing after school? (Are there any clubs, sports, or other activities that your child participated in?)

10. How long has [name of child] attended school? _____.

11. What schools has [name of child] attended? Where are these schools located, and what dates did he/she attend?

    School Name: _____

    Location: _____ Dates Attended: _____

    School Name: _____

    Location: _____ Dates Attended: _____

    School Name: _____

    Location: _____ Dates Attended: _____

12. Was more than one language used to communicate in the student's prior schools? Yes ☐ No ☐

    If yes, what are the languages? Also, please describe when and how these were used.

13. What did classrooms in the student's prior school(s) look like? (Try to get a feel for the student's prior classrooms by learning about the student-teacher ratio, desk arrangements, and other information that helps you to form a visual picture of the student's prior classrooms.)

14. Please describe the school day (length of day, daily schedule, etc.).

15. In what ways did parents/guardians participate in the student's prior school?

16. Were the student's teachers concerned about the student's progress? If yes, please describe the concerns.

17. Do you have any concerns about your child, including academic, social, and emotional?

18. What questions do you wish I had asked and would like to be sure are included?

 Available for download at **resources.corwin.com/transformingschoolsformultilinguallearners**

RESOURCE 3.4

Survey of Students' Interests and Strengths

Newly identified MLs should be asked about their interests and strengths to assist in building an asset-based instructional program. The following survey is intended for this purpose. It should be adapted to support your instructional program and MLs.

Name:

What activities (sports, hobbies, games) do you like to play for fun?

What activities do you like to play with others for fun?

What activities do you like to do with your family?

What activities (sports, hobbies, games) would you like to do, if you could, outside of school?

For older students: It's also helpful to survey students' perceptions of their strengths as learners. Here is a sampling of questions that are intended to support them in building on their strengths as editors, readers, writers, and collaborators.

One of my strengths as an editor is:

One of the areas I would like to work on as an editor is:

One of my strengths as a writer is:

One of the areas I would like to work on as a writer is:

One of my strengths as a reader is:

One of the areas I would like to work on as a reader is:

One of my strengths as a collaborator is:

One of the areas I would like to work on as a collaborator is:

 Available for download at **resources.corwin.com/transformingschoolsformultilinguallearners**

online resources **RESOURCE 3.5**

School/District Analysis of Newly Identified and Returning MLs

[District Name]

Note: A separate form should be used for each school in a district. A school may separate these categories further by completing each form by teacher.

Name of school: _____

Languages spoken by the identified MLs: _____

GRADE	PK	K	1	2	3	4	5	6	7	8	9	10	11	12

Countries of origin among the identified MLs: _____

COUNTRY	PK	K	1	2	3	4	5	6	7	8	9	10	11	12

English proficiency levels among identified MLs

GRADE	PK	K	1	2	3	4	5	6	7	8	9	10	11	12
Level 1														
Level 2														
Level 3														
Level 4														
Level 5														

MLs with interrupted and/or limited prior schooling*

GRADE	1	2	3	4	5	6	7	8	9	10	11	12

*This information is essential for planning effective programs for students in Grades 1–12, and specialized programming should be considered for such students at all grade levels.

MLs on free or reduced-priced lunch*

GRADE	PK	K	1	2	3	4	5	6	7	8	9	10	11	12

*This is a general means for identifying students who live in poverty.

MLs receiving Title I services

GRADE	PK	K	1	2	3	4	5	6	7	8	9	10	11	12

MLs whose families declined (opted out of) language education services

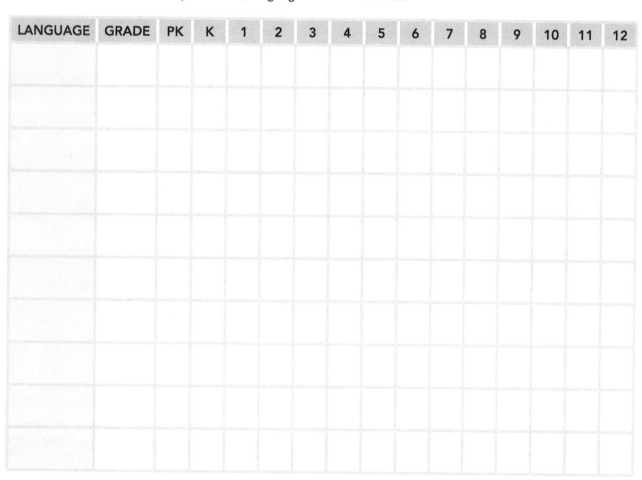

LANGUAGE	GRADE	PK	K	1	2	3	4	5	6	7	8	9	10	11	12

 Available for download at **resources.corwin.com/transformingschoolsformultilinguallearners**

online resources ⬚ **RESOURCE 3.6**

Suggested Readings

Each of these books and resources is intended to support high-quality professional growth for educators and other stakeholders of multilingual learners (MLs).

Teaching MLs

Calderon, M. E., Dove, M. G., Staehr Fenner, D., Gottlieb, M., Hongisfeld, A., Ward Singer, T., Slakk, S., Soto, I., & Zacarian, D. (2017). *Breaking down the wall: Essential shifts for English Learners' success.* Corwin.

Haynes, J., & Zacarian, D. (2010). *Teaching English language learners across the content areas.* Association for Supervision and Curriculum Development.

Zacarian, D., & Haynes, J. (2012). *The essential guide for educating beginning English learners.* Corwin.

Creating programming for MLs

U.S. Department of Justice & U.S. Department of Education. (2015, January 7). *Dear colleague.* https://www2.ed.gov/about/offices/list/ocr/letters/colleague-el-201501.pdf

U.S. Department of Education, Office of Civil Rights. (2005). *Programs for English language learners: Part IV: Glossary.* http://www.ed.gov/about/offices/list/ocr/ell/edlite-glossary.html

MLs in general education classroom settings

Faltis, C. (2007). *Teaching English language learners in mainstream classrooms: A joinfostering approach* (4th ed.). Pearson.

Haynes, J., & Zacarian, D. (2010). *Teaching English language learners across the content areas.* Association for Supervision and Curriculum Development.

Kaplan. E. (2019). 6 essential strategies for teaching English language learners. https://www.edutopia.org/article/6-essential-strategies-teaching-english-language-learners

New Levine, L., & McCloskey, M. (2008). *Teaching English language learners in mainstream classrooms (K–8).* Allyn & Bacon/Merrill.

Zacarian, D., & Soto, I. (2020). *Responsive schooling for culturally and linguistically diverse students.* Norton Education.

Zacarian, D., & Silverstone, M. A. (2020). *Teaching to empower: Taking action to foster student agency, self-confidence, and collaboration.* ASCD.

SIOP model

Echevarria, J., Vogt, M. E., & Short, D. (2017). *Making content comprehensible for English learners: The SIOP model* (5th ed.). Center for Applied Linguistics.

Echevarria, J., Vogt, M. E., & Short, D. (2020). *Developing academic literacy and language in the content areas.* Center for Applied Linguistics. https://www.calstore.cal.org/k-12-resources-inventory/developing-academic-literacy-and-language -in-the-content-areas

Planning and implementing bilingual immersion programming

Center for Applied Linguistics. (n.d.). *Two-way immersion.* https://www.cal.org/twi/

Howard, E. R., & Christian, D. (2002). *Two-way immersion 101: Designing and implementing a two-way immersion program at the elementary level.* Center for Research on Education, Diversity and Excellence. https://www.cal.org/twi/pdfs/two-way-immersion-101.pdf

Soltero, S. W. (2016). *Dual language education: Program design and implementation.* Heinemann.

Teaching students living with adversity

Zacarian, D., Alvarez-Ortiz, L., Haynes, J. (2017). *Teaching to strengths: Supporting students living with trauma, violence, and chronic stress.* ASCD.

Teaching students with limited or interrupted formal education

Calderón, M. E., & Minaya-Rowe, L. (2010). *Preventing long-term ELs: Transforming schools to meet core standards.* Corwin.

Calderón, M. E., & Montenegro, H. (2021). *Empowering long-term with social emotional learning, language, and literacy.* Valazquez Press.

Custodio, B., & O'Loughlin, J. (2017). *Students with interrupted formal education: Bridging where they are and what they need.* Corwin.

Decapua, A., Marshall, H. W., & Tang, L. F. (2020). *Meeting the needs of SLIFE: A guide for educators* (2nd ed.). University of Michigan Press.

Pransky, K. (2008). *Beneath the surface: The hidden realities of teaching culturally and linguistically diverse young learners, K–6.* Heinemann.

Salva, C., & Matis, A. (2017). *Boosting achievement: Reaching students with interrupted or minimal education.* Seidlitz Education.

 Available for download at **resources.corwin.com/transformingschoolsformultilinguallearners**

 **RESOURCE 3.7**

Sample Parent Letter About Newly Identified MLs

[District Name]

[School Name]

[School Contact Information]

Date: _____

Dear Parent/Guardian of [Name of student]:

Welcome to [name of school]. Your child was assessed to determine if they are a multilingual learner and whether they need a specific language assistance program designed to meet their English learning needs. Based on these assessments,

☐ Your child appears to be fluent in English and will not require coursework that is designed for students who are learning English as a new language.

☐ It appears that your child is a multilingual learner at level __ and would benefit from taking courses that are designed for students who are learning English.

This includes classes in English as a second language. It also includes a course of instruction that is specifically for multilingual learners to be actively engaged in learning content and English. It is recommended that your child receive a course of instruction in math ☐, science ☐, social studies ☐ for the purpose of learning English and academic content.

Your child would also benefit from receiving bilingual language clarification in math ☐, science ☐, social studies ☐ to assist them in understanding subject matter.

You have the right to decline this specifically designed English language education course of study. Please contact me if you have any questions about these recommendations and/or your right to decline. I may be reached at [telephone number] _____.

Thank you.

Sincerely,

[Signature]

[Position]

 Available for download at **resources.corwin.com/transformingschoolsformultilinguallearners**

RESOURCE 3.8

Sample Progress Report in Learning [Name of Language]

[Name of School]

Progress reports are written during the time in which each school completes student progress and report cards. They are intended to provide families with information about their child's progress in learning [name of language(s)]. Note: In bilingual and dual-language programs, this form may be duplicated to reflect the languages being learned.

Student Name: _____ Grade: _____ Academic Year: _____

Teacher: _____ Position: _____ Date: _____

Quarter: 1st ☐ 2nd ☐ 3rd ☐ 4th ☐

Section 1: Please rate the student's academic progress in learning English using the following code based on our state department of education standards:

1. Entering
2. Emerging
3. Developing
4. Expanding
5. Bridging
6. Reaching

	1ST QUARTER	2ND QUARTER	3RD QUARTER	4TH QUARTER

I. Listening/speaking
  A. One-to-one interactions
    1. With peers				

2. With adults				
B. Small-group discussion				
II. Reading A. Reading comprehension				
B. Reading for information				
C. Oral reading				

(Continued)

(Continued)

	1ST QUARTER	2ND QUARTER	3RD QUARTER	4TH QUARTER
D. Functional reading in the classroom (directions, etc.)				
E. Additional information about reading				
III. Writing				
A. Functional writing				
B. Journal writing				
C. Writing for reports				
D. Note-taking				
E. Fictional writing				
F. Additional information about writing				

_____ Additional Support Services _____

_____

Comments/Concerns:

1st Quarter _____

2nd Quarter _____

3rd Quarter _____

4th Quarter _____

 Available for download at **resources.corwin.com/transformingschoolsformultilinguallearners**

RESOURCE 3.9

[School District] Monitor Report

Note: This report deals with students who have been reclassified from ML to former ML.

From: _____ (Position): _____

To: _____

Date student was reclassified: _____ Report Year: 1 ☐ 2 ☐ of two

Student Name: _____ Grade: _____ Academic Year: _____

Teacher: _____ Subject Matter: _____

[Name of student] demonstrated the ability to do ordinary classroom work in English and has been reclassified from an ML to a former ML. The student's performance and progress will be monitored for four consecutive school years to ensure a successful reclassification. Please rate the student's academic progress in English language arts using the code below:

1. A significant strength

2. Secure in communicating grade-level concepts and skills

3. Developing communication in grade-level concepts and skills

4. Working on meeting grade-level concepts and skills and will be provided with support and time to develop communicative skills and concepts (as detailed in the *additional support services section* of this document).

	1ST QUARTER	2ND QUARTER	3RD QUARTER	4TH QUARTER
I. Listening/speaking				
A. One-to-one interactions				
1. With peers				
2. With adults				
B. Small-group discussion				
II. Reading				
A. Reading comprehension				
B. Reading for information				
C. Oral reading				

(Continued)

(Continued)

	1ST QUARTER	2ND QUARTER	3RD QUARTER	4TH QUARTER
D. Functional reading in the classroom (directions, etc.)				
III. Writing				
A. Functional writing				
B. Journal writing				
C. Writing for reports				
D. Note-taking				
E. Fictional writing				

_____ Title I _____

_____

_____ Additional Support Services _____

_____

_____ Special Education Services in the Following Areas: _____

_____

Comments/Concerns:

1st Quarter _____

2nd Quarter _____

3rd Quarter _____

4th Quarter _____

 Available for download at **resources.corwin.com/transformingschoolsformultilinguallearners**

References

Cohen, E., & Lotan, R. (2014). *Designing groupwork strategies for the heterogeneous classroom* (3rd ed.). Teachers College Press.

Collier, V., & Thomas, W. (2020). *Why dual language works for everyone PK–12.* https://www.gocabe.org/wp-content/uploads/2020/02/CABE-ME-MAG2020WEB.pdf

Constantino de Cohen, C., & Clewell, B. (2007). *Putting English language learners on the educational map.* Urban Institute.

Davin, K. J., & Heineke, A. J. (2018). The seal of biliteracy: Adding students' voices to the conversation. *Bilingual Research Journal, 41*(3), 312–328. https://doi.org/10.1080/15235882.2018.1481896

Dove, M. G., & Honigsfeld, A. (2018). *Co-teaching for English learners: A guide to collaborative planning, instruction, assessment, and reflection.* Corwin.

Dove, M. G., & Honigsfeld, A. (2020). From isolation to collaboration. In M. E. Calderón, M. G. Dove, D. S. Fenner, M. Gottlieb, A. Honigsfeld, T. W. Singer, S. Slakk, I. Soto, & D. Zacarian (Eds.), *Breaking down the wall: Essential shifts for English learners' success* (pp. 73–88). Corwin.

Gándara, P. (2010). Overcoming triple segregation: Latino students often face language, cultural, and economic isolation. *Educational Leadership, 68*(3), 60–65.

George Global Studies School. (n.d.). *About us.* https://george.bpsma.org/about-us

Güver, S., & Motschnig, R. (2017). Effects of diversity in teams and workgroups: A qualitative systematic review. *International Journal of Business, Humanities and Technology, 7*(2), 6–34.

MacDonald, E. B. (2022). *Intentional moves: How skillful leaders impact learning.* Corwin.

Massachusetts Department of Elementary and Secondary Education. (2022). *Guidance on the initial identification of English learners.* https://www.doe.mass.edu/ele/guidance/general/identification.docx

New York State Department of Education. (2015–16). *Subpart 154-2: Services for English learners for programs operated in the 2015–2016 school year and thereafter.* http://www.nysed.gov/common/nysed/files/programs/bilingual-ed/terms-154-2-effective-2015-16-and-after.pdf

U.S. Department of Education. (2016, November). *Tools and resources for monitoring and exiting English learners from EL programs and services.* https://www2.ed.gov/about/offices/list/oela/english-learner-toolkit/chap8.pdf

U.S. Department of Education. (2020). *Developing programs for English language learners: Plan development.* https://www2.ed.gov/about/offices/list/ocr/ell/plandev.html

U.S. Department of Justice & U.S. Department of Education. (2015, January 7). *Dear colleague.* https://www2.ed.gov/about/offices/list/ocr/letters/colleague-el-201501.pdf

Zacarian, D, Calderón, M. E., & Gottlieb, M. (2021). *Beyond crises: Overcoming linguistic and cultural inequities in communities, schools, and classrooms.* Corwin.

Zacarian, D., & Dove, M. G. (2020). *From nobody cares to everyone/every community cares.* In M. E. Calderón, M. G. Dove, D. S. Fenner, M. Gottlieb, A. Honigsfeld, T. W. Singer, S. Slakk, I. Soto, & D. Zacarian (Eds.), *Breaking down the wall: Essential shifts for English learners' success* (pp. 183–199). Corwin.

Zacarian, D., & Silverstone, M. A. (2015). *In it together: How student, family, and community partnerships advance engagement and achievement in diverse classrooms.* Corwin.

Zacarian, D., & Silverstone, M. A. (2020). *Teaching to empower: Taking action to foster student agency, self-confidence, and collaboration.* Corwin.

Zacarian, D., & Soto, I. (2020). *Responsive schooling for culturally and linguistically diverse students.* Norton Education.

Designing, Implementing, and Strengthening the English Language Development Component

Hoa Li was excited to move to the United States. Her family had decided to live near her favorite aunt, uncle, and cousins, who lived in a small city in New England. During her first month in the United States, she and her family lived with their relatives, and she enrolled in the same middle school as her cousins. Because Hoa Li did not speak any English, the school employed a retired English teacher, Mrs. Janus, to work with her for one half hour every day. Mrs. Janus was told to attend Hoa Li's English class and to work with Hoa Li's English teacher, Mr. Lindquist.

Mr. Lindquist asked Mrs. Janus to sit next to Hoa Li and help her understand the novel that his class was reading. Not sure how to do this without interrupting Mr. Lindquist's class, Mrs. Janus silently used her pointer finger to follow along the text as he and Hoa Li's classmates read aloud from it. She had never worked with a multilingual learner (ML), did not speak Mandarin, and didn't want to disturb Mr. Lindquist's class. She figured that following along silently was the best solution for Hoa Li. Unfortunately, Hoa Li did not understand anything that was occurring and felt miserably lost and alone. While Mrs. Janus was worried about disturbing the class, her attempts to help Hoa Li were wholly inadequate.

Two months later, Hoa Li's family found a temporary apartment in another part of the city. At her new school, Hoa Li was placed in an English as a second language[1] (ESL) class for an hour every day. This class met in a small room on the first floor of the school. Hoa Li's schedule required her to attend the first 15 minutes of her grade-level English class, which was on the second floor, leave while the English class was in

---

[1] The terms *English as a second language* and *English language development* are used interchangeably to describe a type of instruction that is targeted for the learning of English.

session, walk to the first floor to attend the ESL class, and then return to the English class while it was still in session.

Hoa Li found that she was the only Mandarin speaker in the ESL class and that most of her classmates knew a lot more English than she did. She found it difficult to understand the lessons and keep pace with her peers in the ESL class. As she had done in the previous school, she spent most of her time feeling lost and alone. This was even truer when she left her ESL class and rejoined her English class.

At the end of the semester, her family moved yet again, this time to a more permanent apartment in a different part of the city. Hoa Li's parents, like many parents, did not realize that when they moved, their daughter would be attending a different school. While they were upset that she would be starting out at another new school and concerned about her making another transition, they hoped that Hoa Li would acclimate. Her new school enrolled her in a general English language arts class. Once again, she was unable to follow what occurred in it. She was also assigned to an ESL class. It met for 2 hours every day during the time that she would have had math and science. In the ESL class, she was surrounded by beginning learners of English like herself. The class was devoted to learning how to speak in English for everyday social conversations. At the end of the school year, Hoa Li's teachers were pleased by how much progress she had made in learning to speak in English. However, Hoa Li and her parents were worried about the math and science courses that she had missed and how behind she was in English language arts.

The three different schooling experiences of Hoa Li should raise our level of urgency to be transformative about what we can and will do to support MLs' success. This occurs when we tap into the personal, cultural, linguistic, and life experiences of MLs and continuously support the expansion of their oral and written language development. One of the many spaces for doing this is the English language development or ESL class. It is here that we can support and even inspire MLs to use English to listen, speak, read, and write to fully engage with content and interact with others.

Various research panels have shown the importance of providing instruction that is developmentally age appropriate and integrates all that we do so that learning spaces are not silos unto themselves—rather, they are part of an interconnected (and even interdependent) whole. One recent committee that examined "how evidence based on research relevant to the development of dual language learners/MLs from birth to age 21 can inform education and health policies and related practices that can result in better educational outcomes" is the National Academies of Science, Engineering, and Medicine (2017, p. 2). It drew three important conclusions for educators in elementary, middle, and high school contexts to consider in designing and implementing instructional programming for MLs:

Educators of Elementary School MLs

Providing explicit instruction focused on developing key aspects of literacy; developing academic language during content area instruction; providing support to make core content comprehensible; encouraging peer-assisted learning opportunities; capitalizing on students' home language, knowledge, and cultural assets; screening for language and literacy challenges and monitoring progress; and providing small-group academic support for students to learn grade-level core content. (p. 326)

Educators of Middle School MLs

"Research on [English learners'] language and academic subject learning is consistent with findings from studies conducted with children in the previous grades and supports the identification of promising practices during the primary grades (pre-K to 5). However, the developmental needs of young adolescent MLs—specifically their cognitive and social development—and their adaptation to a different organizational structure and expectations for student independence in middle school are important factors to consider in designing and implementing instructional strategies in middle school. The processes of identity formation and social awareness, which increase during adolescence, point to the importance of teacher beliefs about MLs and their attitudes toward learning English when working with middle school MLs. (pp. 326–327)

Educators of High School MLs

[S]ome promising practices include a focus on academic language development that embraces all facets of academic language and includes both oral and written language across content areas; structured reading and writing instruction using a cognitive strategies approach and explicit instruction in reading comprehension strategies; opportunities for extended discussion of text and its meaning between teachers and students and in peer groups that may foster motivation and engagement in literacy learning; provision of peer-assisted learning opportunities; and rigorous, focused, and relevant support for long-term MLs. (p. 327)

What is English as a Second Language?

ESL describes a type of instruction for learning English. It is often, but not always, taught by an instructor who has been specifically trained to teach English to students who are speakers of other languages at home and are not yet able to do ordinary class work in English.

Each of the three scenarios that Hoa Li experienced reflects the types of situations in which many MLs in the United States find themselves. They present an all-too-familiar dilemma: None addressed the specific English learning needs of students such as Hoa Li, and there is little uniformity among the amount, type, and effectiveness of ESL instruction that MLs receive. Further, there is often a lack of uniformity and consistency in ESL classes across districts, and even across schools in the same district, leading to these classes not being as effective and successful as they could be (National Academies for Science, Engineering, and Medicine, 2017). For example, a beginning learner of English in the third grade might receive an hour of ESL instruction, whereas a fourth grader in the same school might receive 2 hours and a fifth grader 30 minutes.

This difference was dramatically demonstrated in a survey I conducted of 26 districts in Massachusetts in 2011. In some, beginning learners of English received over 2.5 hours per day of ESL, while in others, these students received less than a half hour per week! Further, some ESL teachers were relegated to sitting next to the MLs in their regular classrooms and working quietly at the back of the room while the general education teacher conducted a lesson for the whole class. Separate ESL classes, commonly referred to as *pull-out*, took students out of general classes such as English, math, science, and social studies as well as during recess and even lunchtime. Most districts reported that the amount of instruction in ESL was not consistent and depended on many variables that had little to do with students' language learning needs, such as the inability of an understaffed ESL program to provide appropriate language services for MLs in all grades, scheduling issues, and space limitations. All in all, each of the school administrators and ESL teacher leaders surveyed reported that they were not able to either schedule or deliver the type of instructional programming that they believed would be the most effective. Programs that are successful must base their programming decisions on the English proficiency levels of students and their learning needs. They must also organize scheduling that allows for the appropriate amount of time for MLs to learn English and subject matter.

In schools where ESL classes are delivered in a separate setting or in a general classroom setting, ESL and content teachers must also pay focused, intentional, and simultaneous attention to each of four interdependent processes for learning language and content. Drawing from Zacarian and Soto (2020), Zacarian (2012), Goldenberg and Coleman (2010), August and Shanahan (2006, 2008), Genesee et al. (2006), and Collier (1995), these processes consist of the following and are discussed in more detail in Chapter 5:

Four Interdependent Processes of Language and Content Learning

1. Learning language is a sociocultural process. It involves building meaningful connections with MLs' prior personal, social, cultural, and life experiences. It also involves supporting their understanding of the dominant and school cultures.

2. Learning language is a developmental process. Teachers must consider the various proficiency levels of the MLs with whom they work and target instruction, homework, and assessment to these specific levels. Doing this requires knowing and following the English proficiency standards of the state education agency (SEA).

3. Learning language and content is a process that occurs best when it builds on the prior academic experiences of students and when the academic and language goals and objectives are made explicit.

4. Learning language includes developing a high level of cognitive thinking skills. These must be intentionally taught.

Developing the Organizational Model
of the ESL Component of a Program

Thus, while the ESL component is a critical element, it must be aligned with (1) these four processes; (2) the findings from the National Academies of Science, Engineering, and Medicine (2017) on instructing elementary, middle, and high school MLs; and (3) the English language proficiency standards put forth by each state department of education.

There is general agreement in the field that there are five to six levels of English proficiency. TESOL (2006) created a five-level set of ESL standards for students in prekindergarten through Grade 12, and the World-Class Instructional Design and Assessment Consortium created a six-level format (WIDA, 2020). Drawing from Haynes and Zacarian (2010), the following describes one way to conceptualize the English language development levels of MLs.[2]

Knowing the English Proficiency Levels
and Learning Needs of Students

Stage 1: Starting

This is often referred to as a preproduction stage. Students are able to speak in English with one- or two-word responses as they are just beginning to listen in English. Visuals, body language, and activities that are geared for building vocabulary to navigate the school day are essential. Instructional attention should be focused on building students' listening comprehension through body language, demonstrations, modeling, drawings, and other visuals.

Stage 2: Emerging

This stage usually occurs when students have learned English for 6 months to 1 year and are interacting in English. English is generally learned through visual support and demonstrated by responding to yes/no or either/or questions, naming or categorizing information, and writing very simple sentences to go with pictures. Graphic organizers, charts, drawings, demonstrations, and other visuals are essential for learning to occur (Haynes & Zacarian, 2010).

Stage 3: Developing

Students at this stage are beginning to communicate more actively in English using longer and more descriptive sentences. In 1 to 2 years, students generally have conversational skills that can be readily used in most social activities. At the same time, the ability to communicate using academic language in English is emerging. Students can usually follow simple academic directions, discussions, and tasks when the visual, physical, and *controlled vocabulary* supports are continuously present (Goldenberg & Coleman, 2010). Cummins (1984, 1994) describes an important distinction

---

[2]From *Teaching English Language Learners Across the Content Areas* (pp. 10–12), by J. Haynes and D. Zacarian, 2010, Alexandria, VA: ASCD. Copyright 2010 by ASCD. Used with permission. Visit ASCD at www.ascd.org.

between social and academic language: The ability to speak conversationally in social situations (e.g., during recess, at lunch, on the school bus) usually occurs by Stage 3, but the much-needed and essential academic English language that is needed takes much longer and occurs in Stages 4 and 5. (Refer back to the Chapter 2 discussion of basic interpersonal communication skills versus cognitive academic language proficiency.) Students at Stage 3 require content materials to be modified so that they can be easily accessed through visuals; graphic organizers; connections to their personal, social, cultural, and prior schooling experiences; and other means by which students can make meaning.

Stage 4: Expanding

Students are becoming more proficient in English at this stage. Generally, they can secure key information in a text, use graphic organizers independently, and skim material for specific information. They are also more able to readily use critical thinking skills to analyze, create, debate, predict, and hypothesize in English. As will be discussed later, literacy-oriented MLs are able to do this with increasing grade-level proficiency and sophistication as their English improves, but non-literacy-oriented and culturally disrupted students are not.

Stage 5: Bridging

Students at this stage are close to being able to perform ordinary classroom work in English. Support may be needed with oral and written use of complex vocabulary, sentence structure, and writing for various purposes and in different academic registers. Students are continuing to learn English. During this important stage, teacher support is needed to fine-tune important grammatical aspects of language and, more essentially, to ensure that students have developed higher order thinking and communicative skills in English.

In practice, students are much more able to begin to navigate a general academic setting when they can communicate in English. This usually occurs when students move from Stage 2 to Stage 3 and beyond. However, as was discussed in Chapters 2 and 3, students from non-literacy-oriented and culturally disrupted backgrounds need much more support and time to develop these skills, and each stage is not equal in terms of the amount of time it takes for students to complete it before moving to the next stage.

The first step for determining the appropriate ESL or English language development model is to review the various English proficiency levels and learning needs of the MLs in a school. In Chapter 3, we discussed the importance of taking these steps and a process for doing so. Most students at the beginning stages of learning English are not able to participate meaningfully in a general English language arts classroom. For example, while kindergarten and primary-grade teachers may reasonably believe that there are classroom activities that can be accomplished with students who are at the preproduction stage, these can be made much more possible with an ESL teacher who is familiar with the developmental stages of learning English as an additional language and can help organize the classroom environment and implement tasks and activities that are appropriate for beginning-level MLs. Understandably, teachers of older students may not believe that content can be taught meaningfully to students at the earliest stages in the general classroom unless it is co-modified, co-adapted, or cotaught with in-class support from an ESL teacher. In addition, as we learned in Chapter 2, MLs with limited or interrupted formal prior education present a unique set of circumstances that must be carefully examined before implementing ESL programming.

Organizing a Schedule That Allows Time to Learn English

ESL programming is generally offered in the general classroom (sometimes referred to as *push-in*) or out of the general classroom (sometimes referred to as *pull-out*). Whether it is for learning English or for simultaneously learning English and subject matter, the two settings where these classes occur often fail because students receive very little direct and/or comprehensive instruction to learn English (Zacarian, 2009). Further, they often lead to working in silos or a reductionist approach (Zacarian et al., 2021). In the remainder of this chapter, we revisit the three schools that Hoa Li attended so we can look more closely at the models and the organizational structures and resources that are needed for providing the most effective ESL instruction.

ESL in the General Classroom Model

One organizational model is when ESL is provided in the general education classroom. Usually, it involves an ESL provider going into a general classroom to deliver, support the delivery of, or co-deliver instruction. It may include content area classes such as English, math, science, and social studies. While there are multiple contexts in which to enact this model, it is generally found in elementary schools (DelliCarpini, 2009).

This description of this organizational model alone does not provide school leaders, specialists, teachers, and other stakeholders with enough information about the specific structures and organizational approaches that are needed for this model to be effective. For example, in the first school that Hoa Li attended, a retired English teacher, Mrs. Janus, was hired to work with her during a portion of her English class. On the surface, Mrs. Janus provided Hoa Li with additional support every day for 30 minutes. However, Hoa Li did not receive any specific instruction for learning English. Rather, she was expected to learn the language by sitting passively with her peers. Mrs. Janus did not provide Hoa Li with support that was comprehensible or meaningful. Further, Mrs. Janus was not allotted any time to plan with Hoa Li's teacher. Also, it was expected that a half hour a day was enough for Hoa Li to learn English. In this sense, Mrs. Janus was a supporter of the English teacher's program, and the English teacher was responsible for planning and delivering the program.

While Mrs. Janus might not have been credentialed in ESL, she was hired to provide an in-class model of support ESL. In practice, many ESL teachers are employed to provide this support service. Typically, they work with individual or small groups of students and follow the general education teacher's lead (DelliCarpini, 2009). That is, they do not coplan with the teacher or deliver the instruction. They often feel relegated to an inferior role and believe that their capacity to deliver quality instruction is disregarded by the general teacher. In these situations, it is also not surprising for the ML to be regarded as inferior as this parallels how the ESL teacher is regarded. The ways in which teachers communicate with students and colleagues greatly reflects the image that we have of our community and society. Cummins (1994) refers to this as the power that teachers have to form the identity and social standing of their students and their colleagues. In the case of Hoa Li, Mrs. Janus was certainly relegated to a position far less important than that of the general English teacher. For all these reasons, when the ESL model is enacted in this way, it is not likely to be effective.

An additional type of this model occurs when ESL teachers collaboratively plan and deliver instruction with the general education teacher. Both are responsible for the instructional program and take leading roles and responsibilities in implementing it. In these classrooms, according to DelliCarpini (2009), students frequently are not aware of the different roles of their ESL and grade-level teachers. Both teachers value the other as an equal and interdependent partner. In addition, the ESL teacher and general teacher both deliver instruction for the entire time that the subject matter is taught. This method of enacting the model is much more likely to work. Indeed, Maria Dove and Andrea Honigsfeld (2018), renowned experts in the field of coteaching MLs, describe the essentialness of this model to truly be successful with MLs.

There are many advantages for using a coteaching model. It might provide an ideal situation for

- allowing all students to become active members of the class community,

- learning to occur,

- bringing together professionals from different disciplines to create and implement an educational program that is differentiated and individualized for language learning and content learning,

- keeping MLs with English-fluent classmates, and

- creating space where teachers and students become responsible for the learning.

This model can only occur effectively when we provide organizational structures that allow for critical activities including collaborative planning, assessment of student learning, reflection, trust, and agency. Each of these attributes, according to Dove and Honigsfeld (2018), requires a sense of optimism that we can co-create positive outcomes. In addition to providing the resources that are needed for the ESL program to work in the general classrooms where it is implemented, professional development and time to coplan are also required.

A word of caution about coteaching MLs: Research on kindergarten MLs found that separate ESL classes yielded slightly higher performance outcomes (Saunders et al., 2006).

Training General Education Teachers for a Coteaching Model

If a coteaching model is the preferred approach, there are several must-dos. In addition to ESL teachers being trained and credentialed to teach ESL, general education teachers must be trained in three critical areas:

1. The principles of second language acquisition that apply to students at different age levels, with a focus on linguistics, the essential role of culture and cultural differences, and the factors that influence successful bilingualism and multiculturalism

2. Methods for delivering effective English instruction to MLs and teaching the four domains of listening, speaking, reading, and writing for the purpose of becoming proficient and literate users of English in school

3. Assessment and evaluation of English learning

Many teacher preparation programs, including those offered by institutions of higher education, educational service agencies, state departments of education, and local schools, do not include this critical element for content teachers of MLs. According to the Education Commission of the States (2022), "At least 39 states provide for training, professional development, teaching standards, certification, or endorsements for EL-specific teachers in statute or regulation" (para. 6).

Teacher preparation requirements, however, do not consider what is or needs to be occurring for in-service teachers. While teacher preparation programs often serve preservice and in-service teachers, they should not be regarded as the sole means by which teachers will be or are prepared to teach a growing population of MLs. Most classroom teachers have not had training to teach MLs, as seen in Chapter 1. Professional learning to build capacity is a critical need.

To build effective programs for MLs, school leaders, ESL instructional specialists, coaches, and other stakeholders must ensure that general content teachers are trained in the three areas noted above. A variety of steps can and should be included to ensure that this occurs. First, a district or school-based team of leaders, ESL specialist teachers, instructional and curriculum coaches, and other stakeholders should refer to the guidelines of their SEA to ensure that their school's teachers are appropriately and properly credentialed. Once this occurs, a variety of professional growth models should be explored so that the one that is selected and implemented is the best fit. This may include enrolling general education teachers in programs offered by a local university, the state department of education, an educational service agency, or a school-based program that provides professional development in the three areas noted. Also, school leaders should ensure that they have qualified or, where required, appropriately licensed ESL teachers. In addition, professional learning about collaboration is a must for a coteaching model to be highly effective. The term *highly effective* means that teachers have depth of knowledge for achieving student outcomes and students are successful learners of English and content (Wei et al., 2009).

Training ESL Teachers to Coteach Content

A coteaching model often occurs during content instruction such as math, science, and social studies. Yet many ESL teachers have had no formal training to teach these subjects. In a cotaught model, both teachers—content and ESL—must have a solid understanding of content and language learning. In the case of the ESL teacher, content knowledge is essential. ESL teachers require professional development in the following:

- the content curriculum

- the instructional materials that will be used to teach the content

- effective methods for teaching the content

Think of a math class that is focused on quadrilaterals. Instruction of MLs in a cotaught classroom must include the efforts of the math and ESL teachers and requires that both have a fundamental understanding of the other's work. Training ESL teachers in content areas is a crucial component for creating an effective coteaching model. Teacher preparation, educational service agencies, and others can provide training in content areas. Additionally, many schools can provide peer mentoring and study group formats for this purpose.

Training to Coteach

A coteaching model requires teachers to learn how to use a cooperative model of coteaching. It requires a willingness, on the part of teachers and others with whom they work, to work together and co-"do" the right things to achieve the desired outcomes. While universities, educational service agencies, and other institutions offer powerful opportunities for individual teachers to become prepared to teach MLs, a coteaching model requires a deepening of thinking about how to do this as a cooperative endeavor. And the model must be specific to the individual students for whom it is implemented and to the school in which it is occurring.

Most important, it must be sustained long enough to transform the culture of the classroom to be a space in which linguistic and cultural diversity is an asset that is part of the core of the curriculum and in which a coteaching model is valued as the most optimal method. Therefore, teacher knowledge about the principles of second language acquisition, methods for teaching MLs, and effective assessment and evaluation of MLs is but one piece of the coteaching model. For the model to be employed successfully in the United States, it is also critical to study it in the context of a general classroom populated by native speakers of American English as well as MLs.

Implementing a coteaching model does not happen by merely putting an ESL teacher in the grade-level or subject matter classroom. It happens when there is a reciprocal and interdependent relationship among the teachers and others who work with students. Professional learning about a coteaching model is a must and requires a depth of knowledge on the part of teachers—ESL and grade-level or subject matter alike—about the three core areas discussed earlier as well as a deep sense of and belief in a coteaching model.

An effective coteaching model also requires coplanning time for teachers to effectively prepare instruction for an integrated classroom of MLs and monolingual English speakers. Coteaching models that work involve allotting specific and sustained daily or, at the very least, weekly coplanning time.

English Language Instruction in an ESL Setting

Some students receive instruction in ESL in a setting devoted entirely to ESL. Typically, these students spend a scheduled amount of time receiving this instruction. Often, but not always, the schedule parallels the student's level of English proficiency whereby Stage 1 (Starting) students spend the longest amount of time in this separate setting of ESL instruction, and Stage 5 (Bridging) students the least. Figure 4.1 shows a depiction of the type of schedule used in ESL classroom settings. Each increment represents a prescribed amount of time for ESL per day, such as Starting students receiving 2.5 hours, Emerging students 2 hours, Developing students 1.5 hours, Expanding students 1 hour, and Bridging students 0.5 hour.

ESL models that involve students attending ESL classes are implemented for a variety of reasons. Some educators believe them to be more efficient than coteaching models. They select it as a means of teaching MLs from a range of grades and/or general classrooms. This approach is often seen as particularly helpful partly because, on the surface, it provides a way to economically distribute services. An example of this would be an elementary school with four second-grade classrooms, in which the school leader decides to assign MLs to each of these classrooms with the idea that they will receive ESL instruction using the type of increments shown in Figure 4.1.

Figure 4.1   Transitional Model of English Language Development in an ESL Setting

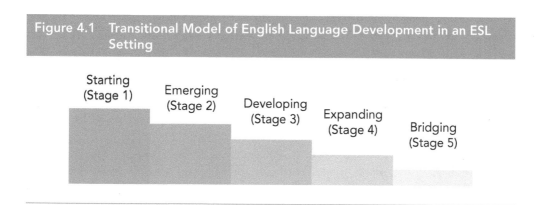

For students at the Starting stage, who are just beginning to learn English, a separate ESL classroom model may provide the easiest access. It is typical in these beginning-level classrooms for students to listen and respond to their teacher's simple commands with appropriate physical movements (e.g., *Go to the door, Open the door, Shut the door*).

In Starting classrooms, students need instruction to help them develop concrete vocabulary words that refer to familiar objects or concrete actions that can be demonstrated by the teacher and acted out by students. Vocabulary is usually introduced in the context in which it is used (e.g., *This is the blackboard, It is lunchtime, Please put your book on the floor, Where is . . . ?*). As students develop more English, they begin to move up the ladder of proficiency levels. Students at the Developing stage may especially benefit from a pull-out class for the same reasons that students at the Starting stage benefit from it.

Classes devoted entirely to ESL are most prevalent at the secondary level (DelliCarpini, 2009). Students are assigned to ESL classes and generally meet in them for the full class period. Scheduling classes according to proficiency levels at the secondary level may be viewed as a clear way to provide instruction that is specifically tailored to students. Yet inherent in this model are several productive tensions, if not recipes for failure, that must be considered.

ESL classes work best when they meet during English classes

School leaders should allocate time for ESL during English classes. This allows students much-needed time to learn the language and not miss critical content instruction such as math, science, and social studies. In one of the scenarios presented at the beginning of this chapter, Hoa Li missed her math and science classes to attend her ESL class. This is not a characteristic of an effective program.

Content-based ESL classes work best when they are taught by appropriately credentialed teachers

Content such as science, math, and social studies can be taught while students are learning English. This is often a fine choice as it provides students with instruction that is specifically planned and delivered for learning content and English simultaneously. The Sheltered Instruction Observation Protocol (SIOP; Echevarria et al., 2017) and Expediting Comprehension for English Language Learners Protocol (Calderón, 2007; Calderón & Minaya-Rowe, 2010) are nationally known models that incorporate content and language learning. In classrooms implementing these, teachers must be credentialed to teach content and ESL, meaning that licensed ESL teachers should not be expected to teach math, science, or social studies unless they are credentialed in the subjects and have had the specific training to do so.

Content-based ESL classes should meet during the same time as the content classes for which they are being substituted

Students should not be pulled from one content class, such as math, to an unrelated content class, such as social studies. In content-based ESL classes, MLs should learn the same subject matter as they would have had had they remained in the general classroom. For example, students have ESL in lieu of English, ESL science in lieu of science, and so forth.

Schools must be organized for a smooth exit and reentry to the general education classroom

Students cannot simply leave and reenter a classroom without some thought as to when and how this will occur. As seen in the scenario presented earlier, Hoa Li was required to leave during her English class and return to it while it was still in session. A first step for organizing the pull-out model is to determine, schoolwide, when students will exit and reenter and how this will occur. This means that teachers of students at various proficiency levels must agree on the times that specific ML students will leave and reenter the classroom. It is not enough to schedule the beginning and ending times of ESL classes. Teachers must collaborate to create time segments that will work smoothly.

Teachers must collaboratively plan what will occur in general education and ESL classes so that the instructional program is as smooth and seamless as possible

Students need to develop an understanding about what is occurring in the general classroom in order to be participants in it. ESL classes can be ideal spaces for students to learn the vocabulary and concepts that are needed. For this to happen, teachers must work collaboratively so that MLs will have as seamless and connected a program as possible. Earlier in this chapter, it was suggested that teachers be trained in how to collaborate. While a model involving ESL classes is not reliant on a coteaching model, it is reliant on each teacher (ESL, grade level, subject matter, and others) having a good grasp of what is occurring in each other's work, MLs' level of English language development, and building such connections for the benefit of students.

Students should not receive decreasing amounts of ESL as they progress from one stage to the next

The scheduled amount of time for ESL classes should be based on the instructional time needed for students to matriculate from one stage of acquisition to the next. For example, students at Stage 3 may need the same amount of daily time as those at Stage 1. Further, a transitional model of ESL may not work well for students from non-literacy-oriented and culturally disrupted backgrounds or those with interrupted prior schooling. It is much more ideal to provide ESL for a longer period each day (often as much as students in the beginning phases of ESL) to better ensure that literacy development occurs well. This is not to say that Starting learners of English should learn alongside Bridging learners, but students at each of these levels may require the maximum amount of ESL that is possible, such as 2.5 or more hours daily.

Whether a school chooses ESL stand-alone or coteaching models, certain things must occur. According to Goldenberg and Coleman (2010), these include the following:

- ESL classes must occur "the moment students walk into the school" (p. 78).

- ESL classes must include a daily focus on listening and speaking in English, direct teaching of English including "vocabulary, syntax, social and conversational conventions, and strategies for how to learn the language" (p. 78).

- Students must be given the opportunity to learn English "authentically and functionally" (p. 78).

- Academic language must be taught across all the content areas (p. 78).

- Students must be prepared to interact with English-speaking peers (p. 79).

Which model is the one that describes your ESL class? To address our students' needs, we should look at the model that we use to provide ESL and ensure that students are receiving the optimal type and length of instruction. In the next chapter, we will continue to discuss academic programming for MLs, delving more deeply into content instruction and the interdependent connections among the sociocultural, developmental, academic, and cognitive processes of learning language and content.

References

August, D., & Shanahan, T. (2006). *Literacy in second language learners: Report of the National Literacy Panel on Language Minority Children and Youth.* Lawrence Erlbaum.

August, D., & Shanahan, T. (2008). *Developing reading and writing in second language learners: Lessons from a report of the National Literacy Panel on Language Minority Children and Youth.* Routledge.

Calderón, M. (2007). *Teaching reading to English language learners 6–12: A framework for improving achievement in content areas.* Corwin.

Calderón, M. E., & Minaya-Rowe, L. (2010). *Preventing long-term MLs: Transforming schools to meet core standards.* Corwin.

Collier, V. (1995). Acquiring a second language for school. *Directions in Language and Education, 1*(4). http://www.eric.ed.gov/ERICWebPortal/detail?accno=ED394301

Cummins, J. (1984). *Bilingualism and special education: Issues in assessment and pedagogy.* Multilingual Matters.

Cummins, J. (1994). Knowledge, power, and identity in teaching English as a second language. In F. Genesee (Ed.), *Educating second language children: The whole child, the whole curriculum, the whole community* (pp. 33–58). Cambridge University Press.

DelliCarpini, M. (2009). Dialogues across disciplines: Preparing English-as-a-second-language teachers for interdisciplinary collaboration. *Current Issues in Education, 11*(2). https://cie.asu.edu/ojs/index.php/cieatasu/issue/view/39

Dove, M. G., & Honigsfeld, A. (2018). *Co-teaching for English learners: A guide to collaborative planning, instruction, assessment, and reflection.* Corwin.

Echevarria, J. A., Vogt, M. E., & Short, D. J. (2017). *Making content comprehensible for English learners: The SIOP model* (5th ed.). Pearson.

Education Commission of the States. (2022). *50 state comparison English learner policies.* https://www.ecs.org/50-state-comparison-english-learner-policies/

Genesee, F., Lindholm-Leary, K., Saunders, W., & Christian, D. (2006). *Educating English language learners.* Cambridge University Press.

Goldenberg, C., & Coleman, R. (2010). *Promoting academic achievement among English learners: A guide to the research.* Corwin.

Haynes, J., & Zacarian, D. (2010). *Teaching content to English language learners.* Association for Supervision and Curriculum Development.

National Academies of Sciences, Engineering, and Medicine. (2017). *Promoting the educational success of children and youth learning English: Promising futures.* National Academies Press. https://doi.org/10.17226/24677

Saunders, W., Foorman, B., & Carlson, C. (2006). Is a separate block of time for oral English language development in program for English learners needed? *Elementary School Journal, 107,* 181–198. https://doi.org/10.1086/510654

TESOL. (2006). *TESOL Pre-K–12 English language proficiency standards framework.* https://www.tesol.org/docs/books/bk_prek-12elpstandards_framework_318 .pdf?sfvrsn=2&sfvrsn=2

Wei, R. C., Darling-Hammond, L., Andree, A., Richardson, N., & Orphanos, S. (2009). *Professional learning in the learning profession: A status report on teacher development in the United States and abroad.* National Staff Development Council.

WIDA. (2020). *WIDA English language development standards framework, 2020 edition: Kindergarten–grade 12.* https://wida.wisc.edu/sites/default/files/resource/WIDA-ELD -Standards-Framework-2020.pdf

Zacarian, D. (2009). How long should ESL classes be? And why? *Essential Teacher, 6*(3/4), 10–11.

Zacarian, D. (2012). *Mastering academic language: A comprehensive framework for supporting student achievement.* Corwin.

Zacarian, D., Calderón, M. E., & Gottlieb, M. (2021). *Beyond crises: Overcoming linguistic and cultural inequities in communities, schools, and classrooms.* Corwin.

Zacarian, D., & Soto, I. (2020). *Responsive schools for culturally and linguistically diverse students.* Norton Education.

CHAPTER 5

Guiding Instruction in Core Content Areas

"What did you notice about your group's work?" Mr. Rodriguez, a high school math teacher, asked his students.

"We understood what Antonio shared with us, and he helped us create a null hypothesis," a student from one of the small groups responded.

"How did you communicate with Antonio? Did you speak in Portuguese?" Mr. Rodriguez asked them.

"Yes and no," they responded.

"While Daniel helped Antonio because he can speak Portuguese, we also listened carefully to your question and used paper to talk through our responses," responded Claire, one of Antonio's teammates. "Having Antonio be the group's illustrator really helped us."

"And what did you learn?" Mr. Rodriguez asked. Marta, another group member, answered the question by saying that the group was able to create their null hypothesis by observing Antonio draw their hypothesis on paper.

"And what is your null hypothesis?" Mr. Rodriguez asked.

"Our hypothesis," Marta answered, "is that multilingual learners are not included in advanced placement courses and that this is not due to chance." Listening carefully to the small group's response, Mr. Rodriguez noted their null hypothesis and talked about the group's work.

He asked each of the six small cooperative learning groups in his math class to make note of how many times each member of the group contributed. To model what he meant by "contributed," he did a think-aloud and suggested one type of contribution. "Let me think about what a contribution would be. I have an idea. If you notice that one member of your group states a way to collect data, this could be called a *contribution*. Let me write this on the board. What else might we consider as a contribution to creating a null hypothesis?" Mr. Rodriguez asked as he wrote, "States a way to collect data."

Some suggested that "drawing it out" was a contribution and referenced Antonio. Others suggested that a contribution was when a teammate pointed to or shared specific pages in the course text to help solve the problem. One group's members whispered to each other and pointed to their spokesperson, who said, "A contribution is when we learn from what's written on the board."

Mr. Rodriguez then suggested that they create a matrix of acceptable contributions. At the end of 5 minutes, the class had created a list of four acceptable contributions. Table 5.1 shows the chart that Mr. Rodriguez and his class created for tallying all the contributions. Mr. Rodriguez then asked one member of each small group to make a tally sheet of that group's contributions. "It will help us in knowing that everyone has something to contribute to our class," he told them.

Table 5.1 Contribution Tally Sheet for Problem Set Solutions

	DRAWING	SAYING AN ANSWER OR SUGGESTION	SUGGESTING A PAGE FROM THE COURSE TEXT	SUGGESTING AN EXAMPLE FROM THE BOARD
Antonio	///			
Thomas		///// /////		//
Marta		/////	//	/////
Claire		///// ////	///	/////

Antonio's small group of four began working on determining how they would collect data to test their null hypothesis. Mr. Rodriguez noted that they leaned forward to the center of their table to watch Antonio draw on a piece of chart paper. He observed one of the members pointing to the board and talking about the problem while also pointing to what Antonio had written.

While Mr. Rodriguez was walking around the classroom and observing his students' responses to the problem set, Ms. Brown, the school principal, dropped into his class. She observed that three objectives had been written on the board. The first was listed as an overarching question: "How is math used to make predictions about our lives?" The second was listed as the day's learning objective: "Today, we will be able to solve a problem using a statistical hypothesis test." The third was stated as the day's language objectives that students would do:

1. In small groups, we will create a null hypothesis problem.

2. In small groups, we will create a means for collecting data to test our null hypothesis.

3. We will track our small group's contributions to the creation of our null hypothesis.

4. We will share our data collection plans with another small group.

Ms. Brown observed several problem sets displayed on the board, above which was a list of vocabulary about the topic of null hypothesis that Mr. Rodriguez and his students had created. The list was separated into categories and was accompanied by student-generated drawings of their meaning. Ms. Brown also observed that there was a tally keeper in each small group who was marking down the type of contribution that each peer was making. She noted that Antonio and other multilingual learners (MLs) in the class were contributing in ways that she had not expected, including the fact that Antonio was illustrating the math problem. Before waving goodbye to Mr. Rodriguez and his class as she prepared to drop into another math class, Ms. Brown whispered to Mr. Rodriguez, "Your students are so engaged. What are you doing to keep them on task and make your lesson so effective?"

What did Mr. Rodriguez do to make his lesson meaningful and effective?

In this chapter, we discuss the various steps that should be involved in teaching content to MLs. The intent is to share how lessons should be taught so that all multilingual learners can succeed in learning.

What constitutes a high-quality content lesson for an ML?

This section presents nine principles for providing high-quality content lessons. These relate to the four interdependent processes of language and content learning introduced in Chapter 4 and drawn from Zacarian et al. (2021), Zacarian and Soto (2020), Zacarian et al. (2017), Goldenberg and Coleman (2010), August and Shanahan (2006, 2008), Genesee et al. (2006), and Collier (1995). Each principle is important to include, whether the language of instruction is the student's primary language, English with support in the student's native language, or solely English. In addition, these principles apply in settings composed of MLs only, MLs and native speakers of English, heritage language learners, long-term MLs, and students with limited and interrupted formal education. Indeed, these principles apply to all settings where MLs are instructed.

Learning is a sociocultural process

Principle 1: Build positive relationships with students

Students greatly benefit from having positive, consistent, reliable, and trusted relationships with their educators (Fischer et al., 2020). It is amplified when we are curious about and have unconditional positive regard for them and take time to learn about their interests, hopes, and desires so that we may connect these to learning (Zacarian & Silverstone, 2020). Resources 3.3 and 3.4 in Chapter 3, which deal with interviewing and surveying MLs and their families, can greatly support our relationship-building efforts. Additionally, it is greatly helpful to share personal experiences with our students to let them know that we are human. It is also important to provide regular and consistent one-on-one check-ins with our students. Indeed, frequent check-ins were found to have a positive impact in supporting MLs during the height of the COVID-19 pandemic when students were learning remotely (U.S. Government Accountability Office, 2022). These strategies, and all that we do to build sustained relationships with MLs, require that we continuously identify students' personal strengths and competencies and create tasks and activities through which they can demonstrate these (Zacarian et al., 2017).

Principle 2: Connect academic learning to socially relevant issues that are personal to students' lives

High-quality lessons must be connected to students' lives in a way that propels and compels students' interest to learn content. Building connections is not as simple as connecting content to what students have learned in the classroom. Rather, learning is a social endeavor that requires a high level of interaction and connection making. It means taking time to learn what students already know and using this information to support the learning of new information in an interactive environment (Bandura, 1977; Gottlieb, 2021; Zacarian, 2013; Zacarian et al., 2021; Zacarian & Soto, 2020). Taking time to learn about students may seem like a daunting task given the number of students that teachers teach and their diverse cultural and language experiences. However, this should not be considered a barrier that cannot be addressed. Selecting issues that are socially relevant for students can be a very effective means for building students' interest to study content. It helps to take something that is important to students and connect it with something that may seem entirely irrelevant or unobtainable.

Connecting curriculum with socially relevant issues provides a means for getting students interested in learning content because it helps the task of learning to be personally connected (Vasquez, 2010; Zacarian et al., 2021; Zacarian & Silverstone, 2020; Zacarian & Soto, 2020). For example, a course in U.S. history may be more easily made relevant for a U.S.-born speaker of English than for an ML who was born and spent their primary years in a nondemocratic country. In the United States, for example, the civil rights work of Martin Luther King Jr. is honored in a number of ways, including celebrating his birth as a national holiday on the third Monday of every January. Many children in the United States learn about King and at least some of the civil rights movement in preschool, before they enter grade school. Thus, a lesson about this topic may be more easily understood and valued by native speakers of English from the United States than others because of the background knowledge that has been built up since they were very young children. Finding value in learning about U.S. history has to be connected to something that is relevant to every student's life, including students who are not from the United States or familiar with its history. The absence of these connections can literally disconnect students from the learning process. This is especially true for MLs and other students who find learning to be challenging.

Lee (2000), award-winning author of *China Boy* (Lee, 1991), has talked about his desire to drop out of school and become a gang member. When he enrolled in ninth grade and attended the first day of his English class, his teacher told the class that they would be reading the book *Pride and Prejudice* throughout the year. The book, written in 1813 by Jane Austen, a white woman who wrote romantic novels set in upper-class settings in England, had little relevance to Lee's life as a Chinese American. Convinced that school was not for him, he went to his English teacher to tell her that he would soon be dropping out of school. His teacher asked Lee what he knew about pride, and when he did not respond, she then asked him what he knew about prejudice. He knew quite a bit and responded to the question. When she told him that they would be learning about prejudice throughout the year and that his personal experience with it would be important, it compelled him to do more than just take the English course; he stayed in school and later developed an illustrious career as an assistant attorney general, author, and featured speaker. Lee's teacher helped him find value in learning the content, an important key principle. Effective lessons should include connections to something that is socially relevant while supporting the learning of content.

Mr. Rodriguez, the high school math teacher referenced at the beginning of this chapter, needed to think about math in terms of his students' lives to make it have value. He found a copy of a study about racial and gender profiling (Northeastern University, 2004) and brought it to class. The report, he hoped, would help spark students' interest in learning math. It provided information about traffic violations by race and gender and included the towns and cities in which these had occurred. Drawing from a mathematics unit created by Blatner (2006), Mr. Rodriguez selected this study because he knew that most of his students were reaching an age at which they would soon be obtaining a driver's license. He selected specific parts of the study and posed the following question: "Do you think that students of color from our town will have a higher chance of receiving a traffic violation than white people?" He selected this question because of its social justice relevance and a belief that learning involves creating a space in which students can discuss social issues that are relevant to them. Drawing from the study, each small group looked at the data and drew various conclusions. After this examination, Mr. Rodriguez asked his students to create a hypothesis that would examine the disparities that they thought existed in their personal lives through conducting a mathematical analysis of them.

With data gathered from the school principal, the small group that hypothesized that "there was no difference between the proportion of MLs in honors classes and the proportion of MLs expected to be in honor classes" conducted a computer simulation of their null hypothesis. They found that the actual placement of MLs in honors classes occurred fewer than 4 times in 1,000 simulated trials and concluded that it was highly unlikely that the situation in their school had occurred by chance.

Mr. Rodriguez found that his students eagerly engaged in their small-group projects. Everyone, including the group that examined the honors classes, examined a socially relevant issue. Mr. Rodriguez went a step further. He encouraged his students to present their findings to their classmates and others, including school administrators.

Learning should be made relevant to students of all ages. An example is a second-grade mathematics lesson in which students are studying basic operations of odd and even numbers based on their state standards. Eight of 25 students in the class are MLs at Levels 3 and 4 of English proficiency based on the standards. At the beginning of the school year, their teacher takes time to meet with families and asks them the questions found in Resource 3.3 ("Interview of Family and/or Newly Identified ML"). He also meets with each of his students during the first 2 weeks of school and asks them the survey questions found in Resource 3.4 ("Survey of Students' Interests and Strengths"). He draws from the responses to create lessons that are meaningful for his students. For example, he learns that most of his students enjoy playing soccer and several enjoy playing video and board games with their families. However, he observes that some students are not being included, are being too bossy, or are feeling upset at others as they play pick-up soccer at recess and math games in class. Drawing from his state's mathematics and English language proficiency standards, he engages students in examining their challenges in collaborating with each. He asks questions such as the following to help them use the language of content and explore the process of working and socializing together.

— We all like to play soccer at recess. To make it fair, it's important to have even teams. I have eight popsicle sticks here that show the names of some of the students in our class. How can they make two teams with the same number of people on each?

— What types of activities would help the two teams play well together?

Connecting curriculum to socially and personally relevant issues creates student interest in learning. It helps to move content from being dry and rote to being of interest and value to students. There are limitless ideas for making content relevant. When teachers take time to seek ways to do this, all students, including MLs, are more compelled to learn.

Principle 3: Build background knowledge by activating prior knowledge

In addition to helping students find value in learning, building background should include four means for activating prior knowledge with content: students' prior personal, social, cultural, and life experiences (Zacarian et al., 2017, 2021; Zacarian & Silverstone, 2020).

Connecting content to students' prior experiences can be accomplished in a myriad of ways. Drawing from ideas about how the brain works, connecting content to a student's personal experiences is an important key for connecting what a student does and does not know (Caine et al., 2005; Hammond, 2014; Jensen & Liesl, 2020). A powerful example of activating MLs' prior knowledge can be found in the

Sheltered Instruction Observation Protocol (SIOP; Echevarria et al., 2017), a lesson planning and delivery model for MLs. In a video that is a companion to texts on the SIOP model (Hubec & Short, 2002), a teacher delivers a lesson about the time in which early European settlers moved to what would become the United States. A large course text can be seen, as can various facts about and maps of this historical time period. To activate her students' knowledge, the teacher asks them a question about their personal experiences: "List the reasons why you and your family or someone you know came to the United States." Thus, while the text and maps are filled with historical facts, the teacher wisely chooses a means for connecting her students' experiences to key content and concept ideas.

A good rule of thumb is to build these types of background connections in the beginning of a unit so that, in addition to creating lessons that are socially relevant to students' lives, building connections to students' personal, social, cultural, and educational experiences accentuates making learning meaningful and comprehensible. It is also essential to support student learning by using a strengths-based approach.

Carol Salva, author, consultant, and former teacher of MLs with limited or interrupted schooling, shared the following about the importance of using an assets-based lens to support students' success.

Working with SLIFE (students with limited or interrupted formal education) used to feel overwhelming to me. Many of my students had just started learning English, they had missed years of formal schooling, and they were often going through some level of culture shock. Despite these very real challenges, I saw my SLIFE learn very quickly. I saw them catch up and even pass up their native-English-speaking peers. I was initially surprised by this. I wasn't expecting it because I failed to recognize the enormous amount of knowledge SLIFE bring and their capacity to learn rapidly. I had to remind myself that that missing formal education is not a cognitive issue. It is a lack of opportunity issue.

Here is what I learned: I needed to focus more on making content relevant to my SLIFE. Once content became relevant, engagement dramatically increased. This is exactly what research suggests: that we focus on interconnectedness and immediate relevance for SLIFE (Decapua & Marshall, 2015). Engaged students working together with plenty of low-stress opportunities to produce English results in their language repertoire expanding quickly (Seidlitz & Perryman, 2021). I also saw that drawing on their funds of knowledge helped keep them engaged (Moll et al., 2006), while collaborative learning helped me create a welcoming environment where all students felt honored and valued for their contributions.

(Continued)

(Continued)

I think this environment truly made the students feel motivated and connected, which enabled them to excel.

Some of the key conditions that promote engagement and connection for SLIFE are

- cooperative learning,

- low-stress opportunities to produce language,

- drawing on what they bring,

- relevant connections to the content.

Through all of this I have learned that SLIFE are absolutely able to learn quickly. We just need to focus on creating the right conditions. (C. Salva, personal communication, April 13, 2022)

Principle 4: Use cooperative learning

Cooperative learning should be a mainstay in any classroom with MLs. The small interactive space of pair and small-group work gives students multiple practice opportunities to use, apply, and learn the language of content (Calderón & Minaya-Rowe, 2010; Cohen & Lotan, 2014; Zacarian & Silverstone, 2015, 2020). It also provides an important space for students to have academic conversations and develop academic language, support each other's learning, problem solve, reach consensus, and more (Soto & Ward Singer, 2020). A national survey of elementary and secondary teachers reported that one of the most helpful strategies for mitigating learning obstacles for MLs during the pandemic was in-person small-group work (U.S. Government Accountability Office, 2022).

Pair and group work should occur after the teacher has introduced the overarching unit objective and the day's content and language objectives. It should also occur after the teacher has provided a model for enacting the type of pair and group work that is assigned. For example, after Mr. Rodriguez displayed and shared his overarching objective and the day's content and language objectives, he gave his students an example, a model and think-aloud, of what constituted a contribution for the group's task. He included a visual display of the vocabulary that he needed to form a mathematical hypothesis. He did this so that his students could see the type of response that he was seeking and have the vocabulary readily available. But keep in mind that providing a model, or think-aloud, is not the only means of engaging students to learn cooperatively and will not necessarily yield the outcomes that are desired.

Group work is a complex endeavor. It involves teachers reducing their authority and control so that students can learn with and from each other (Cohen, & Lotan, 2014; Zacarian & Silverstone, 2020). The rules of engaging in group work are often implied. Think of a teacher who instructs students to "get in their groups" or "talk with a partner." These seemingly simple directions have many hidden expectations, including that students will know what is expected of them when they work in groups—namely, that they will work collegially and participate evenly and equitably. In addition, roles are often not assigned and students are expected to simply work together.

When teachers take time to help their students learn about and work on the process of pair and group work and administrators, instructional coaches, curriculum directors, and other stakeholders support this activity, learning is much more likely to occur among all participants (Zacarian & Silverstone, 2020). Mr. Rodriguez, for example, assigned roles to each member of the group and engaged the groups in taking a tally of the types of responses that each participant contributed to the group's process. These activities, assigning roles and noting a group's communication process, helped to promote the effectiveness of the group work model.

For many reasons, MLs are not as likely to contribute to group or pair work as their peers. They may not yet have the capacity to speak in English with fluency because they may be at a stage of language learning where they are translating ideas from English to their native language in order to comprehend them. In addition, many MLs may be afraid to make errors in front of peers, and the pace of conversation may be too fast for MLs to keep up with. Also, the group's talk may reflect personal, world, or cultural experiences with which MLs are not familiar. Each of these challenges can be addressed when teachers take time to manage the process of group or pair work.

A first and important step is to assign roles that parallel the English proficiency levels of the MLs in the group. Mr. Rodriguez, for example, assigned the role of artist to the MLs who were at a stage of English proficiency that matched this role. Many different roles can support pair and group work, including listener, illustrator, and "ask the teacher." In addition to assigning roles, teachers must take time to explain how roles will be enacted. A second step is to help the group in its interactive process. This may be done in a myriad of ways, including coming to agreement about the types of contributions that count as participation and having a member of the group make note of them. It may include having partners or groups reflect on their work together and make note of their strengths and what needs to occur. It may also include creating a matrix for group processes and having groups self-grade their process of collaborative work.

Pair and group work involves two functions: process and product (Zacarian et al., 2017; Zacarian & Silverstone, 2015, 2020; Zacarian & Soto, 2020). Mr. Rodriguez asked each group to note their contributions to the group's task. This is a process function, whereas creating a null hypothesis is a task or product function. When we gather two or more students to work together, we are asking them to engage in the **collaborative process** of listening to others, having empathy for others, expressing their feelings, mediating their emotions, and resolving conflict productively

(Zacarian & Silverstone, 2020). Each of these process attributes is essential for successful collaborations. We must support students to positively engage in the process of collaborating. One approach for this type of engagement is having students individually and collaboratively examine the ways that they work together (i.e., what Mr. Rodriguez did to ensure students collaboratively acknowledged each other's contributions). It is also important to observe collaborations and respond to the positives we notice. Here are some observations Mr. Rodriguez shared with the small group:

> "I appreciate the ways you are listening to each other!"

> "Antonio, your drawing is very good. You are a great mathematician and artist!"

> "Your group created a powerful null hypothesis. Great collaboration!"

An additional means of reflective examination of a group's process and students' social-emotional growth is engaging MLs in journal writing. It is one of the most powerful tools that we have in supporting students' social-emotional growth (Durlak et al., 2011; Konichi & Park, 2018). Students can engage in a variety of means for journaling including computer-assisted and hand writing, drawing, and other creative means of self-reflection.

Cooperative learning is an important element in an effective lesson. When it incorporates assigning roles, matching tasks and activities to MLs' language development/proficiency level, and paying attention to group process and group product, it can be a powerful teaching method.

Learning language is a developmental process

Principle 5: Deliver lessons that are comprehensible

In an era of high-stakes testing in which high school graduation depends on students passing state exams, many teachers may feel pressured to cover all of the curriculum and to "teach to the test." This can lead to surface coverage of content and a desire to teach as quickly as possible to cover it all. MLs are not able to grasp fast-paced lessons delivered in English as they are learning English and content simultaneously. The quickness of the pace can become an even larger challenge for students with limited or interrupted prior schooling or schooling that does not match that of a U.S. public school. This is true whether the lesson is delivered in English or in a student's native language.

Making lessons comprehensible means making them accessible and understandable. Teachers must factor in the pace of the lesson as well as the volume of text that is required for students to learn content. Mr. Rodriguez was careful to speak slowly and carefully as he delivered his lesson. He also deliberately provided ample practice space when his students worked in small groups. And he required his students to take a tally of who was contributing as a means of ensuring that every student was contributing actively. The means for receiving a tally mark included a wide variety of communicative tasks that matched his MLs' English proficiency level. Thus, whether he was teaching the lesson or his students were engaging in group work related to it, he made sure the pace of the class deliberately and intentionally took into account the MLs in his classroom as well as the students with varying learning styles and differences.

Knowing the English proficiency levels of MLs and creating tasks and activities that parallel these levels is essential. Equally important is considering the use of students' native languages and providing students with opportunities to use their native languages for learning (Gottlieb, 2021; Zacarian et al., 2021). For example, with help from the ESL teacher in his school, Mr. Rodriguez reviewed the WIDA (2022) Can Dos that were pertinent to Antonio's stage of learning English. Based on this information, they brainstormed ways to support Antonio to be more comfortable in the math class. They came up with the plan of having him draw and illustrate his mathematical ideas. Mr. Rodriguez also knew that it was perfectly fine for Antonio to express his ideas in Portuguese, and he encouraged him to do so with a fellow classmate. When Antonio engaged in class, his drawings conveyed his ideas and were a way for Mr. Rodriguez to know that Antonio understood the lesson.

Since Mr. Rodriguez frequently used group work, he also created ways to make the lesson more comprehensible when MLs worked with peers. For example, he made sure to place Antonio in a group with a peer who spoke Portuguese. He also encouraged the group to use drawings to help Antonio understand their ideas with meaning. The importance of making lessons comprehensible goes well beyond looking at what is stated by a teacher to what is done by students in order to use the language of content.

In addition, when Mr. Rodriguez assigned homework to Antonio, he made sure that it involved tasks that Antonio had done successfully in class. While Antonio was able to write and solve mathematical formulas using numbers, he was not able to express these in English in a written format. Mr. Rodriguez assigned Antonio homework that required him to use English at his proficiency level. Designing lessons for understanding must take into account factors such as these.

Principle 6: Plan assessments and homework for and with MLs

MLs must be engaged in learning language as they are learning subject matter such as mathematics and science. Unlike their English-fluent peers, they must engage in both of these processes simultaneously. The same holds true for English-fluent students who are enrolled in dual-language programs. They, too, must engage in learning the target language and content. In planning and enacting lessons and assessing their effectiveness, whether in one language or more than one, there must be a direct connection between

- what is being learned and

- what is being assessed to demonstrate what has been learned.

We must always consider the following: what students should be able to know and do by the end of a lesson, unit, or task; how we will tap into their and their families' funds of knowledge (i.e., their personal, social, cultural, linguistic, and life experiences) to support student learning; and what students will do to demonstrate their learning. Renowned scholar and founder of the WIDA consortium Margo Gottlieb (2021) shares that there should be "a direct connection among curriculum, instruction, and assessment" (p. 65) and stresses the importance of working to "negotiate a final product, project, or performance with students" (p. 67). As important a role as we have, it is essential to empower students as learners. One means of doing this is to support students' creativity in demonstrating their learning. A national survey asked elementary and secondary teachers to share the strategies they used to reduce learning obstacles during the pandemic. One of the most helpful strategies was "flexibility . . . in the media students . . . use to submit assignments" (U.S. Government Accountability Office, 2022, p. 18). We can accomplish a good deal more when we empower students!

A student's language development/proficiency level is key to determining appropriate tasks and assignments. MLs should be assigned tasks and activities that are just a little beyond their language development/proficiency level (Krashen, 2002). Some may argue that this means doing less and "dumbing down" the instructional program and teachers' expectations of students. Actually, it means creatively thinking about what is possible for students to do in order to demonstrate understanding and creating tasks and assessments that match it. For example, Mr. Rodriguez assigned the role of illustrator to Antonio and some of the other students. Their mathematical illustrations of a null hypothesis gave him clear evidence that they had learned and understood the concepts. Thus the assignment ("work in groups to create a null hypothesis") was enacted through a variety of roles that Mr. Rodriguez assigned, including one that he, the MLs, and their peers could assess as it was occurring. Observing the illustration role as it was occurring provided Mr. Rodriguez with an on-the-spot means of assessing students. The end-of-unit summative assessments were also based on MLs' language development/proficiency levels. Thus, the formative on-the-spot and summative assessments were designed and delivered to match his MLs' level(s) of language and academic development.

Differentiating homework tasks is critical for ensuring that MLs not only can do the homework we assign but will not find it too difficult or impossible to accomplish. Another key aspect of homework is that it is a great opportunity for families and local communities to share their expertise. For example, young students learning about different means of measurement can engage in homework tasks with their families to apply what they have learned by measuring the ingredients used in a common meal that they enjoy (e.g., 2 cups of water, 1/4 cup of fine egg noodles, 1 cup of rice, and 1 tablespoon of butter to make rice pilaf). Local community resources can also support student learning in a myriad of ways. An example is a high school statistics course whose students choose local issues to explore. One group decides to explore the accessibility challenges that senior citizens have in obtaining COVID-19 vaccinations. They do this by tapping into the expertise of local pharmacists, public health professionals, and, of course, senior citizens. One aspect that is key for every educator is ensuring that homework matches students' level of language proficiency and content understanding.

How can teachers assign homework for MLs? An important rule of thumb is to design homework that is based on the principles presented in this chapter. Each of these implies that we will differentiate instruction to match the individual needs of our students. After all, homework is completed during a time in which students are out of class and on their own. We have to think about the types of tasks that our MLs are able to complete successfully in class and extend these as homework assignments. For example, Mr. Rodriguez asked students to illustrate another hypothesis and share the idea with a family member. We should engage students in tasks outside of class by considering the following:

1. The *amount* of work assigned: We must think carefully about the amount of time that is needed for each ML to complete the assignment, then assign tasks that will not take an unreasonable amount of time.

2. The *type* of work assigned: Simpler or modified reading and writing tasks are more appropriate for some MLs, as are adapted texts. These give students much-needed time to learn material that is not overwhelming.

3. The *visual displays* that are needed to support and do out-of-class assignments: This might include the overarching content and learning objectives, key vocabulary, and graphic organizers that are used in class as key home supports (Haynes & Zacarian, 2010; Zacarian, 2013).

4. *Feedback from students* about the assigned homework: Asking students about their homework experience can be a critical means for assessing its effectiveness. Ask students to complete statements such as these:

    I was able to understand the homework assignment because _____.

    I found the homework to be too difficult because: _____.

    The homework helped me learn _____.

Learning is an academic process

Principle 7: Define overarching objectives and the day's learning and language objectives

An important principle for making lessons effective is to determine (1) the key content concepts that are essential for students to learn and (2) what they will need to do to learn these key concepts. Gardner (2009) outlines specific abilities that are needed by educators. One is the ability to take a mass of information, sort through it, determine the key information that is important, and convey it succinctly to others. Teachers are the leaders of their classrooms. They are also the deliverers of content. Some content, such as a high school biology or history text, is dense and filled with information.

Other content, such as a picture book used to teach kindergarten students how to read, contains illustrations and other graphics that do not necessarily depict the key idea that is important for students to learn. Teachers have an important role in considering what it is they want students to learn and then conveying this to them. Teachers must also ensure that their students, especially MLs, have access to the content.

Displaying an overarching unit objective is an important first step to making the key content visible (Echevarria et al., 2017; Haynes & Zacarian, 2010). Mr. Rodriguez posted an overarching unit objective on the board: "How is math used to make predictions about our lives?" Writing this in the form of a question was intended to pique his students' interest in solving the question. The overarching question remained on the board throughout the unit of study. Each lesson began and ended with Mr. Rodriguez referring to the overarching unit question. The reason that he displayed this unit objective was to help his students focus on the content to be learned. The presence of an overarching question is an important aspect of an effective lesson.

Displaying the day's learning objective is also important (Echevarria et al., 2017; Haynes & Zacarian, 2010; Zacarian, 2013). It provides a clear idea of what is to be learned and plays an important role in helping students understand the various functions of language, such as using language to hypothesize. For example, Mr. Rodriguez posted this learning objective: "Today, we will be able to solve a problem by using a statistical hypothesis test." He spent time thinking about the content that his students would learn and created this single learning objective for the day's lesson. Many teachers draw from their state and local curriculum standards to design and deliver lessons. These are generally written in teacher language; that is, the standards are written in language aimed at educators that is not student friendly. A good content objective must be written in student-friendly, age-appropriate language. However, a learning objective is not enough to help all learners.

As part of a print-rich environment, short statements about what students will do in order to learn are important to include in the day's objectives. Echevarria et al. (2017) describe these as language objectives. It is important to think of these as how students will communicate to use the language of content or what they will do to listen, speak, read, and write during the lesson.

Mr. Rodriguez listed four language objectives for the day's lesson: (1) In small groups, we will create a null hypothesis problem. (2) We will create a means for collecting data to test it. (3) We will track our small group's contributions to creating our null hypothesis. (4) We will then share our null hypothesis and data collection plans with another small group for feedback.

An overarching unit objective as well as daily content and language objectives are critical to designing and delivering effective content lessons.

Principle 8: Target vocabulary instruction

Haynes and Zacarian (2010) refer to vocabulary as the terms, words, idioms, and phrases (TWIPs) that students need to learn and use. Beck et al. (2013) provide a way for leaders to think about vocabulary in terms of three tiers, or levels. Drawing from Haynes and Zacarian as well as Beck et al., Tier 1 TWIPs reflect common basic one- to two-syllable words or phrases that are typically and frequently used in everyday conversation (e.g., *couch, pencil, chair, school, walk*). While many believe that these are not necessary to teach because of their frequency of use, these are a must for beginning speakers of English. As seen in Chapter 2, teachers of preproduction and emerging learners of English must provide instruction of Tier 1 words. Teaching this level of words is often accompanied with visuals such as labeling the classroom and creating flash cards. In addition, teachers often act out the words using body language and kinesthetic displays to help students use these common everyday words through experiential learning. All MLs need intentional support to learn common everyday TWIPs, especially those with multiple meanings: anaphoric references to replace words or phrases (e.g., *The test was delayed. It was put off.*) and idiomatic expressions (e.g., *put up, put down, put off*).

Content vocabulary is essential for students. Tier 3 TWIPs are unlike those at Tier 1 in that they are not used with high frequency. Indeed, they are used infrequently and are often multisyllabic (Beck et al., 2013). Terms such as *quadratic equation, null hypothesis, hexagon, barometric pressure,* and *iambic pentameter* are examples of Tier 3 TWIPs. They are also academic terms that are not likely to be used outside of the classroom in which the content is being taught. MLs and others need to be taught these words for them to "stick." However, unlike fluent speakers of English, MLs need as many as 20 practice opportunities using these TWIPs in context to learn them (Calderón, 2009; Hinkel, 2009). Mr. Rodriguez posted a word wall of Tier 3 mathematical vocabulary that was essential for his students to learn. Marzano (2010) conducted a study of the academic vocabulary that is needed by most students. While content books are filled with content-specific vocabulary, much less is actually needed and used by students. This is quite important to consider when planning and delivering lessons. For example, prior to teaching the lesson, Mr. Rodriguez reviewed all of the math vocabulary that was used in the course text on the topic of null hypothesis and selected the key terms that he believed were essential for his students. Tier 3 words must be taught to be learned, but it is important to synthesize the key vocabulary that is essential for content learning and peel away what is not. Visuals such as student drawings of the vocabulary (Marzano & Pickering, 2005) and word walls that are sorted by categories (Haynes & Zacarian, 2010), as well as student practice using the vocabulary in context, are essential for learning content vocabulary.

However, everyday basic vocabulary and content vocabulary are not all that students need. Indeed, there is a large volume of other words, those at Tier 2, that are needed to be successful in school. According to Beck et al. (2013), Tier 2 vocabulary refers to synonyms for Tier 1 words. Tier 2 vocabulary is much more specific and descriptive than Tier 1 vocabulary and is often one or two syllables longer than Tier 1 words (e.g., *sofa, love seat, divan*). Tier 2 also includes transition words that are used to mean *and, but,* and *so* and include words such as *also, however,* and *therefore.* These are essential not just for the English language development of MLs but for all students. We must infuse Tier 2 vocabulary (including connectors and transition words as well as words with multiple meanings) and Tier 3 discipline-specific vocabulary into every lesson.

MLs with well-developed vocabularies in their first language are likely to be able to transfer these vocabulary skills into their second language. Generally, students with large Tier 2 first-language vocabularies have had rich exposure to and experiences engaging in literacy (Pransky, 2008; Pransky & Zacarian, 2011). Students who do not have well-developed Tier 2 vocabularies in their native language, including students with limited or interrupted prior schooling, need focused and continuous instruction on this tier. Developing Tier 2 vocabulary should be part of the instructional program of any English language development teacher and content teacher. Unlike Tier 1 words, which occur in high frequency in everyday conversation, Tier 2 words are less likely to be used unless they are directly taught to students and students are given multiple practice opportunities to use these in listening, speaking, reading, and writing contexts (Calderón, 2007; Pransky & Zacarian, 2011). Word walls, handouts, and other visual displays are essential for this type of vocabulary development. A national survey of elementary and secondary teachers affirms the importance of vocabulary building and using visual tools such as these (U.S. Government Accountability Office, 2022). Table 5.2 is a sample of a visual display.

Table 5.2   Visual Display of Synonyms for *And, But,* and *So*

AND	BUT	SO
Also	However	Therefore
In addition	Except	Accordingly
Plus	In spite of	Thus
As well as	Nevertheless	Consequently
Together with	Yet	Hence

Visual displays provide MLs with multiple opportunities to see Tier 2 words. It's also greatly helpful to assign tasks that require their usage such as the sentence stems in Table 5.3, in which students are tasked with creating a sentence using Tier 2 synonyms.

Table 5.3   Sentence Stems Using Synonyms for *And, But,* and *So*

I agree with you [and]

I agree with you [but]

I agree with you [so]

Here is a possible extension activity:

With your group, think of as many words as you can for each of the following three transition words

And:

But:

So:

It is important to note that students with interrupted schooling may need a more intensive form of vocabulary development. Calderón (2007) addresses the need for teachers to focus academic instruction intentionally and purposefully in key areas, including students' word knowledge, reading fluency, understanding of classroom texts, discussion skills, grammar knowledge and use, writing skills, and spelling. Building word knowledge should be at the heart of any academic program for MLs. According to Calderón, comprehension depends on a student knowing 90% to 95% of the words in a text. To support vocabulary learning, she emphasizes the importance of a teacher saying the word aloud, asking students to repeat it three times, providing students with examples of the word in context with content text, supporting dictionary definitions with those that have student-friendly wording, and engaging students in multiple practice opportunities to use the word in context.

Learning is a cognitive process

Principle 9: Support critical thinking

Language is used to convey our thoughts. Whether we use language to listen, speak, read, or write, each of these domains is a means for communicating what we are thinking. School is an environment in which students are expected to use a high level of thinking and cognitive skills. Bloom's Taxonomy is a helpful means for understanding the types of thinking skills that students need (Anderson & Krathwohl, 2001; Bloom & Krathwohl, 1956). These fall into six categories of increasing levels of complexity:

- remembering

- understanding

- applying

- analyzing

- evaluating

- creating

Mr. Rodriguez asked his students to create a null hypothesis, a task that required the very highest level of cognition. His students needed to *remember* information about what a null hypothesis was. They needed to *understand* what this definition meant and what it did not mean. They needed to *apply* the definition to engage in the assigned task. They needed to *analyze* and *evaluate* the means by which they would measure their null hypothesis. They also needed to *create* the null hypothesis, the most complex of the six categories listed above. The means by which these thinking skills are taught are critical. Mr. Rodriguez modeled aloud the thinking skills that were needed. It is important for teachers to identify the thinking skills, such as the following, that students need and to explicitly teach them:

Clarify	Explain	Predict
Consider	Hypothesize	Report
Convince	Illustrate	Request
Create	Imagine	Respond
Describe	Infer	Retell
Direct	Interact	Summarize
Draw	Persuade	Synthesize

Each one of these requires a different type of thinking skill. What is critical is that each be identified and explicitly taught so that every student has the opportunity to learn what each word means in practice.

Using Visuals

Visual displays, as we have discussed in this chapter, are important for delivering high-quality lessons. Along with visibly displaying the overarching unit objective and the day's learning and language objectives and vocabulary, graphic organizers and pictures (including maps, drawings, photographs, graphs, sentence stems, and charts) should also be included. Visuals provide an important means for the brain to "see," or grasp, ideas and concepts (Hyerle & Alper, 2011; Jensen, 2005; Jensen & Liesl, 2020). Indeed, a national survey of elementary and secondary teachers reported that using visuals was a helpful strategy for mitigating learning obstacles during the pandemic (U.S. Government Accountability Office, 2022).

Authentic visuals such as videos, photographs, and drawings of a concept provide helpful access for learning. Field trips to locations where the concept can be seen (e.g., a walking trip to the local post office to see the process of sending and receiving a letter) is a great way to make lessons authentic because students experience the context in which the concept occurs. Conducting these at the beginning of a unit (as opposed to as a culminating activity at the conclusion) is a very helpful way to make the content understandable by situating students in the context from the start.

Graphic organizers are commonly used by teachers, and many course texts include graphic organizers as a means for illustrating and describing an idea or concept. While these can be greatly helpful, they can also be confusing when different ones are used to depict the same concept and when there is little consistency as to how often they are used. It is not uncommon, for example, for elementary school MLs and students with learning differences and learning disabilities to be instructed by more than one teacher. An ML may be taught by a grade-level classroom teacher, an ESL teacher, a bilingual teacher, and a Title 1 teacher. Each of these teachers may choose a different graphic organizer to teach the same concept.

For example, think of the concept *same and different* and apply it to the following: ways in which an elementary school and a middle school are the same and different. One teacher may choose to use a Venn diagram to illustrate this idea (Figure 5.1), whereas another might use a different type of graphic organizer (Figure 5.2), and a third might choose to be creative and design an entirely different visual to illustrate the same concept.

Figure 5.1   Venn Diagram Showing How an Elementary School and a Middle School Are the Same and Different

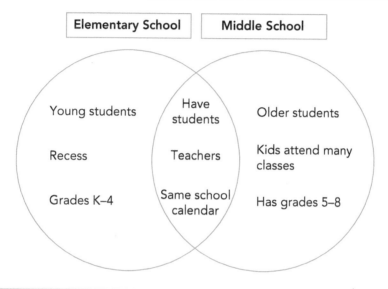

Figure 5.2   Another Visual Showing How an Elementary School and a Middle School Are the Same and Different

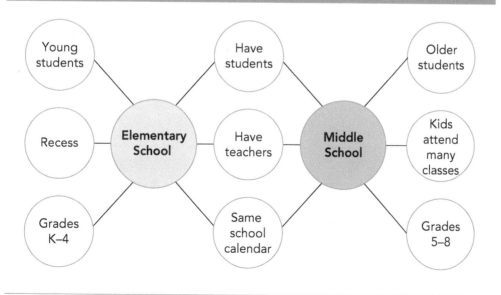

While the intent of a graphic organizer is to help make concepts and ideas more meaningful, school leaders should help teachers select specific organizers that will be used to depict the various concepts, as using more than one can create confusion rather than provide access to MLs. Let's look closely at the various reasons for selecting a graphic organizer.

We use visuals to organize our thoughts, connecting a concept relationship to an idea, in eight ways (Hyerle & Alper, 2011):

- brainstorming

- describing

- sequencing/ordering

- comparing/contrasting

- classifying/grouping

- whole–part relationships

- describing cause–effect relationships

- seeing analogies[1]

While these eight elements are not directly the core curriculum that is taught, they are essential means for teaching the curriculum and, more important, helping students engage in a thinking process in order to learn. In a real sense, each time we use a graphic organizer, we help students visually map concepts. This can break down when there is no consistency among the type of organizers that are used. When the same organizer is used to teach any one of these important eight elements, it provides a good conceptual anchor for students, particularly MLs who are learning new content and language simultaneously and must rely on the familiar to make a connection with new information. Graphic organizers of any sort must be explicitly taught to students. They cannot simply be written on the board. Gathering a team of elementary grade-level, secondary subject matter, resource, and specialist teachers can be a very helpful means for school and district leaders to develop the routine organizer that will be used for each concept. Leaders can play an integral role in ensuring that these important visuals are consistent and, therefore, more accessible for all learners.

Strengths-Based Peer Coaching, Mentoring, and Supervision

Each of these eight principles should be used to effectively deliver a lesson. The checklist found in Resource 5.1 can help teachers, instructional coaches, peer mentors, and supervisors guide the planning and enactment as well as effectiveness of instruction in meeting the needs of our ever-growing and -changing MLs. Two credos are

---

[1] The trademarked term *Thinking Maps* was developed to describe the eight types of thinking processes that are used when engaging in a learning task.

essential to consider: "Feedback is the breakfast of champions" and "You got it wrong before you got it better" (Zacarian et al., 2021, p. 105). Peers, instructional coaches, mentors, and supervisors are invaluable professionals who can help guide us during our worst and best moments to transform our practice. They can help us navigate our toughest and most challenging moments and integrate ideas and strategies for working both online and in person with students and families, use curricula we have never used and culturally responsive practices we have not yet tried, work better without working impossibly harder, use trauma-informed practices, and much more! The idea behind this strengths-based support is that it be with those we trust, respect, and have good rapport with. As importantly, it should be with those who will help us stretch our thinking to try new ideas while simultaneously helping us feel safe and a sense of confidence in doing so. Resource 5.1 can be used as a guide for this purpose of professional growth. The next chapter will discuss the importance of engaging parents in their children's education.

RESOURCE 5.1

Checklist for Designing and Delivering Quality Learning Experiences

IN MY CLASSROOM, . . .	ABSOLUTELY! WHAT IT LOOKS LIKE	WHAT I PLAN TO DO TO SUPPORT IT OCCURRING AND WHAT IT LOOKS LIKE
1. I have taken time to build positive relationships with MLs.		
2. I have taken time to connect the academic learning experience to socially relevant issues that are personal to my students' lives in the following ways:		
3. My lessons connect with students' personal, cultural, language, and prior academic experiences.		
4. I have designed pair and small-group tasks and activities that will engage students in multiple opportunities to practice using and applying the language of content.		
5. I have specifically taught students how to engage in pair and group work.		
6. I have designed activities that will help students examine their group's communicative process in enacting pair and group work.		
7. I have designed activities that will help students assess their group's task, product, or performance.		
8. I know the language development/ proficiency levels of the MLs I teach and have planned activities and tasks that are targeted to these levels.		
9. I have assigned roles that MLs will do in pair and group work that match their level of language development/ proficiency.		
10. I have provided MLs with in-class opportunities to practice the tasks and assignments that they will do at home.		

IN MY CLASSROOM, . . .	ABSOLUTELY! WHAT IT LOOKS LIKE	WHAT I PLAN TO DO TO SUPPORT IT OCCURRING AND WHAT IT LOOKS LIKE
I have also modified these to match each ML's current level of English language development/proficiency.		
11. I have planned and negotiated homework tasks and assessments with MLs to ensure that students have a voice in how to demonstrate their learning.		
12. I have taken time to phrase the overarching objectives of the unit in a meaningful way to help my students understand the unit's purpose.		
13. I have posted my daily lesson's content (i.e., learning) and language objectives (i.e., what students will do to learn) on the board in clear and simple language (and checked for student comprehension).		
14. I have identified the important terms, words, idioms, and phrases (TWIPs) that my students need to learn this subject matter and posted these on the board using categories and illustrations to make them meaningful.		
15. I have identified the graphic organizers that I will use to display the concepts that I want my students to learn. These include organizers that will help my students brainstorm, describe, order, compare/contrast, classify, and/or display whole to part, cause–effect, or analogy relationships.		
16. I have modeled the tasks and activities that my students will do and stated directions in simple language.		
17. I have modeled and explicitly taught the thinking skills that my students will use.		

 Available for download at **resources.corwin.com/transformingschoolsformultilinguallearners**

References

Anderson, L. W., & Krathwohl, D. R. (Eds.). (2001). *A taxonomy for learning, teaching and assessing: A revision of Bloom's Taxonomy of educational objectives: Complete edition.* Longman.

August, D., & Shanahan, T. (2006). *Developing literacy in second-language learners: Report of the National Literacy Panel on Language-Minority Children and Youth.* Lawrence Erlbaum.

August, D., & Shanahan, T. (2008). *Developing reading and writing in second-language learners: Lessons from the report of the National Literacy Panel on Language-Minority Children and Youth.* Routledge.

Bandura, A. (1977). *Social learning theory.* General Learning Press.

Beck, I. L., McKeown, M. G., & Kucan, L. (2013). *Bringing words to life: Robust vocabulary instruction* (2nd ed.). Guilford Press.

Blatner, W. (2006). *Final paper.* Unpublished manuscript, University of Massachusetts at Amherst.

Bloom, B. S., & Krathwohl, D. R. (1956). *Taxonomy of educational objectives: The classification of educational goals, by a committee of college and university examiners. Handbook 1: Cognitive domain.* Longman.

Caine, R. N., Caine, G., McClintic, C., & Klimek, K. (2005). *12 brain/mind learning principles in action: The field book for making connections, teaching, and the human brain.* Corwin.

Calderón, M. (2007). *Teaching reading to English language learners, grades 6–12: A framework for improving achievement in the content areas.* Corwin.

Calderón, M. (2009, March). *Expediting reading comprehension for English language learners.* Paper presented at the annual convention of TESOL, Denver, CO.

Calderón, M. E., & Minaya-Rowe, L. (2010). *Preventing long-term MLs: Transforming schools to meet core standards.* Corwin.

Cohen, E. G., & Lotan, R. (2014). *Designing groupwork: Strategies for the heterogeneous classroom* (10th ed.). Teachers College Press.

Collier, V. (1995). Acquiring a second language for school. *Directions in Language and Education, 1*(4). http://www.eric.ed.gov/ERICWebPortal/recordDetail?accno=ED394301

DeCapua, A., & Marshall, H. W. (2015). Reframing the conversation about students with limited or interrupted formal education: From achievement gap to cultural dissonance. *NASSP Bulletin, 99*(4), 356–370.

Durlak, J. A., Weissberg, R. P., Dymnicki, A. B., Taylor, R. D., & Schellinger, K. B. (2011). The impact of enhancing students' social and emotional learning: A meta-analysis of school based universal interventions. *Child Development, 82*(1), 405–432.

Echevarria, J., Vogt, M., & Short, D. (2017). *Making content comprehensible for English learners: The SIOP model* (5th ed.). Pearson.

Fischer, D., Frey, N., & Hattie, J. (2020). *The distance learning handbook: Grades K–12: Teaching for engagement and impact in any setting.* Corwin.

Gardner, H. (2009). *Five minds for the future.* Harvard University Press.

Genesee, F., Lindholm-Leary, K., Saunders, W., & Christian, D. (2006). *Educating English language learners.* Cambridge University Press.

Goldenberg, C., & Coleman, R. (2010). *Promoting academic achievement among English learners: A guide to the research.* Corwin.

Gottlieb, M. (2021). *Classroom assessment in multiple languages: A handbook for teachers.* Corwin.

Hammond, Z. L. (2014). *Culturally responsive teaching and the brain: Promoting authentic engagement and rigor among culturally and linguistically diverse students.* Corwin.

Haynes, J., & Zacarian, D. (2010). *Teaching English language learners across the content areas.* Association for Supervision and Curriculum Development.

Hinkel, E. (2009, March). *Teaching academic vocabulary and helping students retain it.* Paper presented at the annual convention of TESOL, Denver, CO.

Hubec, J., & Short, D. (Producers). (2002). *The SIOP model: Sheltered instruction for academic achievement* [Videotape]. Authors.

Hyerle, D., & Alper, L. (2011). *Student successes with Thinking Maps®: School-based research, results, and models for achievement using visual tools* (2nd ed.). Sage.

Jensen, E. (2005). *Teaching with the brain in mind* (2nd ed.). Association for Supervision and Curriculum Development.

Jensen, E., & Liesl, M. (2020). *Brain based learning: Teaching the way students really learn* (3rd ed.). Corwin.

Konichi, C., & Park, S. (2018). Promoting children's healthy social-emotional growth: Dialogue journal. *Journal of Education and Learning, 7*(1), 246–253. https://doi.org/10.5539/jel.v6n2p246

Krashen, S. D. (2002). *Second language acquisition and second language learning.* http://www.sdkrashen.com/content/books/sl_acquisition_and_learning.pdf

Lee, G. (1991). *China boy.* Random House.

Lee, G. (2000, May). *Keynote speech.* Paper presented at the annual conference of MATSOL, Leominster, MA.

Marzano, R. (2010, March). *Building academic background knowledge in English language learners.* Workshop at the annual convention of TESOL, Boston.

Marzano, R. J., & Pickering, D. J. (2005). *Building academic vocabulary: Teacher's manual.* Association for Supervision and Curriculum Development.

Moll, L., Amanti, C., Neff, D., & González, N. (2006). Funds of knowledge for teaching: Using a qualitative approach to connect homes and classrooms. In N. Gonzalez, L. C. Moll, & C. Amanti (Eds.), *Funds of knowledge: Theorizing practices in households, communities, and classrooms* (pp. 83–100). Routledge.

Northeastern University, Institute on Race and Justice. (2004). *Massachusetts racial and gender profiling technical report.* https://www.boston.com/images/daily/04/profiling_finalreport.pdf

Pransky, K. (2008). *Beneath the surface: The hidden realities of teaching culturally and linguistically diverse young learners, K–6.* Heinemann.

Pransky, K., & Zacarian, D. (2011). *Teacher's guide to providing rich vocabulary instruction.* Collaborative for Educational Services.

Seidlitz, J., & Perryman, B. (2021). *7 steps to a language-rich interactive classroom* (2nd ed.). Seidlitz Education.

Soto, I., & Ward Singer, T. (2020). From silence to conversation. In M. E. Calderón, M. G. Dove, D. Staehr Fenner, M. Gottlieb, A. Honigsfeld, T. Ward Singer, S. Slakk, I. Soto, & D. Zacarian (Eds.), *Breaking down the wall: Essential shifts for English learners' success* (pp. 89–100). Corwin.

U.S. Government Accountability Office. (2022, May). *Pandemic learning: Teachers reported many obstacles for high-poverty students and English learners as well as some mitigating factors.* https://www.gao.gov/assets/gao-22-105815.pdf

Vasquez, V. (2010). *Getting beyond "I like the book": Creating space for critical literacy in K–6 classrooms* (2nd ed.). International Reading Association.

WIDA. (2022). *Can do descriptors: Key uses edition, grades 9–12.* https://wida.wisc.edu/sites/default/files/resource/CanDo-KeyUses-Gr-9-12.pdf

Zacarian, D. (2013). *Mastering academic language: A framework for supporting student achievement.* Corwin.

Zacarian, D., Alvarez-Ortiz, L. A., & Haynes, J. (2017). *Teaching to strengths: Supporting students living with trauma, violence, and chronic stress.* Association for Supervision and Curriculum Development.

Zacarian, D., Calderón, M. E., & Gottlieb, M. (2021). *Beyond crises: Overcoming linguistic and cultural inequities in communities, schools, and classrooms.* Corwin.

Zacarian, D., & Silverstone, M. A. (2015). *In it together: How student, family, and community partnerships advance engagement and achievement in diverse classrooms.* Corwin.

Zacarian, D., & Silverstone, M. A. (2020). *Teaching to empower: Taking action to foster student agency, collaboration, and reflection.* Association for Supervision and Curriculum Development.

Zacarian, D., & Soto, I. (2020). *Responsive schooling for culturally and linguistically diverse learners.* Norton Professional Books.

CHAPTER 6

Emphasizing the Importance of Family Engagement

When Sokhem arrived to take the SAT, he was 15 minutes late. The public transportation that he normally took to school during the week ran on a different schedule on the weekend. When he arrived at 8:15, the monitor would not let him in. She told Sokhem that the testing had begun at 8:00 and the door was closed. He almost broke down in tears as she shut the door, refusing him entry. He returned to the bus stop and waited over an hour for the bus to return him to his house. When he finally arrived home and told his mother what happened, he cried, "Now, I will never go to college!"

Sokhem's mother was not sure what to do. She knew that his school was having an Open House for parents soon. Thinking that would be a good time to ask his teachers for help, she took time off from work to help her son—though she would miss a much-needed day of pay. On Open House night, she waited anxiously in a line that was marked for parents of 11th graders whose last name began with the letters A through G. When she reached the sign-in table, she tried to muster the courage to seek help for her son. But before she could, she was shuttled off to Sokhem's first-period math class. She politely waited while the math teacher described the math course to all the parents so she could speak with him about Sokhem. However, the teacher spoke so quickly that she could not keep up with him. Suddenly, at the end of 10 minutes, a bell rang, and the school principal announced over the loudspeaker that parents should go to their child's next class. Sokhem's mother reluctantly got up from her seat and tried to get the math teacher's attention. However, all he did was reach for the course schedule that she was holding and tell her where to go for Sokhem's second-period class. This same scenario continued throughout the Open House event. Sokhem's mother went from class to class hoping that she could get advice from one of his teachers. By the last class, she was exhausted. She had been rushed from one classroom to the next, one side of the building to the other, and had not been able to ask her important question. She was not empowered enough to stop the flow of the Open House night like a more empowered parent from the dominant culture might have been, nor did she have enough English language skill to do so.

When the bell rang for the last time, the school principal thanked everyone for coming, announced that the Open House was over, and bid everyone goodnight. So that she wouldn't be leaving without hearing anything to help her son, Sokhem's mother mustered the courage to speak to his last-period instructor, who happened to be his ESL teacher. The ESL teacher, though anxious to go home, took time to talk with her about Sokhem's problem. The teacher helped her understand that she and her son needn't worry, and that there would be other opportunities to take the SAT. The next day, the ESL teacher found Sokhem and helped him make plans to take the SAT the next time the test was offered in the area.

The following year, when Sokhem had scored well on the SAT, had graduated from high school, and was excitedly getting ready to attend a local college, he told his ESL teacher that he could not have done it without her and his mother's help. She began to reflect on the experience that she had had with Sokhem's mother. Could she and the school have been more proactive to help students and their parents with the college application process?

The Importance of Family Engagement

The importance of family–school engagement is well documented (Delpit, 1995; Epstein et al., 2019; Espinosa, 2015; Gonzalez et al., 2005; Henderson et al., 2007; Lawrence-Lightfoot, 1999, 2003; Robles de Mélendez & Beck, 2019). Additionally, federal regulations explicitly state that schools and state education agencies are obligated "to ensure that LEP [limited English proficient] parents and guardians have meaningful access to district and school-related information" (U.S. Department of Justice & U.S. Department of Education, 2015, p. 37). Further, federal regulations specify:

> This essential information includes but is not limited to information regarding: language assistance programs, special education and related services, IEP meetings, grievance procedures, notices of nondiscrimination, student discipline policies and procedures, registration and enrollment, report cards, requests for parent permission for student participation in district or school activities, parent-teacher conferences, parent handbooks, gifted and talented programs, magnet and charter schools, and any other school and program choice options. (U.S. Department of Justice & U.S. Department of Education, 2015, p. 38)

The research and regulations affirm that all parents and guardians (hereafter families), including two-parent, single parent, grandparent, stepparent, foster parent, custodial parent, extrafamilial member, and others in our ever-changing society, are important partners in their child's education and that we must take the steps needed to engage families. Every family constellation, regardless of configuration, is foundational to a child's development, understanding of the world around them, social interactions, and cultural identity.

Kristina Robertson is the English Language Program supervisor at St. Paul Public Schools, in Minnesota. She provides important information about our obligations:

> We should provide interpreter support so that families and educators can connect with each other. Partnerships require a two-way communication process. It's important to select the type of communication that will work best. For example, some families may not have had the opportunity to learn to read and, as a result, are unable to understand written translated messages. Alternatives, such as translated miniconferences, phone calls, and oral and video messaging, may help.

> Establishing relationships with families should be an important objective and priority for educators at all grade levels. While much has been written about family partnerships at the early childhood level (Ballantyne et al., 2008; Espinosa, 2015; Robles de Mélendez & Beck, 2019; Tabors, 1998), maintaining strong partnerships with the families of multilingual learners (MLs) should continue through high school. Moreover, we should understand the important role that many multilingual children of all ages play on their families' behalf and consider how we might support such families.

Kristina also provides us with a rich example of the important role that a student played on behalf of her family:

> A Karen refugee high school student (whom I refer to with the pseudonym Paw Ku) was responsible for her schoolwork, navigating school systems, understanding college preparation, as well as acting as the main interpreter in her home for adult tasks such as telehealth visits with her grandmother, talking with the landlord, and calling the bank to help her mother ask about the account. As a 16-year-old high school student, she acted as her own parent and household manager like an adult because her parents didn't have meaningful access to information. Paw Ku took on these responsibilities without expecting additional support or more bilingual connections for her family, and she was stressed out all the time with so much to do.

> She saw it as her duty and wouldn't complain: "I know English, so I have to help my family." When told her parents should have access to information in their native language, she replied, "That would be good, but they still don't understand. They don't understand school." (K. Robertson, personal communication, May 25, 2022)

While we are familiar with the importance of family involvement, we sometimes overlook its special relevance for families from linguistically and culturally diverse backgrounds. Indeed, many educators are not familiar with the various cultural norms of MLs and their families. Conversely, many families of MLs are not familiar with the culture of the U.S. public school system, in terms of its implied ways of thinking, being, and acting by the dominant culture's notion of "school culture." Misconceptions and misunderstandings abound on both sides, and these differences can easily become impenetrable barriers that divide and separate one group from another.

Differences can also be exacerbated by the realities of (1) a largely untrained educational community in such important areas as second/multilanguage acquisition; culturally and linguistically responsive practices; working with families who have experienced significant trauma, violence, and chronic stress; positive assets-based messaging about the assets of home language(s); and methods for working with MLs and their families, and (2) families who are not familiar with U.S. public school practices (Haynes & Zacarian, 2010; Zacarian et al. 2021; Zacarian & Silverstone, 2015, 2020; Zacarian & Soto, 2020). Moreover, families and educators may hold a variety of misconceptions about what it takes to educate MLs successfully. For example, they may think that using more than one language is a problem instead of a resource (Espinosa, 2015; Stechuk et al., 2006). As a result, students' best interests can be lost in a sea of misinformation and misassumptions about language learning as well as the cultural divide (Zacarian & Soto, 2020).

The Open House example from the beginning of the chapter is a common one in public schools across the United States. Of course, many families do understand the norms and expectations of this event—because it is a very familiar facet of our culture and has existed for generations (Lawrence-Lightfoot, 2003). For example, most families of secondary students know that they will be standing in line for their child's schedule at the Open House night. And if they don't know what is going on, they can freely ask a peer for help. Let's look at the following exchange between an American English-fluent father of a freshman and a peer who has a freshman and an older child attending the high school.

Father: So, what do we do now?

Parent 2: You'll get Janet's Monday class schedule. The bell'll ring, and you'll hear Mr. Martin [the school principal] announce that we'll go to our kids' first-period class. It'll last about 10 minutes. Bell'll ring again and we'll go to our kids' second class. If Janet has a study hall, you can go to the cafeteria for cookies and coffee and to learn about the Parent Council. Definitely stop there. The cookies are usually good!

In this book, the terms *culture* and *cultural way of being* are used to refer to two groups: (1) MLs and their families who are from diverse cultural experiences other than the dominant monolingual American English-speaking culture and (2) monolingual American English-speaking students, educators, parents, and community members. Drawing from seminal scholars Trueba et al. (1981), these terms are used to describe

> a form of communication with learned and shared, explicit, and implicit
> rules for perceiving, believing, evaluating, and acting. . . . What people
> talk about and are specific about, such as traditional customs and laws,
> constitutes their overt or explicit culture. What they take for granted, or
> what exists beyond conscious awareness, is their implicit culture. (pp. 4–5)

In this short exchange, the first parent learns that he will attend an abbreviated school day and listen to a quick overview of his child's classes and that there are good snacks as well as information about the parent council in the cafeteria. It's likely that this parent already knew that an Open House is not a time to ask questions about one's own child, as he has been to all his child's Open Houses since kindergarten. He has been "trained" to ask questions about his child during another routine cultural event: parent conferences. It's also likely that he has attended parent conferences since his child was in kindergarten. Thus, in the above exchange, a lot of implied rules have already been learned, and it is likely that the inquiring parent quickly understands the rules and can follow them easily because he has so much applicable background experience. In this sense, he is well positioned to adapt to the new context and participate meaningfully in it.

Let's look at another example of culture as a way of being and acting. Consider the rapid shift from in-person to remote schooling that was made when COVID-19 struck. One example is Wolfe Street School, in Baltimore, Maryland. Its after-school programming had been an integral part of students' lives. Rather than forgo this mainstay, Wolfe Street quickly and adeptly launched several after-school remote activities including yoga, robotics, art, and debate classes taught by staff, families, and members of the local community (Zacarian, 2021; Zacarian et al., 2021).

While the herculean efforts of educators and families, including Wolfe Street's, should be resoundingly applauded for the flexibility, care, and amazing creativity that they demonstrated, much of what occurred during the pandemic was an extension of what was understood about the implied rules and ways of being of our various school communities' cultures. This depth of familiarity cannot be assumed of many parents of MLs. School programs, services, activities, and events are often unfamiliar to many parents of MLs and can even seem unwelcoming at times. In addition, many families often do not have access to the same peer resources (including cultural and linguistic) that families from the dominant group have.

It is typical for families to learn about school practices from peers who are like themselves. As in all human societies, we tend to associate with others like ourselves. We feel more comfortable and safer with, and ask questions of, others from our own group when possible; this is particularly true among minority groups (Allport, 1979; Roets & Van Hiel, 2011; Tatum, 1997). So naturally, it is typical for families to learn about school practices from peers who are like them. This reality is highly relevant for all educators to consider for two reasons. First, U.S. public school practices reflect dominant culture norms, which include a host of implied rules for acting and being. Most families of MLs are not so familiar with U.S. dominant culture norms, thus they are not very familiar with the hidden rules of U.S. public schools and are likely to be uncomfortable asking for help from others outside of their own cultural group. Second, unless schools create safe places in which the implied rules are explained explicitly until they are well understood, families may feel and be disconnected from their child's school. One of the primary reasons for Wolfe Street's success is the steps that it takes to partner with and empower families (Zacarian et al., 2021; Zacarian & Silverstone, 2015).

Indeed, almost all school events, programs, and activities, including parent conferences, potluck suppers, football games, field trips, driver's education, school plays, and signing up for basketball and soccer, are cultural activities. Successful interactions involve knowing the appropriate rules for engaging in these activities as well as what is and is not expected. Routine events that are emblematic of a school are familiar and welcoming for English-fluent American families and anyone else who knows the event's predictable routines, practices, and outcomes. However, these events pose unique challenges for families and teachers of MLs alike when neither is familiar with the other's cultural expectations and rules.

It should be clear by now that educators must create and implement new routines and practices that consider the unique needs of their ML parent population in order to ensure that all are welcomed and can become active members of the school community. In the example at the beginning of the chapter, Sokhem and his mother were at a clear disadvantage. They did not know the rules for taking the SAT and were entirely reliant on Sokhem's school to make this knowledge explicit. At the same time, it was only luck that connected Sokhem's mother with his empathetic ESL teacher. Schools should be proactive about creating meaningful connections to families, not reactive or leaving it to luck. In a certain sense, commonly occurring events such as the one in this example puts MLs, their families, and others in a lower status position than that of the dominant group because they lack familiarity with and knowledge about those common practices. This lack of familiarity can perpetuate the status quo of being in a powerless position. Ideally, we must create spaces that are built on mutual respect and ensure the allocation of equal status for all. This requires educators to think carefully, empathetically, and proactively about the ways in which families can become active members and partners in their child's education.

We have a much better chance to partner with families on behalf of children when we take steps to

- make school practices known by all;

- welcome and embrace families from cultures other than our own;

- transform our practices to integrate the unique representatives of our school, district, family, and local communities; and

- create meaningful partnerships with families.

Creating Meaningful Partnerships With Families

All families should be considered as rich resources, as people who have something important to contribute. Educators need to set the right tone for this to be possible, which requires them to have a deep belief in, and commitment to, the notion that families are important contributors to ensuring the success of all students.

Contribution, in a broad sense, refers to having a high level of respect for, deep appreciation of, and interest in cultural differences as rich and valuable assets with which to build partnerships. Drawing from Henderson et al. (2007), Espinosa (2015), Delpit (1995), and Zacarian and Silverstone (2015), four elements form the framework for creating strong parent–school partnerships. The four elements cannot be accomplished in isolation; each is dependent on and interconnected to the others.

Framework for Family–School Partner Schools

1. **Bridging the cultural divide**

   - Make routines and practices transparent, meaningful, and accessible for families of MLs.

   - Create events and activities that pay particular attention to families of MLs and their cultural ways of being.

   - Encourage family involvement throughout all grade levels in a manner that is respectful of parents.

2. **Infusing family advocacy as part of the core**

   - Help families become a powerful influence in their child's education.

   - Understand the ML community and its need to support ML family advocacy.

   - Copower families as partners

3. **Linking parent involvement to learning**

   - Connect family activities with learning.

   - Connect learning to what is happening at home and in the community.

4. **Working together for the common good of students**

   - Educators and families work together to create a welcoming climate.

   - Educators and families work with the community to improve student outcomes and their connections with and service to the community.

The following example illustrates this framework.

When a group of elementary-age students from El Salvador and Puerto Rico enrolled in Crocker Farm School, in Amherst, Massachusetts, they and their families were unable to communicate in English. In addition, some of the students had only limited documents about their prior schooling. Bilingual bicultural translators conducted interviews with all the parents to learn as much as possible about the children's prior schooling experiences (see Chapter 3, Resource 3.3, for suggested interview questions). The interview was conducted in Spanish to allow for a free flow of comfortable conversation. During the interview, it was learned that some of the children had had limited prior schooling. They had attended school for just a few hours a day and were unable to attend on a regular basis.

In addition, the bilingual bicultural translators learned that it would have been inappropriate for families to be involved in their child's schooling in their native countries. Their cultural beliefs were that teachers and the school were the all-knowing authority and that it was not a family's place to question teachers about their child's educational programming. However, the translators knew that it was appropriate for families to be involved in any social programming and events, as this was a commonly held practice in their own cultures, and they knew to ask about it during the family interviews.

Based on these interviews, Crocker Farm School's principal, assistant principal, counselor, teachers, specialists, and other stakeholders saw three challenges. First, they needed to create a program that would benefit students with interrupted schooling. Second, they wanted to create a program in which Latinx students would not be isolated from their American monolingual English-fluent peers. Third, to build community, they knew that they needed to honor and build on the assets of the MLs' family community.

To build community and honor families as assets, they decided to organize a play that students would perform entirely in Spanish. With the complete support of the school principal and staff, a small group of mixed monolingual English and bilingual Spanish/English staff held tryouts for the play. The teachers distributed bilingual Spanish/English flyers to the school community about the play and the tryouts. They held an art contest for the advertising that would be included in the playbill. The tryouts occurred after school and finished in time for students to catch the "late" bus. The play had 20 speaking parts, and over 50 Spanish- and English-speaking students came to the tryouts. In response, the teachers decided to expand the play to include singing, dancing, and acting parts so that everyone could be selected and have an important role in the play. English- and Spanish-speaking students learned Latin ballroom dancing, a Spanish song, and dialogue in Spanish. During the initial interviews, the translators learned that some of the parents of MLs were seamstresses. When they shared this with the staff, they reached out to the parents for help in creating the costumes. The parents happily agreed and solicited further support from additional parents of MLs and community members. Other parents of MLs and local businesspeople from the town's Latinx restaurants were recruited to help in additional ways, including providing the snacks that would be served during the play's conclusion. Within a short period of time, parents and community members who had never been involved in their child's schooling gladly volunteered to help. The school bustled with activities related to the play, and there was a steady stream of English-fluent and non-English-speaking parents working side by side helping with the play's preparation.

On opening night, the auditorium was filled to capacity. Knowing that many of the parents of MLs worked morning, afternoon, and sometimes evening shifts, several performances were held, before, during, and after school. Each was well attended and, often, at standing-room-only capacity. Quickly, word about the wonderful play spread through the town, and within a few days two of the town's other schools asked if the students could perform the play in their school. By the play's end, the number of family volunteers swelled to the highest in the school's history, as did the play's attendance. In addition, some of the newcomer Spanish-speaking students became renowned in the school and, more important, their families became more comfortable in their child's school. There were many other successes worth noting, including two in particular: Students and families from all cultures involved in the play engaged more actively with each other, and monolingual English-fluent students learned Spanish. So, what did the school do that worked so well?

Bridging the Cultural Divide

Family outreach is critical. Whether schools have high or low ML populations, partnerships can be built only when families have working knowledge about a school's routines and practices, and when school leaders, teachers, and other staff have working knowledge of students' and families' culture and language. Bi/multilingual outreach workers are essential for building this important knowledge. Outreach workers need the following skills:

- strong communication skills in both English and the families' home language

- insider knowledge about the school system and how it works

- a high level of trust in the family community

- depth of knowledge about the local community to support students' health and well-being and engagement in after- and out-of-school activities

Dr. Jennifer Love, director of language access for Prince George's County Public Schools, in Maryland, shared the following about the importance of being committed to communicating with families in an authentic way.

Prince George's County Public Schools has long demonstrated a commitment to language access for equitable engagement of culturally and linguistically diverse families. The early 1990s paved the way for the development of an interpreter bank to support interpreting services across the school district for families who were not native speakers of English. The evolution of services to families has been a continuous and intentional journey, providing professional and efficient language interpretation for families in dozens of languages, bridging vital communication between school staff and families. At the heart of this sustainable district model are language access policies and procedures that acknowledge and perpetuate a shared responsibility for authentic communication with families. The DOJ/DOE/OCR [Department of Justice/Department of Education/Office of Civil Rights] guidance of 2015 solidified the translation arm of the district's language access program, bringing a long-held vision to life with a full-time

(Continued)

(Continued)

translation team and coordinator. There is now an inherent accessibility of all systemic communication, from e-blasts and outreach videos to social media and the system website, that remains focused on the linguistic needs of the community and overcoming language obstacles to engagement. Language access cards with their native language indicated on the card are provided to families, giving them peace of mind and acknowledging families' right to language services for school communication.

The district has moved from language access as an add-on to fully embracing multilingual communication as part of a Professional Language Access Community (PLAC; Love, 2019). This community is focused on streamlined hiring and assessment practices to identify capable and qualified interpreters and translators to join the team. Central to the PLAC is building investment and context for interpreters and translators through professional development and training. It is critical to their success in the field and in supporting families that the language services team have full knowledge of their responsibilities, training in effective practices, and opportunities for reflective practice. The PLAC also prioritizes nurturing the growth and leadership of language access professionals in service to linguistically diverse families across the district. (J. Love, personal communication March 25, 2022)

It is important to be as proactive as possible with bi/multilingual outreach. It should begin at enrollment because doing so makes it much more likely that parents will feel welcomed. As seen in Chapter 1, some parents of MLs have prior educational experiences that are like or matched with their child's, whereas others do not. Schools need to be culturally sensitive and responsive to ensure that diverse communities of families are fully integrated in and empowered members of the school community. Outreach is an important element for building community. The value of outreach is threefold:

- It helps families understand the routines and practices of school.

- It helps the school community understand the family community.

- It brings together the collective assets of families, educators, and local communities on behalf of students' physical and social-emotional well-being and academic success.

When a school has identified MLs, it is important to then proactively provide outreach. Some schools have trained bi/multilingual bi/multicultural outreach workers on their staff. While their roles might be titled *liaison, coordinator, outreach worker,* and more, the work of this critical role "involves someone who is designated to help families, schools, and communities use their collective assets in the interest of students" (Zacarian et al., 2021, p. 36). Generally, these professionals have advanced knowledge and skills in counseling, community service, or a related field and are members of the culture and language group of a school's dominant ML population.

Kristina Robertson, the English Language Program supervisor at St. Paul Public Schools, in Minnesota, states the following about the liaisons in her district:

> Our cultural liaisons are invaluable, and we wouldn't be able to support our students without their direct connection and trust in the communities they serve. It's important to note that cultural liaisons do not replace direct educator-to-parent communication; they enhance it. (K. Robertson, personal communication, May 25, 2022)

Other schools solicit help from family volunteers, support staff, teachers, guidance counselors, and other educators to perform this important role. It is essential that it be performed by a family community "insider" who also has depth of knowledge about how a school works and its educational programming, MLs' family community, as well as the local community. When the family's culture is fully integrated into the school's and local community's preferred ways of being and acting, it is very fortunate to get a direct pipeline to an "outsider" perspective on their school, which otherwise it might never see. This includes both the implicit as well as the school's more obvious and explicit ways of being and acting.

An example of bi/multilingual outreach is from Becky Corr, team lead of the Language, Culture and Equity Department of Douglas County Public Schools, in Colorado. Let's examine what Becky shares about the importance of this involvement and the role that bi/multilingual liaisons play with all families, not just those of MLs.

> In Douglas County, Colorado, our team of liaisons are ambassadors who are integral in supporting families who are new to our district. Our liaisons are bilingual, but they serve families of all linguistic and cultural backgrounds. We find that parents who are fluent English speakers, in fact, benefit from the support of a liaison at times. The primary focus of our liaisons is to build relationships with families and educators, and it is through these relationships that our liaisons create bridges. Our liaisons are ambassadors who seek to understand families and educators to create the best outcome for students.
>
> Several times per year, our liaisons survey families and organize coffee chats. The surveys provide data about potential topics as well as the best days and times to meet. During the coffee chats, families connect with each other, enjoy refreshments, have an opportunity to learn about a particular aspect of a school, and meet with leadership to discuss topics of interest. A liaison in our district held a coffee chat and invited school counselors to discuss what they do and how they support students. Parents had time to connect with each other, ask questions, and meet leaders from the school.
>
> As a result of our liaison team and their great work, parents have reported having more confidence to interact with the school, and they report having a better

(Continued)

(Continued)

understanding of how they can help their children in school. Our families also reported that their children felt more connected to the schools.

Recently, families gathered at a local state park to participate in a ranger-led hike to learn about different species in the area. Regional English language development teachers coordinated efforts to organize the event and it was very well received. Students were able to learn alongside their caretakers and build relationships with educators and the larger community. The state park granted free access to the park, while the Language, Culture and Equity Department provided food and refreshments. Year after year this event continues to grow in popularity and supports relationship building outside the classroom. (B. Corr, personal communication, May 20, 2022)

Being able to take an outsider's point of view allows educators to look at the whole of what occurs in and outside of school and establish a means for building strong partnerships to support students to succeed in their lives. In the example at the beginning of the chapter, for example, Sokhem and his mother would have been better informed had the school been able to take an outsider's view about the college application process. This would have happened had an outreach worker established positive relationships with the mother and school personnel and taken steps to copower them in supporting Sokhem's post-high school aspirations.

For example, the school enrollment process involves families filling out a wide range of documents and receiving a lot of varied information about the school. The purpose of asking for much of what is gathered from families is only implied. The school emergency card, for example, is a frequently used form that enables the school to contact parents or their designee in the event of an emergency. Some parents of MLs may not be familiar with what constitutes an emergency, and the words *emergency* and *designee* may be misconstrued. A bi/multilingual bi/multicultural outreach worker would be trained to explicitly explain the purpose of this important document and to respond to questions about it.

OUTREACH AS AN ESSENTIAL ENROLLMENT COMPONENT

Outreach workers should do the following:

1. Assist families with the registration process by explaining the following to students and their families:

   Student's class schedule

   School schedule

Extracurricular activities (including after and out of school) available to all students

Lunch procedure and the process by which students may participate in free or reduced-price lunch

Students' right to equal access to an education

Emergency card purpose and form

Student handbook and code of conduct

2. Establish a routine means of communication to accomplish Step 3.

3. Encourage parents to be active empowered members of the school community:

Address concerns that parents have.

Ensure that families are routinely apprised of their child's academic progress.

Notify families about important school-related information or extracurricular activities that were not communicated at enrollment.

Familiarize families with school-related activities and procedures.

Support families to identify school-to-school and school-to-breaks transitions as well as postgraduate plans that routinely occur for all students.

4. Empower families as essential partners in children's education:

Be curious about families by asking questions such as the ones in Chapter 3, Resource 3.3.

Take an outsider perspective on what it means to become a member of a school community.

Take time to engage families in various groups, including school, classroom, and parent advisory councils and volunteer groups.

It is better to have ongoing outreach programs over the course of a school year than to have just one orientation meeting, especially since many MLs enroll throughout the school year. A second important element for bridging the cultural divide is to create activities that pay particular attention to families of MLs and their cultural ways of being. The arts, including plays, music, dance, and other performance modes, are wonderful resources for involving parents. They are fun, engaging, and rouse parents' interest in participating in their child's schooling (Henderson et al., 2007). It is also helpful to infuse families' varied and valuable expertise into learning.

Earlier in the chapter, we were introduced to an example from Crocker Farm School. When bi/multilingual bi/multicultural counselors noted that two of the mothers of MLs were seamstresses, they shared this information with the group that organized the school play. The teachers reached out to these parents, and they eagerly helped create the costumes. The mothers also solicited the help of other families and community members in this effort. They became more familiar and comfortable with the school and its staff and students through the costume-making activity. This is an example of an asset-based model. To launch this type of model requires all educators, including school leaders, teachers, specialists, counselors, support staff, and other stakeholders, to set the tone for involving families actively and comfortably in their child's school and involving their child as well. In the school play example, the event was delivered entirely in Spanish. The language used promoted the assets of the minority group. It allowed native speakers of Spanish to be powerful mentors of English-fluent peers and the dominant community to enjoy the benefits of a performance, albeit in a language with which they were not familiar. The entire school community's leadership throughout this process greatly helped to bridge the cultural divide and forge new and meaningful partnerships. This type of leadership and advocacy was also encouraged by the district's leaders, especially the superintendent, as part of the district's commitment to involving families in their child's education. Families can and should be involved in a myriad of ways that enrich everyone's opportunities for learning.

Infusing Family Advocacy as Part of the Core

A child's biggest advocate is their family. The family knows their child very well and wants the best for them. However, schools are complex institutions that can be difficult for even the most seasoned family to navigate well, let alone families of MLs. Educators must be proactive in empowering and supporting families of MLs to advocate for their child. One way of doing this is for educators to be fully committed to helping families be comfortably and meaningfully integrated into the school community. The more contact that a school has with families in a positive way, the more opportunities for advocacy to occur. To be transformational, it is time to move beyond perceiving that the families who are involved in their child's schooling care about their child and those who are not involved do not care (Finders & Lewis, 1994; Henderson et al., 2007). That perception is deficit based and keeps us locked in a sealed silo where we might perceive particular groups of families as not caring for their child and, more importantly, we might miss the opportunities that they can offer. Family involvement in their child's schooling is a type of advocacy. And an important one! The more opportunities that families have to be involved in ways in which they are comfortable, the more they can advocate for their child. Active and continuous involvement helps families gain an insider's view through repeated exposure to the culture and practices of U.S. public schools and become empowered as equal partners on behalf of children's education.

An asset-based partner model is one in which the school provides explicit knowledge to families about their child's schooling so that families can gain the knowledge that they need to do what they do best: advocate for their own child. Unless families are given multiple and continuous opportunities to engage in this advocacy role, schools may find it challenging to regard families as legitimate and valued partners in their child's education.

Advocacy should have a broad meaning so that it includes whatever is needed to help a student be committed to learning and doing well in school and a family be invested in helping the child do so. An important distinction must be made between students and families who are members of the dominant U.S. culture, which values independence and competition highly, versus the preponderance of MLs and families from underrepresented cultures where group harmony and interpersonal relationships take precedence over all else (DeCapua & Marshall, 2015; Hofstede, 2011; Hofstede et al., 2005; Tyler et al., 2008).

Although these cultural differences are not set in stone, as so many people represent hybrid experiences, we may lean toward using approaches that represent U.S. dominant culture, such as individual responsibility for self, independence, self-reliance, self-esteem, individual achievement, and task orientation (over social or process orientation; Rothstein-Fisch & Trumbull, 2008, pp. 10–11), because it matches our frame of reference (Tyler et al., 2008; Zacarian & Soto, 2020). If we look at two hypothetical classrooms, the first representing an individualistic culture and the second a collectivist culture, here is what we would see: According to the American Psychological Association (2003) and Tyler et al. (2008), the first prefers a relatively quiet classroom, few student interactions, and assigning tasks to be done independently, whereas the second represents many interactions that involve students and teachers being interdependent, interconnected, and highly relationship driven.

Taking an outsider's view here is important, once again. Knowing that personal relationships are important for building partnerships with families from collectivist cultures, it is important to create socializing activities at the beginning of the school year that give families the opportunity to get to know their child's educators in a more personal way and to continue offering social activities throughout the school year. Educators should carefully consider all the events that typically occur during the school year that relate to the academic side of students' education, such as parent conferences, report card periods, and Open Houses, and precede these with activities that provide a more personal and social means for getting to know the families of MLs. Some schools do this through home visits, potluck suppers, telemeetings using parents' preference for connecting (e.g., WhatsApp), and multicultural activities. This approach to building personal relationships with families parallels the cultural frame in which families are familiar and comfortable.

It can be helpful to seek expert supports in building family advocacy groups. Becky Corr, team lead of the Language, Culture and Equity Department of Douglas County Schools, a large suburban school district of about 90 schools, 900 square miles, 64,000 students, and about 3,800 MLs, shares an example of the expert support that Douglas County received.

> In Douglas County, Colorado, we had some false starts with our parent advocacy groups where we tried some activities, and they didn't work. So, we worked with Patsy Roybal, a consultant in the Denver area specializing in family engagement, to

(Continued)

(Continued)

offer a series of workshops for families to learn about how they can advocate for their children in a multitude of ways. Workshops [were on] topics such as the leadership structure of the district, school report cards, public speaking, and the role of parent advocacy in student success. At the conclusion, parents volunteered to lead future workshops after they attend a full-day trainer-of-trainers session. One parent, as a result of the workshops, petitioned the district to establish a new bus stop.

As our district prepared to implement a new telephone interpretation service with educators from 60 schools, we knew we had to take a multifaceted approach. We leveraged our in-district communication and training streams, but we also empowered parents to request interpretation through the distribution of iSpeak cards. The cards provide a way for families to request interpretation and for educators to recall the information needed to access an interpreter. The iSpeak cards were distributed at local sporting events and schools that our multilingual families attended. The cards empower families to access information and advocate for their children. (B. Corr, personal communication, May 20, 2022)

SAMPLING OF ACTIVITIES TARGETED FOR BUILDING RELATIONSHIPS WITH FAMILIES

September 5: Family picnic—Families, children, and staff are invited to bring a picnic dinner or snack and enjoy it on the school grounds. Cookies and fruit punch are furnished by the school. Bi/multilingual bi/multicultural staff and volunteers contact families about the event, support transportation plans to and from the event, and attend the event to ensure as smooth an activity as possible.

September 15: Multicultural potluck supper—Families, children, and staff gather for a potluck supper, bringing various dishes to share. Bi/multilingual bi/multicultural staff and volunteers contact families about the event and attend it to ensure as smooth an activity as possible. Music from the various communities of MLs is also shared.

An example of this type of activity occurring remotely comes from second-grade teacher Michael Silverstone. His students did not want to miss the annual ritual during the COVID-19 pandemic, and they brainstormed ideas for an alternative. With support from Mr. Silverstone, they developed a remote potluck dinner that involved students, their families, and the teacher creating a meal at home and enjoying it together online as a class. Students also created a class cookbook of the dishes they shared at the remote potluck.

October 1: Open House—Families of MLs are invited an hour before the general family population to learn about the evening's events. Bi/multilingual bi/multicultural staff and volunteers contact families and attend the Open House to ensure its success.

Becky Corr, team lead of the Language, Culture and Equity Department of Douglas County Public Schools, shares some powerful experiences about building family–school partnerships.

> There are times when family engagement for multilingual learners can be part of the larger context of the school plan, and there are times when it is best as a separate event.
>
> As an example, for parent–teacher conferences, our English language development teachers partner with liaisons and interpreters, they hang multilingual signs to signal where interpretation is available, and they provide a schedule to interpreters. Some schools offer a preconference dinner before parent–teacher conferences for families where they provide time for families to connect and share potential questions they may consider asking of teachers. Some schools offer regional math and literacy nights specific to multilingual learners and their families. For back-to-school nights, some schools have their multilingual families attend the opening remarks by the principal, which are interpreted as necessary. Then, families who are new have an opportunity to meet with the English language development teachers to learn about processes and topics they are interested in, such as how to volunteer at the school, upcoming events, how to check their child's grades, contact information for each teacher, and so on. At the forefront is always creating a welcoming and inclusive environment for all families that builds trusting partnerships with our families.
>
> One of the most impactful, according to the Flamboyan Foundation, and least time-consuming strategies involves making positive phone calls home. Some of our schools have held parent–teacher conferences and then spent the last hour making positive phone calls and sending positive text messages to caregivers. It was a win-win for families and teachers alike. Making positive phone calls home has supported behavior and academics as well as fostered trusting relationships with families. (B. Corr, personal communication, May 20, 2022)

It is also important to provide families with support in advocating for their child's education and for all MLs to succeed. The California Association of Bilingual Education has been implementing a family leadership program that supports families as partners in their child's education. Known as Project2Inspire, it "provide[s] high-quality education, resources and leadership development" (California Association of Bilingual Education, 2021). It includes a sequence of course modules that support districts in creating "parent experts" who will engage families as well as school and district personnel in creating and sustaining effective language assistance programs (Zacarian & Soto, 2020). It also includes trainer-of-trainer modules for school and district personnel on such topics as family engagement, cultural proficiency, and writing action plans for family engagement (Zacarian & Soto, 2020). It begins, as all asset-based models do, with honoring and valuing the cultural and linguistic capital of families and school personnel as well as the depth of knowledge, skills, and attributes that all can contribute to the group's work.

Linking Parent Involvement to Learning

More often than not, we worry that families who are not fluent in English cannot connect with or support their child's education and we find ourselves worrying more about families who we believe cannot understand academic text and help their child understand it. We may think this because we believe that learning is entirely academic. An alternate view is important here. Learning involves building connections between what students already know and what is being learned. However, not all connections occur through academic experiences. They occur also via students' personal, social, cultural, linguistic, and life experiences (Haynes & Zacarian, 2010; Zacarian et al., 2021). Rousing students' interest to learn must include making connections with their prior experiences. Indeed, these connectors may be far more successful than drawing strictly from academic knowledge. Families have a good deal to contribute to their child's intellectual development. When parents are empowered, their knowledge can be used in powerful ways (Gonzalez et al., 2005; Moll, 1992; Zacarian et al., 2021). For example, when a school principal noted that many of the fathers of the school's MLs were fishermen, she encouraged their teachers to develop a unit of study on the fishing industry. With help from the fathers and other members of the fishing community, various teachers designed and delivered successful interdisciplinary science, social studies, and language arts lessons on this topic. The same is true for a high school chemistry teacher who engaged students in the study of thermal reaction. Knowing some parents of MLs were welders, he solicited their help in demonstrating an authentic model of the concept. Viewing parents as resources allows us to be much more open to the possibilities of building connections that can be readily integrated in school and at home.

While this is a helpful means for connecting to families, much of academic text is built on implied understandings about U.S. society. Think of the social studies teacher who asks the important question, "What is the relevance of Barack Obama being the first African American president?" This question requires depth of knowledge about race in the United States that many MLs do not possess. Helping to build connections to learning through students' and their families' prior experiences can be more easily accomplished if we consider the relevance of the other connection makers and include families in the process. Drawing from Gonzalez et al. (2005) and Moll (1992), we must encourage educators to consider how parents' knowledge will be encouraged and empowered. In this sense, learning occurs when it is connected to what is happening at home and in the community. It is personal and cultural and built on students' and their families' views of the world. For example, asking students to interview their parents about a time in which they were not treated well and/or were discriminated against can activate students' interest to study the relevance of the first African American president.

This asset-based model of connecting curriculum to MLs' personal, social, cultural, language, and world experiences provides opportunities for families to help in their child's schooling by using the rich resources that they possess. When schools build systematic connections to students' and their families' lives, there is a much greater chance that academic learning will occur.

Working Together for the Common Good of Students

Schools do not exist in a vacuum. They reside in communities in which students travel from one side of a city or town to their school, walk to school, or both. Creating a welcoming environment for an ML community and its culture(s) requires a high level of commitment in the student and family community as well as the community at large, and it requires more than celebrating cultural holidays and events. In an example described earlier, the school involved community members in the production of a play. Local restaurant workers, seamstresses, and other community members became involved with the performance for the common good of the children, and their collective contributions are what made the performance successful. This type of effort requires a much broader lens. It involves a willingness on the part of the school, as well as the community, to look closely at itself.

It means taking time to learn about how the school's MLs are or are not participating in events and activities that are common among the dominant group.

An example of supporting family involvement comes from Becky Corr, team lead of the Language, Culture and Equity Department of Douglas County Public Schools. She shares what the district has done to support families, including a group of immigrants who recently moved to the district.

> The annual Language, Culture and Equity celebration in Douglas County, Colorado, brings together families and educators from across the district to celebrate the accomplishments of our students and the diversity of our community. Each year, there is a focus on a theme. Students create projects including artwork, written pieces, and presentations centered around the theme. Families enjoy viewing the artwork, a slideshow of the year's highlights, and performances by student groups, and teachers are honored as ambassadors for multilingual families. Parents are invited to be guest speakers and are partners in the planning process. Caretakers/parents are also invited to host craft tables where they teach a craft to students. At the end of the evening, families enjoy a meal together.
>
> Recently, one geographic area of our district experienced tremendous growth of families from India. Our leaders and teachers expressed interest in understanding more about their culture and how to come together to support our students. We had an existing partnership with a local nonprofit of Indian American families and wanted to partner with them to build a deeper understanding of our MLs and their families. So, we organized a focus group to build partnerships and relationships with the new community and our school. Then, families presented what's going well for them and some ideas to explore to refine our practices. As a result, we are now partnering with the nonprofit to organize presentations that will inform about partnership led by families. This is the beginning of the partnership, but it is exciting to continue to build upon these successes. (B. Corr, personal communication, May 20, 2022)

Expanding Beyond the School

Town or city sports and driver's education programs, Girl and Boy Scouts, dance classes, and Boys and Girls Clubs, though generally not part of a school program, are often activities and groups that students engage in and that are part of their development. Because these are so common, teachers may draw from them to build connections to the curriculum. Think of a classroom teacher who uses a soccer example to illustrate a math problem. MLs and others may not be exposed to activities like playing on a soccer team for many reasons, including lack of awareness about the after- or out-of-school activities that the dominant culture of children participate in and lack of financial means to support their participation.

Building partnerships with families requires opening the circle of opportunity and involving all educators in making this an important and sustained priority. Figure 6.1 shows the steps that can be taken to better ensure that we take time to identify, recruit, and continuously cultivate the resources needed to support the assets, interests, and needs of MLs and their families in our schools.

Figure 6.1   Identifying and Cultivating External Supports and Resources

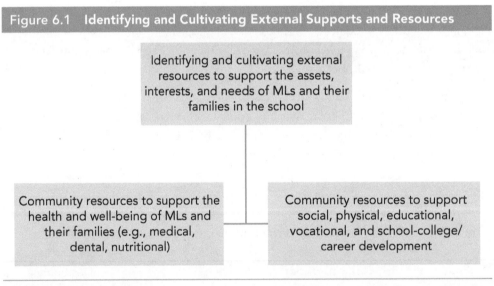

Source: Zacarian et al. (2021).

One way to identify and cultivate external resources to support the assets, interests, and needs of MLs is to survey staff and families. Resources 6.1 and 6.2 from Zacarian et al. (2021) are intended for this purpose.

RESOURCE 6.1

Staff Survey

The purpose of this survey is to help us understand the health and well-being and social interests and desires of our students and build strong community partnerships on behalf of our students. Our collective responses will greatly help us in these efforts.

Please select your classification below:

☐ School administrator

☐ Schoolteacher

☐ School support staff (counselor, social worker, custodian, lunch staff, etc.)

☐ Other:

Please check the resources that you believe are most needed by the students in your classes:

☐ Medical

☐ Dental

☐ Eye care

☐ Housing

☐ Nutritional

☐ Counseling

☐ Other (please list):

Please briefly describe why you believe these resources are needed.

Please check the three family–school partnership activities that you think would be most helpful to our students:

☐ Family gatherings for social purposes

☐ Family gatherings for students to showcase their learning

☐ Ways for families to share resources

☐ Creating a shared home–school culture of learning

☐ Other (please describe):

(Continued)

(Continued)

Please briefly describe why you believe these activities are needed.

Please check three activities that you believe would be most beneficial to students:

☐ After-school clubs and recreational activities

☐ Before/after-school programs

☐ Field trips

☐ Buddy programs

☐ Other (please describe):

Please briefly describe why you believe these activities are needed.

Zacarian, D., Calderón, M. E., & Gottlieb, M. (2021). *Beyond crises: Overcoming linguistic and cultural inequities in communities, schools, and classrooms* (pp. 61–62). Corwin.

 Available for download at **resources.corwin.com/transformingschoolsformultilinguallearners**

RESOURCE 6.2

Family Survey

The purpose of this survey is to help us understand the health and well-being and social interests and desires of your child and to build strong family–school partnerships. Your responses will greatly help us in these efforts. Thank you!

Please check the resources that you believe are most needed:

☐ Medical

☐ Dental

☐ Eye care

☐ Housing

☐ Nutritional

☐ Counseling

☐ Other (please list):

Please check the three family–school partnership activities that you think would be most helpful to your child:

☐ Family gatherings for social purposes

☐ Family gatherings for students to showcase their learning

☐ Ways for families to share resources

☐ Creating a shared home–school culture of learning

☐ Other (please describe):

Please briefly describe why you believe these activities are needed.

What is the best means to contact you to support our efforts?

Please check three activities that you believe would be most beneficial to your child:

☐ After-school clubs and recreational activities

☐ Before/after-school programs

☐ Field trips

☐ Buddy programs

☐ Other (please describe):

Please briefly describe why you believe these activities are needed.

 Available for download at **resources.corwin.com/transformingschoolsformultilinguallearners**

An equally important goal is empowering MLs intellectually, socially, and emotionally in making meaningful contributions to the community. Commonly referred to as *service learning*, its purpose is twofold: (1) providing students with an authentic experience to apply learning and (2) encouraging students to be responsible for and committed to the community. In 2008, the Education Commission of the States synthesized 20 years of research about service learning and found that it greatly supports "young people develop[ing] civic skills, attitudes and behaviors" (Pickeral et al., 2008, p. 1). This approach to learning was enacted broadly with passage of the National Community Service Act in 1990 by President George H. W. Bush and the National Community and Service Trust Act in 1993 by President Bill Clinton (Ryan, 2012). While economic downturns led to the decline of service learning in low-income communities across the nation despite its efficacy, renewed interest is sparking its return (Zacarian & Silverstone, 2020; Zacarian & Soto, 2020). An example is Brockton Public Schools, in Massachusetts. As the city of Brockton became more diverse, the need for medical interpreters grew. In response, Brockton High School, with the support of families and community members, implemented a medical interpretation-translation certification program for its multilingual Spanish, Haitian, and Cape Verdean students and others. Students participate in a 2-year program of study in anatomy, physiology, human systems, and the art of communicating and intern at a neighborhood health center where several graduates have been employed full-time (Zacarian & Soto, 2020). The district is now considering adding a program in legal studies in response to a community need. This district shows us what's possible when we draw on students' strengths and assets and work with families to support MLs' success.

Families of MLs can be more engaged in their child's education and school community when each of four frames is employed intentionally by school leaders—bridging the cultural divide, infusing family advocacy as part of the core, linking family involvement to learning, and working together for the common good of students. In the next chapter, we will explore ways to identify and work with MLs with learning differences and learning disabilities.

Suggested Reading

California Association of Bilingual Education. (2021). *Parents*. https://www.gocabe.org/index.php/parents-3/project-2-inspire-i3-development-grant/

Zacarian, D., & Soto, I. (2020). Service-learning as a culturally responsive practice. In *Responsive schooling for culturally and linguistically diverse students* (pp. 135–156). Norton Professional Books.

References

Allport, D. (1979). *The nature of prejudice: The classic study of the roots of discrimination* (25th anniv. ed.). Basic Books.

American Psychological Association. (2003). Guidelines on multicultural education, training, research, practice, and organizational change for psychologists. *American Psychologist, 58*, 377–402. https://doi.org/10.1037/0003-066X.58.5.377

Ballantyne, K. B., Sanderman, A. R., & McLaughlin, N. (2008). *Dual language learners in the early years: Getting ready to succeed in school.* National Clearinghouse for English Language Acquisition. https://files.eric.ed.gov/fulltext/ED512635.pdf

California Association of Bilingual Education. (2021). Project2Inspire. *Parents.* https://www.gocabe.org/index.php/parents-3/project-2-inspire-i3-development-grant/

DeCapua, A., & Marshall, H. W. (2015). Reframing the conversation about students with limited or interrupted formal education: From achievement gap to cultural dissonance. *NASSP Bulletin, 99*(4), 356–370. https://doi.org/10.1177/0192636515620662

Delpit, L. (1995). *Other people's children: Cultural conflict in the classroom.* New Press.

Epstein, J. L., Greenfeld, M. D., Hutchins, D. J., Williams, K. J., & Sanders, M. G. (2019). *School, family, and community partnerships: Your handbook for action* (4th ed.). Corwin.

Espinosa, L. (2015). *Getting it right for young children from diverse backgrounds: Applying research to improve practice with a focus on dual language learners* (2nd ed.). Pearson.

Finders, M., & Lewis, C. (1994). Why some parents don't come to school. *Educating for Diversity, 51*(8), 50–54.

Gonzalez, N., Moll, L. C., & Amanti, C. (Eds.). (2005). *Funds of knowledge: Theorizing practices in households, communities, and classrooms.* Lawrence Erlbaum.

Haynes, J., & Zacarian, D. (2010). *Teaching English language learners across the content areas.* Association for Supervision and Curriculum Development.

Henderson, A. T., Mapp, K. L., Johnson, V. R., & Davies, D. (2007). *Beyond the bake sale: The essential guide to family-school partnerships.* New Press.

Hofstede, G. (2011). Dimensionalizing cultures: The Hofstede model in context. *Online Readings in Psychology and Culture, 2*(1). https://doi.org/10.9707/2307-0919.1014

Hofstede, G., Hofstede, G. J., & Minkov, M. (2005). *Cultures and organizations: Software of the mind* (3rd ed., pp. 90–91). McGraw-Hill.

Lawrence-Lightfoot, S. (1999). *Respect: An exploration.* Perseus Books.

Lawrence-Lightfoot, S. (2003). *The essential conversation: What parents and teachers can learn from each other.* Random House.

Love, J. (2019). *Illuminating promising practice: A phenomenological study on the engagement of culturally and linguistically diverse families of children with exceptionalities.* (Publication No. 27964446) [Doctoral dissertation, Bowie State University]. ProQuest Dissertations and Theses Global.

Moll, L. (1992). Bilingual classroom studies and community analysis: Some recent trends. *Educational Researcher, 21*, 20–24.

Pickeral, T., Lennon, T., & Piscatelli, J. (2008). *Service-learning policies and practices: A research-based advocacy paper.* National Center for Learning and Citizenship.

Robles de Mélendez, W., & Beck, V. (2019). *Teaching young children in multicultural classrooms: Issues, concepts, and strategies* (5th ed.). Cengage Learning.

Roets, A., & Van Hiel, A. (2011). Allport's prejudiced personality today: Need for closure as the motivated cognitive basis of prejudice. *Current Directions in Psychological Science, 20*(6), 349–354. https://doi.org/10.1177/0963721411424894

Rothstein-Fisch, C., & Trumbull, E. (2008). *Managing diverse classrooms: How to build on students' cultural strengths.* Association for Supervision and Curriculum Development.

Ryan, M. (2012). *Service learning after Learn and Serve America: How five states are moving forward.* Education Commission of the States. http://www.ecs.org/clearinghouse/01/02/87/10287.pdf

Stechuk, R. A., Burns, M. S., & Yandian, S. E. (2006). *Bilingual infant/toddler environments: Supporting language and learning in our youngest children: A guide for migrant and seasonal head start programs.* Academy for Educational Development. https://files .eric.ed.gov/fulltext/ED520113.pdf

Tabors, P. O. (1998, November). What early childhood educators need to know: Developing effective programs for linguistically diverse children and families. *Young Children* (pp. 20–26).

Tatum, B. D. (1997). *"Why are all of the Black kids sitting together in the cafeteria?" And other conversations about race.* Basic Books.

Trueba, H., Guthrie, G. P., & Au, K. H. (1981). *Culture and the classroom: Studies in classroom ethnography.* Newbury House.

Tyler, K. M., Uqdah, A. L., Dillihunt, M. L., Beatty-Hazelbaker, R., Conner, T., Gadson, N. C., Henchy, A. M., Hughes, T., Mulder, S., Owens, E., Roan-Belle, C., Smith, L., & Stevens, R. (2008). Cultural discontinuity: Towards the empirical inquiry of a major hypothesis in education. *Educational Researcher, 37,* 280–297.

U.S. Department of Justice & U.S. Department of Education. (2015, January 7). *Dear colleague.* https://www2.ed.gov/about/offices/list/ocr/letters/colleague-el-201501.pdf

Zacarian, D. (2021). *Responsive schooling for culturally and linguistically diverse students* [Webinar]. https://home.edweb.net/webinar/clrt20210127/

Zacarian, D., Calderon, M. E., & Gottlieb, M. (2021). *Beyond crises: Overcoming linguistic and cultural inequities in communities, schools, and classrooms.* Corwin.

Zacarian, D., & Silverstone, M. A. (2015). *In it together: How student, family, and community partnerships advance engagement and achievement in diverse classrooms.* Corwin.

Zacarian, D., & Silverstone, M. A. (2020). *Teaching to empower: Take action to support student agency, collaboration, and reflection.* Association for Supervision and Curriculum Development.

Zacarian, D., & Soto, I. (2020). Service-learning as a culturally responsive practice. In *Responsive schooling for culturally and linguistically diverse students* (pp. 135–156). Norton Professional Books.

CHAPTER 7

Identifying and Working With Multilingual Learners With Learning Differences and Learning Disabilities

Carlos enrolled in Mrs. Monahan's third-grade class during the spring term. Prior to enrolling, he had attended school in a neighboring city for less than a year and been referred for a special education evaluation because of his poor academic progress in English. Prior to that time, Carlos had had limited prior schooling in his home country as his parents could not afford to pay for the education that was available to him. When he enrolled in Mrs. Monahan's class, Carlos was tested by a monolingual English-speaking school psychologist and a speech language pathologist to formally determine the type of learning disability that he had. The testing was conducted in English, as was the family and social history interview with his parents. The interview was conducted by the school's guidance counselor, who noted that Carlos's parents were unable to answer many of the questions "in full."

After the testing process was completed, a meeting was held with his parents to review the results of the special education evaluation. The time allotted for the meeting was the same as it was for all special education evaluation meetings. In attendance were the school psychologist, a special educator, a guidance counselor, Carlos's teacher, and a translator employed by the school to translate the meeting. The school psychologist and special educator confirmed that they suspected Carlos had a language learning disability. During their explanation of the test findings, they looked directly at the translator and made very little eye contact with Carlos's parents. One of the services that they recommended was for Carlos to receive instruction from a special educator in lieu of ESL classes because they thought it would be a more effective way for him to learn the compensatory skills that he needed to cope with his disability. Carlos's parents respected the school's findings and recommendations. They felt out of place at the meeting, as they did not really understand most of the technical language that was being used. They politely nodded in agreement with all that was stated and recommended.

Do you believe that the steps taken to determine whether Carlos had a disability were appropriate? Is there anything that you would change in the process? What would you change regarding the meeting held with his parents to discuss the findings and recommendations for their child?

When Abad enrolled in the third grade in the United States, he did so after having been enrolled in school in his native country. In his native country, while he spoke Arabic at home and was instructed in Arabic, he had had a good deal of difficulty in school and often did not comprehend what was being taught. His teachers and parents had been concerned about his academic progress and suspected that he might have a language delay. While Abad was a very well-behaved child, he struggled in school and often came home crying in frustration. When he moved to the United States, his parents continued to be concerned about his academic progress. When they expressed their concerns to his teacher, she responded that it was important to give Abad time to learn English. Thinking that his teacher knew the right thing to do, his parents did not continue to express their concerns or pursue a referral. Rather, they waited and waited and waited. By the end of his first year in the United States, Abad was failing his classes miserably. However, his teacher and most of the school problem-solving team continued to believe that his failure was due to his lack of English proficiency.

Were team members correct in making these assumptions about Abad? What different steps might you have taken to support Abad's learning? What would you have changed in the learning environment?

What are some trends regarding multilingual learners and special education in the United States?

The U.S. Department of Education (2022b) posted some facts about multilingual learners (MLs) that are important to consider. These include that MLs

- grew by close to 30% between SY [school year] 2012 and SY 2020;
- were more likely to drop out of school, less likely to graduate with a high school diploma, and more likely to receive a certificate as compared to all students served under IDEA [Individuals with Disabilities Education Act], Part B;
- were less likely to be served inside regular class 80% more of the day as compared to all school-aged students served on IDEA, Part B;
- were more likely to be identified with specific learning disability or speech or language impairment and less likely to be identified with other health impairment, autism, or emotional disturbance as compared school-aged students served on IDEA, Part B.

The concern about overidentifying and underidentifying MLs with disabilities has existed for years (Artiles & Ortiz, 2002; Haas & Esperanza Brown, 2019; Hamayan et al., 2022). In some schools, when MLs don't seem to be making the same academic progress as their peers or learning English rapidly, they are referred for a special education evaluation. The dilemma of overidentifying students, such as in the case of Carlos, leads to a high and disproportionate number of culturally and linguistically diverse learners being referred for a special education evaluation and, ultimately, diagnosed with a learning disability. Overrepresentation is a chronic issue that requires our attention.

On many levels, as seen in Chapter 1, this is likely occurring due to the need to expand educators' expertise, knowledge, familiarity, and preparedness to teach diverse populations. That is, students who are "different" from their teachers are all too often regarded as having disabilities. The educational needs of MLs require that we understand the diversity among our student populations and plan and deliver instruction that is tailored to their individual needs (Artiles & Ortiz, 2002; Haager et al., 2007; Haas & Esparza Brown, 2019; Haynes & Zacarian, 2010; Sánchez López & Young, 2018). It calls for educators to provide evidence-based instruction that fully embraces a strength-based ideology, integrate the whole of students' backgrounds and experiences, and provide the resources and supports needed for the social-emotional and academic language development of students. It is imperative to individually and collectively examine and reexamine our practices so that we are more secure in making distinctions between and among learning acquisition, differences, and disabilities. Additionally, it is critical that school-based teams gather information about ML students to provide context for and get a better sense of why they may be experiencing challenges in school (Hamayan et al., 2022). Until this is done, it is likely that we will continue to overidentify many students as having disabilities when they do not.

Simultaneously, some schools fear that they might be referring MLs too quickly and that time is needed for a student to learn English before a special education referral is made and completed. This "wait till the student fails" and "stall for time" approach, as seen in the case of Abad, can prevent implementation of the interventions that are needed (Fuchs et al., 2003). The extent to which MLs are underidentified cannot be minimized. Some schools stall the process for such a long period of time that when the referral and identification process finally occurs, it is too late to provide the types of interventions that would have helped the student most effectively (Esparza Brown & Doolittle, 2008; Haas & Esparza Brown, 2019).

Thus, the pendulum swings from one extreme to the other and rarely stops in a balanced "just right" position. The process needed to create a more effective means for identifying MLs with disabilities and, more important, for providing an instructional program that is effective for all MLs requires leaders to address the disproportionate representation of MLs in special education by using a multistep scale of response commonly referred to as *Multi-Tiered Systems of Support* (MTSS). Before moving into a discussion about MTSS, however, it is important to understand the main law pertaining to students with disabilities and how schools gather data about

- the effectiveness of school programming for the general population of MLs (i.e., the effectiveness of the language assistance program as a whole),

- MLs who struggle to learn and are subsequently referred for a special education evaluation, and

- MLs who are diagnosed with disabilities.

What is the Individuals with Disabilities Education Act?

In 1975, Congress enacted the Individuals with Disabilities Education Act, which addresses the rights and educational needs of children with disabilities. The law has been amended several times, most recently in 2004 and as the Every Student Succeeds Act in 2015. IDEA spans students' education from birth to age 21. Its intent, according to the U.S. Department of Education (n.d.-a), is the following: "Improving educational results for children with disabilities is an essential element of our national policy of ensuring equality of opportunity, full participation, independent living, and economic self-sufficiency for individuals with disabilities" (para. 6).

Under IDEA regulations, each state is responsible for ensuring that its children receive a free evaluation to determine whether there is a disability and the types of services that are needed when a disability is found. It also requires that free services be provided when a disability is identified (U.S. Department of Education, 2022a). IDEA applies to any state or local educational agency that accepts federal funding.

IDEA addresses several types of disabilities:

Under IDEA, §1401 Section 3:

(A) In general

The term "child with a disability" means a child—

(i) with intellectual disabilities, hearing impairments (including deafness), speech or language impairments, visual impairments (including blindness), serious emotional disturbance (referred to in this chapter as "emotional disturbance"), orthopedic impairments, autism, traumatic brain injury, other health impairments, or specific learning disabilities; and

(ii) who, by reason thereof, needs special education and related services.

(B) Child[ren] aged 3 through 9

The term "child with a disability" for a child aged 3 through 9 (or any subset of that age range, including ages 3 through 5), may, at the discretion of the State and the local educational agency, include a child—

(i) experiencing developmental delays, as defined by the State and as measured by appropriate diagnostic instruments and procedures, in 1 or more of the following areas: physical development; cognitive development; communication development; social or emotional development; or adaptive development; and

(ii) who, by reason thereof, needs special education and related services.

Source: U.S. Department of Education (n.d.-b).

English language learning is not a disability and cannot be regarded as such. However, one of the most significant reasons that MLs are often misdiagnosed as having a disability is that some disability types (e.g., emotional and behavioral disabilities, mild to moderate cognitive disabilities, speech impairment, developmental language disorder) are socially constructed categories (Hamayan et al., 2022) and depend largely on the clinical judgment of practitioners (school psychologists, special educators, speech-language pathologists) to identify. That is, these disabilities are often diagnosed based on perceptions about how students interact with their environment or, conversely, how the environment interacts with them. All too often, when the environment is not conducive to the linguistic and cultural needs of students, it is more likely that a student will be referred for a special education evaluation and that a disability will be diagnosed (Hamayan et al., 2022; Harry & Klingner, 2022).

Prior to the most recent reauthorization of IDEA, students could not receive supports or interventions unless they were diagnosed with a disability. This traditionally included the application of the Wechsler Intelligence Scale for Children (WISC-IV) and an evaluation of student performance in class, on report cards, and on other standardized tests. The intent of these evaluation protocols was to measure students' potential in relation to their performance. Proponents of the reauthorization argued that these tests were often biased against students from diverse cultural and linguistic communities. For MLs this was problematic in that the tests were often normed on monolingual English-speaking students and administered only in English by monolingual English-speaking school psychologists. This resulted in the misdiagnosis and labeling of students with disabilities (Artiles et al., 2004; Donovan & Cross, 2002; Klingner & Edwards, 2006). The most recent reauthorization of IDEA allows schools to provide interventions before a student is referred for a special education evaluation. The purpose of these early interventions is to enhance the learning environment for all students and better ensure that students who experience challenges receive the supports that they need when they are needed so that fewer students will be referred and misdiagnosed as having a disability, especially students from culturally and linguistically diverse backgrounds.

Let's look at two scenarios of the same student, a 5-year-old kindergartener named Li, to illustrate the types of interventions that are now allowed under IDEA. As you read the first scenario, ask yourself if you think that Li's challenges are due to a disability or whether the difficulties are socially constructed and primarily due to the learning environment. If it is the latter, what might the school have done to provide for Li's instructional needs more effectively? As you read the second scenario, pay close attention to the steps that Li's teacher takes to provide interventions that she and others think will be helpful. We begin with a short description of Li, which is followed by a description of the two different responses that the school took to address observable behaviors.

Li was born in a rural province outside of Beijing. Shortly after she was born, her parents moved to the United States to complete their graduate studies and left Li in China, entrusting her to the care of her paternal grandparents. During her first 5 years, Li spoke solely in Mandarin, her grandparents were her sole caretakers, and she did not attend preschool. In August of her fifth year, her grandparents lovingly put Li on a plane bound for the United States, where she was reunited with her parents. Her parents' plan was for Li to begin attending kindergarten in the local public school a few weeks after her arrival. Thinking that it was important for Li to begin speaking in English, her parents decided that it was important for them to communicate with her solely in English.

When Li arrived in the United States, she was unable to understand her parents or the English-speaking environment in which they lived. In frustration, she spent her first few weeks crying, having temper tantrums, and begging to return to her grandparents. When Li began attending kindergarten, she was placed in an English-only classroom where she was the sole Mandarin speaker. Because of limited time and scheduling conflicts, Li's school allotted one 20-minute block of time per week for Li to receive ESL classes. The school justified this action based on the belief that kindergarten classes included a language-rich environment where MLs would flourish and that 5-year-olds learned English quickly and without much help.

During Li's first month in school, she rarely interacted with her peers, and when she did, it was usually to grab something from them. Her teacher frequently observed Li kicking other students and being unable to perform most of the tasks that were assigned. At the end of Li's first month in school, her teacher held a parent conference to express her concerns about Li's poor academic progress and inappropriate behavior. At the meeting, Li's parents told the teacher that Li was a "difficult" child.

Example 1: Thinking that a referral might be helpful, the teacher suggested that Li be referred to see whether she had a special education need. Her parents agreed with the teacher, thinking that the school knew what was best for their child. During the ensuing weeks, Li was tested in English by the school psychologist, speech and language therapist, and special educator to determine whether she had a disability. By the end of her first term in kindergarten, Li was diagnosed as having significant emotional and cognitive disabilities. In addition to her kindergarten teacher, she began working with a speech and language therapist, the school counselor, and a special educator in an all-English learning environment. She rarely attended her kindergarten class with her peers. Rather, the specialists with whom she worked took Li out of class, where she received a variety of supports that they believed were targeted for addressing her disabilities. When her teachers met with Li's parents at the end of the school year, they recommended that Li repeat kindergarten. Her parents agreed with this plan.

Example 2: Li's teacher asked the school counselor, psychologist, speech and language therapist, and special educator to join her in meeting with Li's parents. Wanting more information about Li, the group asked her parents to describe what she had been like as a younger child. When they learned that Li had lived with her grandparents in China and had not lived with her parents until just prior to enrolling in kindergarten, they asked if Li had heard or spoken English prior to arriving in the United States. They also asked Li's parents if she had attended preschool. The teachers and specialists learned that Li spoke only in Mandarin, had not attended preschool, and had not had much contact with her parents during her first 5 years of life. A much clearer picture of Li emerged because of the meeting. Several prereferral interventions were recommended, including that Li speak in Mandarin at home and that her parents meet with the school counselor to discuss various parenting strategies. In addition, a Chinese interpreter was employed to work in Li's kindergarten class to help Li understand her kindergarten environment, to support her in communicating with her teacher and peers, and to preview content area concepts in Mandarin before they were presented in English. The school psychologist, counselor, and interpreter often visited with Li during her lunch to work on her social-emotional well-being and to help her deal with her sadness at leaving her grandparents. They also engaged her in role-playing to help her engage more appropriately with her peers. The English language development instruction she received from the ESL teacher was increased to an hour per day. The kindergarten and ESL teachers collaborated closely and often codelivered lessons that they thought would benefit Li and her classmates. For example, during a unit about what makes a family, Li and her peers were encouraged to bring in family photos, draw pictures of their home, and use these visuals to talk about their family. Li brought in several photos of her grandparents and parents and drew some beautiful pictures of her home in China and in the United States. She readily shared these with her peers and began to converse in English more fluently. By the close of her kindergarten year, Li was able to communicate in English, was working well with her peers, and was making remarkable progress. Her parents and teachers were delighted with her accomplishments, and plans were made for her to attend the first grade.

The two scenarios about the same student provide us with very helpful information about what is allowed under IDEA as well as the types of interventions that are important to consider. In the first scenario, Li's teacher observed her behavior and performance in class and decided to refer her for a special education evaluation for two reasons: inappropriate behavior and poor school performance. When Li's parents commented that she was a "difficult" child, it confirmed the kindergarten teacher's assumptions that Li had behavioral issues. Li was also tested solely in English despite the reality that she had not yet had the opportunity to learn English and was not able to do ordinary classwork in English. It is likely that she was tested using a discrepancy model whereby her performance on tests (such as the WISC-IV) was used to compare how well she did in comparison with particular test norms. As stated earlier, the process of misidentifying and making assumptions about MLs is a common dilemma and has led to national concern about the high incidence of overidentifying MLs as having disabilities. The first scenario provides an example of misidentifying an EL as having a disability as well as a rush to judgment.

The second scenario shows us the steps that can be taken to help a student such as Li be successful in school.

Providing Sound General Education Programming Before Referring Students for a Special Education Evaluation

In the second scenario, Li's school problem-solving team took time to examine the effectiveness of their programming, elements of the learning environment, and information about a range of factors that might explain her performance in school (Artiles & Ortiz, 2002; Hamayan et al., 2022; Ortiz et al., 2011). The team found that MLs in kindergarten were not receiving enough ESL instructional time. They increased Li's ESL class time from 20 minutes per week to an hour per day. Also, they saw that Li could not grasp the instructional program because it was delivered solely in English. A bilingual Mandarin/English-speaking translator was employed to preview content in Mandarin to help Li meaningfully understand the instruction and then worked to support Li in her communication with her peers and teacher. The school did this because it needed to look more closely at the type of programming that has been found to be the most successful, as described in Chapter 2, and its application of this proven-effective model.

Various specialists intervened immediately in the general classroom setting to help Li behave more appropriately with her peers and to learn. The interventions that were employed reflect the types of activities that are allowed under IDEA. The intent of interventions is to prevent students from being overidentified as having disabilities by immediately providing supports that will help them be successful in school. With Li, the school provided a Multi-Tiered System of Supports. Each of the interventions occurred in all her general classes and did not require her to be referred for special education or diagnosed with a disability.

What is Multi-Tiered System of Supports?

MTSS is a schoolwide system that is implemented to proactively provide supports and interventions when they are needed to prevent students from failing. The intent of MTSS is to offer levels of interventions for addressing students' challenges as they occur or even proactively before the students experience significant challenges and without waiting for a special education evaluation (Hamayan et al., 2022). MTSS uses proven practices that are asset-based, developmentally appropriate, culturally and linguistically responsive, and student centered for the social-emotional, behavioral, and academic growth of students (Hoover et al., 2016).

Generally, MTSS includes three levels of intervention (see Figure 7.1). The first two occur in the general classroom, and the third, the most intensive and individualized intervention, can occur outside of the classroom before a referral to special education or when a student has been identified as having disabilities and special education services are provided. Li was provided with the first two tiers of interventions. These were part of the general classroom and included various specialists' responses to what was believed would be effective.

In the model seen in Figure 7.1, the tiers of support within MTSS are meant to be flexible in that the amount of intervention(s) may be increased and decreased depending on the particular context, the difficulties the student is experiencing,

Figure 7.1   Three-Tiered MTSS Model

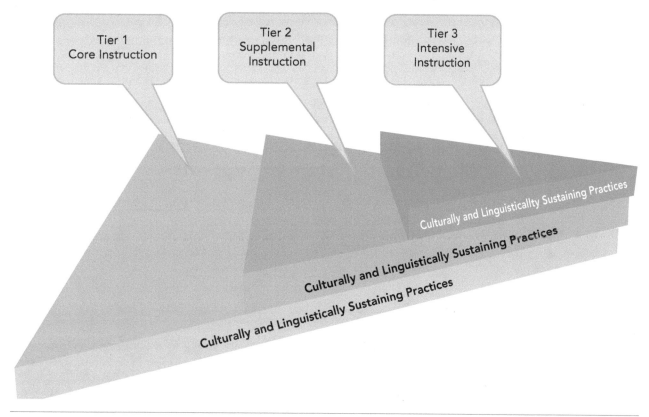

Culturally and Linguistically Sustaining Multi-Tiered System of Supports

Tier 1
Core Instruction

Tier 2
Supplemental
Instruction

Tier 3
Intensive
Instruction

Culturally and Linguisticallty Sustaining Practices

Culturally and Linguistically Sustaining Practices

Culturally and Linguistically Sustaining Practices

Source: Adapted from Batsch (2017) by Sánchez López & Young (2019).

and when challenges are resolved and students begin to experience success. As such, the infusion of proven interventions is intentionally targeted to bolster students' social-emotional, behavioral, and academic growth.

MTSS can strengthen our practice!

What is learned from an ML's success at different levels of MTSS can advance our understanding and professional practice about working with MLs (such as those who are learning a new language and/or experiencing differences in the form of physical, social-emotional, or academic development). An example of the application of the MTSS model and lessons learned is Clara, an ML who experienced the trauma of civil crisis in her home country, where she observed the tortuous murder of her family. During her first month of living in the United States with distant relatives and attending a new school, Clara was observed to be profoundly withdrawn in and out of school. In partnership with Clara's new family of distant relatives, her school-based team developed a 1-month proactive intervention protocol using evidence-based strategies for students living with adversity. It included Clara receiving daily one-on-one social-emotional support from a bilingual psychologist, Clara's teacher receiving daily instructional coaching from a bilingual teacher trained in trauma-informed practices with refugees, and Clara's family receiving weekly counseling from a practitioner at a local agency who had extensive professional training in working with students experiencing trauma, violence, and chronic stress. The plan also called for the team to reconvene after 1 month to determine whether the interventions would remain the same, be reduced, or be increased depending on Clara's needs. Figure 7.2 depicts the flexibility of the MTSS model to address the individual needs of a student such as Clara.

Figure 7.2   Flexibility of the Three-Tiered MTSS Model

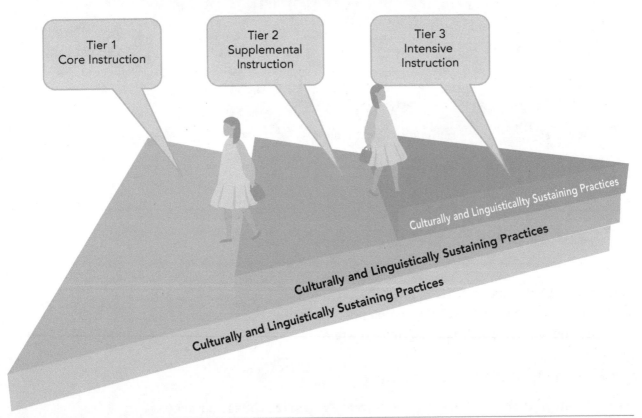

Source: Adapted from Sánchez López & Young (2022).

According to the Center on Multi-Tiered Systems of Support (2022), there are four components to an MTSS model:

1. Screening is generally conducted three times per year to identify students who may be at risk of poor outcomes and need additional academic, social, emotional, or behavioral supports.

2. Progress monitoring uses valid and reliable tools and processes to assess performance, quantify improvement or responsiveness to intervention and

instruction, and evaluate the effectiveness of instruction, interventions, and supports.

3. Multi-level prevention system includes a continuum (Tiers 1, 2, and 3) of integrated academic, social, emotional, and behavioral instruction and intervention supports that are evidence based and culturally and linguistically responsive.

4. Data-based decision making includes data analysis and problem solving through teaming to make decisions about instruction, intervention, implementation, and disability identification (in accordance with state law).

At the heart of an MTSS model is making decisions that are based on information gathered about the student's physical and social-emotional as well as linguistic, literacy, and academic development. Gathering authentic classroom-based information helps school-based MTSS teams identify the students who may be at risk of doing poorly and, more important, providing them with effective and meaningful intervention in a timely manner. In this scnsc, an MTSS model is intended to be a deliberate and proactive means for addressing potential difficulties before they occur by intervening early. When MTSS is designed with MLs in mind and implemented in culturally and linguistically responsive and sustaining ways, it is also a means to better identify ML students who also have disabilities. An MTSS model also uses increasing levels of supports whereby students who indeed have disabilities receive the most support. What is important to note is that the intensity of supports can decrease and increase depending on a student's progress.

Many MTSS models provide two levels of screenings at the beginning of the school year—or in the case of kindergarten, a prescreening—to identify the students who may be at risk of doing poorly (Center on Multi-Tiered Systems of Support, 2022). After the first screening is completed, a second screening occurs for students who have been identified in order to gather more information about them and to determine which ones are the most likely to struggle. Some schools conduct this type of screening at different intervals during the same school year to best ensure that students at risk of failing will be identified before failure occurs and that changes in the Tier 1 learning environment are made to enhance instruction for MLs and add any appropriate interventions as needed. Student progress is monitored throughout the school year, and interventions are provided when needed. A true MTSS model must ensure that its tests and measures of student progress and behavior are reliable and valid for MLs.

An MTSS model must use interventions that have been scientifically proven to be sound for MLs. They must be research based and known to be effective for the students for whom they are being used. When an ML student does not appear to respond, the team must be certain that the supports put into place were appropriate for MLs before making any decisions about the reasons for the ML's response to these interventions and before moving on to more intensive interventions. Generally,

MTSS models use increasing levels of intensity of support, from Tiers 1 to 3, as they are needed.

As seen in the second example of Li's case, her teacher and others provided interventions without referring her for a special education evaluation. In addition, her programming for learning English was evaluated and strengthened. The following interventions or rapid responses were provided in Li's general education classes:

1. A bilingual translator was employed to help Li communicate with her peers and teacher.

2. The school increased Li's ESL instruction from 20 minutes per week to an hour per day and made sure it was coordinated with what was occurring in her content area classes.

3. The school counselor supported Li's parents.

4. The school counselor and the psychologist provided support in Li's classroom to help her interact more appropriately with others and during lunchtime to give her opportunities to discuss her feelings about leaving her grandparents and getting to know her parents in this new and unfamiliar setting.

Each of these responses supported Li in learning English and content and matriculating successfully to the first grade.

Factors to Consider When Using an MTSS Model With MLs

On the face of it, MTSS may seem like an ideal model for providing the kind of individualized help that is needed when it is needed. It allows schools to provide interventions to students without the obstacle of having to wait for a special education evaluation to be completed. This alone should make schools relieved, especially those that find waiting to refer an ML to be detrimental to the overall success of students. With all these good reasons, why should schools be concerned about applying an MTSS model with MLs? The viability of applying an MTSS model with MLs demands our attention for several reasons:

- Interventions at all levels require educators to use culturally and linguistically sustaining approaches that draw from MLs' personal, social, cultural, linguistic, academic, and intellectual referents so they are empowered as learners (Zacarian & Soto, 2020). However, many of the actual interventions that are applied are not enough and/or do not address the specific needs of students from diverse linguistic and cultural experiences.

- Some schools and states don't offer instruction or support in a student's home language(s) or have eliminated bilingual education programming, making English the only language of instruction that is available for MLs.

- Many schools have limited programming and resources for MLs. Rather than providing the most basic of programming for English language and content development, schools with limited services and staff provide much less than what is needed. As a result, MLs do not get the type of programming that they should and do poorly because they are not provided with the type of Tier 1 learning environments and educational programming to which they are entitled.

- Many schools and states do not adequately address the unique needs of MLs who have had limited or interrupted prior schooling and do not give these students the time or specific instruction they need to learn literacy and grade-level content skills.

The reasons listed above illustrate scenarios where an ML might not be any better off participating in an MTSS process. This is not to say that MTSS is an ineffective model, rather, that it must be applied appropriately for MLs. Moreover, teaching MLs should mean that schools have a solid grounding in second language development and differences, the resources needed for teaching culturally and linguistically diverse students, and depth of understanding about the specific cultures and cultural ways of being of students so that instruction is culturally and linguistically responsive and sustaining (Hoover et al., 2007, 2016; Zacarian & Soto, 2020). Fundamentally, schools' general education programming must be responsive to the varied linguistic and cultural representatives found among their MLs so that the students who struggle are not struggling due to inadequate programming.

A Tier 1 response is high-quality, scientifically proven general education programming

One of the core elements of Tier 1 of an MTSS model is that core learning environments for all learners are effective. An MTSS model is heavily dependent on high-quality services being provided in the general education classroom and schools taking time to ensure that this is occurring. Language assistance programming is not considered special education; it is part of the general education model. Creating effective programming for individual students means providing language programming that is scientifically known to be sound and effective with the supports that are needed for the MLs who are struggling. Most teachers have not been trained to teach MLs, therefore the decision to refer an ML for a special education evaluation is most likely being made by a teacher who has had little training to work with MLs. In addition, as seen earlier in this book, programming is often dictated by the availability of limited resources and not necessarily the needs of MLs. Indeed, programming for learning English and content may be inadequate.

A quick response sequence that is effective for MLs who are struggling should be a top priority. As stated earlier, an MTSS model must include a systematic gathering of information, both qualitative and quantitative, on a range of factors (for a discussion of factors that impact MLs' performance in school, see Hamayan et al., 2022) to determine the reasons why a student is experiencing challenges and to identify a set of individualized responses for addressing the challenges effectively. More important, rather than provide one type of intervention, multiple intervening steps, such as the ones employed with Li in the second example, can and should occur using an MTSS model. However, how is a school to know what is best for MLs?

Gathering Data to Understand the Effectiveness of Language Assistance Programming for the General Population of MLs

Determining whether a student's difficulties are due to second language learning, a disability, or both is challenging for many districts. An important step is for a school to examine the effectiveness of its language assistance programming. Educators must implement language assistance programming models that are scientifically based and known to yield the best results. Chapters 2 and 3 provide a synopsis of the related federal laws, regulations, and legal decisions (including the seminal *Castañeda v. Pickard*); programming models that have been found to be the most effective; and a means for selecting and applying the model that is the most appropriate for individual school circumstances. Educators must also gather data about MLs who are struggling to learn in order to determine whether the difficulties students are experiencing are due to the typical developmental process involved in learning English while also learning academic content or an underlying learning disability that occurs in both the home language and English. When difficulties are only seen in an English-only instructional context and not in the student's primary or home language, it is less likely that there is an underlying disability. When difficulties occur across all or most settings and in both languages, it is more likely that a referral for a special education evaluation may be an appropriate course of action (Hamayan et al., 2022).

Schools must examine the likelihood of MLs being referred because of inadequate programming or lack of understanding about the process of second language acquisition. That is, when students are placed in programs without, or with less than, the proper resources, it is far more likely that they will be referred for a special education evaluation and diagnosed with a disability. In Li's case, she had been provided with 20 minutes of weekly instruction in ESL—many times less than what was needed—so the rest of her instructional day was not comprehensible, nor was there attention to teaching language objectives in her content area classes. Inappropriate core learning environments and inadequate language assistance programming are commonplace and must be remedied, if for nothing else than to address the disproportionate number of MLs who are misdiagnosed as having disabilities.

Examining the Effectiveness of Language Assistance Programming and MTSS With MLs

Careful examination of the frequency with which and reasons that MLs are and are not being referred can be very helpful. Such an evaluation greatly aids in understanding whether MLs are being referred due to external causes, such as ineffective programming, or individual disabilities. Resource 7.1 provides school leaders with a format for conducting this type of evaluation.

School leaders should not wait for MLs to fail in order to launch into a tiered MTSS model. There are many initial steps that leaders should routinely use to ensure that MLs are receiving effective programming in their core learning environments.

Creating a Data Analysis Team of Language Assistance and Special Education Staff

Implementing programming models that are scientifically proven to be sound is no guarantee that all students will do well or that a school will appropriately refer and evaluate students for potential disabilities. A systemic team approach is needed. School leaders should gather a team of specialists, special educators, ESL teachers, bilingual teachers, and parents for the purpose of analyzing the school's prereferral, referral, and disability services (see Resource 7.1). Using the results gathered from this evaluation, the team may discover that over- or underidentification is occurring because the language assistance programming is under-resourced (Hamayan et al., 2022). Remedies for this may involve doing the following:

- increasing professional development so that more teachers and specialists are trained and have a better understanding of the school's ML population from a cultural and linguistic perspective

- implementing daily ESL instruction so that students receive a greater continuum of English language development

- offering instruction or support in the student's home language(s) so that they have increased access to the curriculum

- inviting students to discuss and preview concepts and content in their home language(s) before English instruction

- hiring more specialists who are bilingual and bicultural in students' home languages and cultures

- creating a districtwide approach to curriculum planning and delivery that at the design level incorporates content and language objectives, students' cultural resources, as well as linguistic and other supports that MLs require

- using a systemic team approach for evaluating the learning environment through a multilingual/multicultural lens for MLs

Conducting an ongoing evaluation of the school's special education referral, identification, and services process for MLs; enriching the core learning environment; and enhancing language assistance are important ways of providing MLs with greater and more equitable access to the curriculum. The purpose of the evaluation is to better ensure that students receive appropriate and effective programming for learning English and content, address the problem of a disproportionate number of MLs in special education, and ensure that MLs are more properly referred for special education evaluation and diagnosed with a special education disability when it is necessary. Once this is done, it is critical to immediately apply the following kinds of interventions, if warranted:

- developing more culturally and linguistically appropriate core learning environments for MLs

- supporting educators in a timely and ongoing manner on ML-appropriate instructional approaches

- providing help to individual students when they first appear to struggle to learn

- identifying the students who have disabilities

- supporting individual students with interventions that are proven to work

- evaluating the success of the supports and interventions so that additional or more intensive interventions may be applied if needed

- providing special education referral and service delivery

Ensuring Equality for All Students

When students receive quality core instruction and interventions as needed, they are more likely to be successful. The application of effective programming improves outcomes for MLs. When these students are seen to be making progress, they are much less likely to be referred for special education services. Key to any quality program is collaboration. The rate of referral for MLs should be the same as it is for the general population of students. When students require a much higher level of intervention or modification, a special education referral may be needed. This could occur as a Tier 3 response.

The American Speech-Language-Hearing Association (ASHA; 1985) recognizes that not all speech and language therapists have the training and skills needed to serve MLs. It suggests that districts use a variety of strategies for evaluating and working with MLs. ASHA's suggestions are helpful for any specialist who is charged with evaluating and working with MLs.

First, reach out to schools, associations, and institutions to secure specialists who can be employed to evaluate and work with MLs. Colleges and universities are fine sources and resources for this work, as are professional associations, such as ASHA and the American Association for School Psychologists, as well as their state affiliates. Schools may find that recent graduates who are bi/multilingual bi/multicultural in English and students' home language(s) and culture(s) can help with this important work. They may also find bi/multilingual bi/multicultural graduate students who need practicum experiences. This can be an ideal pairing for schools that need this type of support. Reaching out to others is especially helpful for schools that need bi/multilingual bi/multicultural specialists who speak the same home languages as the schools' MLs.

Second, develop a collaborative or cooperative of districts. Collaboration among districts can be a fine means for finding specialists who can identify and work with MLs with disabilities. State education agencies and boards of cooperative educational services can be particularly helpful in establishing collaboratives.

Third, it may be helpful to secure a bi/multilingual bi/multicultural professional who is knowledgeable about the process of identifying and working with MLs with disabilities and can work closely with specialists. The American Association for Speech-Language-Hearing (n.d.) affirms the importance of collaborating with interpreters, transliterators, and translators. It is important for the specialist to review the assessment process that will take place and to receive input about its appropriateness for students from the particular language group for which it will be administered.

If a referral to special education services is required, instruction and intervention should be considered an extension of the high-quality instruction that is occurring in the core learning environment and the interventions that have been provided to the student. It is important that the interventions provided be research based and known to be effective for the MLs in question (Sánchez López & Young, 2018). The models that have been found to be the most successful are those that integrate students' home language(s), cultural resources, peer interactions and collaboration, and oral language development into instruction and intervention (Sánchez López & Young, 2018).

Key to identifying and working with MLs with learning differences and learning disabilities is the quality of the programming and how districts evaluate the effectiveness of that programming. In the next chapter, we will discuss making data-informed decisions based on effective measures of student performance.

online resources ▸ **RESOURCE 7.1**

[School District] Evaluation of Multilingual Learners
Referred for Special Education Evaluation and Diagnosed With a Disability

A team of English language and special education teachers and specialists should convene periodically to review and analyze data about the students who have been referred and evaluated for special education services.

Analysis of the ML Population

1. The total number of identified MLs in the school is _____. The total number of MLs who were referred during this school year for a special education evaluation in the school is _____. The total percentage of MLs referred for a special education evaluation during this school year is _____.

2. Is the proportion of MLs who have been referred the same as the proportion of the general population of students who have been referred? Yes ☐ No ☐ If no, what is the difference noted?

3. Is the proportion of MLs who have been identified as having disabilities the same as the proportion of the general population of students who have been identified? Yes ☐ No ☐ If no, describe the differences.

4. The languages spoken by the MLs in the school are:

5. The languages spoken by the MLs who were referred for a special education evaluation are:

6. Are there commonalities among the languages spoken by MLs and the reasons for referral or diagnosis of disability? Yes ☐ No ☐ If yes, what is the commonality?

Reasons That MLs Have Been Referred

7. The reasons, by total number of occurrences, that MLs were referred for a special education evaluation this year are:

   ———— autism

   ———— cognitive disability

   ———— deaf-blindness

   ———— deafness

   ———— emotional disturbance

   ———— hearing impairment

   ———— multiple disabilities

   ———— orthopedic impairment

   ———— other health impairment

   ———— specific learning disability

——————— speech/language impairment

——————— traumatic brain injury

——————— visual impairment, including blindness

8. The most common reason that MLs were referred for a special education evaluation this year is:

9. Anecdotally, describe any additional commonalities among the MLs who were referred (e.g., interrupted formal education).

Teachers and Specialists

10. Have the assessors received instruction and ongoing professional learning in second language acquisition and linguistic and cultural diversity? Yes ☐ No ☐ If no, what steps is the school taking to ensure that its evaluators—including school psychologists, speech and language therapists, and special education staff—are being equipped with the appropriate theory, research, and techniques?

Assessments

11. Do the assessments used to identify MLs with disabilities make use of relevant and actual behaviors in classroom contexts? Yes ☐ No ☐

12. Are assessments being provided in the students' home language(s) by staff who have trained in second language acquisition and practices for teaching MLs? Yes ☐ No ☐ If no, what steps has the school taken to ensure that actual data are used?

Language Assistance Programming Services

13. Do the MLs who have been referred receive effective programming for learning English, including the following:

    a. an English language development program from a licensed ESL or bilingual teacher? Yes ☐ No ☐

    b. an appropriate amount of daily instruction of English language development for MLs? Yes ☐ No ☐

    c. content instruction from a teacher who is trained to teach MLs? Yes ☐ No ☐

    d. curriculum that is specifically connected to MLs' personal, cultural, linguistic, and world experiences and knowledge so that it is meaningful, relevant, and comprehensible? Yes ☐ No ☐

    e. An education program for students with interrupted formal education? Yes ☐ No ☐

14. If any of the responses to Question 13 are "no," what are the steps the school is taking to ensure that its programming for MLs is properly resourced?

 Available for download at **resources.corwin.com/transformingschoolsformultilinguallearners**

References

American Speech-Language-Hearing Association. (n.d.). *Collaborating with interpreters, transliterators, and translators.* https://www.asha.org/practice-portal/professional-issues/collaborating-with-interpreters/

American Speech-Language-Hearing Association. (1985). *Clinical management of communicatively handicapped minority language populations* [Position statement]. https://4alxhe1ewli9359s702rvpks-wpengine.netdna-ssl.com/wp-content/uploads/2018/01/G.-ASHA-position-stmt.pdf

Artiles, A., & Ortiz. A. (Eds.). (2002). *English language learners with special education needs: Assessment, identification, and instruction.* Center for Applied Linguistics.

Artiles, A. J., Trent, S. C., & Palmer, J. (2004). Culturally diverse students in special education: Legacies and prospects. In J. A. Banks & C. M. Banks (Eds.), *Handbook of research on multicultural education* (2nd ed., pp. 716–735). Jossey-Bass.

Center on Multi-Tiered Systems of Support at the American Institutes for Research. (2022). https://mtss4success.org/

Donovan, S., & Cross, C. (2002). *Minority students in special and gifted education.* National Academy Press.

Esparza Brown, J., & Doolittle, J. (2008). *A cultural, linguistic, and ecological framework for response to intervention with English language learners.* National Center for Culturally Responsive Educational Systems.

Fuchs, D., Mock, D., Morgan, P. L., & Young, C. L. (2003). Responsiveness-to-intervention: Definitions, evidence, and implications for the learning disabilities construct. *Learning Disabilities Research & Practice, 18*(3), 157–171.

Haager, D., Klingner, J. K., & Vaughn, S. (Eds.). (2007). *Validated reading practices for three tiers of intervention.* Brookes.

Haas, E. M., & Esparza Brown, J. (2019). *Supporting English learners in the classroom: Best practices for distinguishing language acquisition from disabilities.* Teachers College Press.

Hamayan, E., Marler, B., Sánchez López, C., & Damico, J. (2022). *Special education considerations for English language learners: Delivering a continuum of services* (3rd ed.). Brookes.

Harry, B., & Klingner, J. (2022). *Why are so many students of color in special education? Understanding race and disability in schools* (3rd ed.). Teachers College Press.

Haynes, J., & Zacarian, D. (2010). *Teaching English language learners across the content areas.* Association for Supervision and Curriculum Development.

Hoover, J. J., Baca, L. M., & Klingner, J. K. (2016). *Why do English learners struggle with reading? Distinguishing language acquisition from learning disabilities.* Corwin.

Hoover, J., Klingner, J., Baca, L., & Patton, J. (2007). *Methods for teaching culturally and linguistically diverse exceptional learners.* Merrill/Prentice Hall.

Klingner, J. K., & Edwards, P. A. (2006). Cultural considerations with response to intervention models. *Reading Research Quarterly, 41*(1), 108–117.

Ortiz, A. A., Robertson, P. M., Wilkinson, C. Y., Liu, Y., McGhee, B. D., & Kushner, M. I. (2011). The role of bilingual education teachers in preventing inappropriate referrals of ELLs to special education: Implications for response to intervention. *Bilingual Research Journal, 34,* 316–333.

Sánchez López, C., & Young, T. (2018). *Focus on special educational needs.* Oxford University Press.

Sánchez López, C., & Young, T. (2019, November). *Culturally and linguistically responsive problem-solving within MTSS/RtI for multilingual learners.* Presentation at the La Cosecha conference, Santa Fe, NM.

U.S. Department of Education. (2022a). *43rd annual report to Congress on the implementation of the Individuals with Disabilities act, 2021.* Office of Special Education and Rehabilitative Services. https://sites.ed.gov/idea/files/43rd-arc-for-idea.pdf

U.S. Department of Education. (2022b). OSEP fast facts: Students with disabilities who are English learners (ELs) served under IDEA Part B. https://sites.ed.gov/idea/osep-fast-facts-students-with-disabilities-english-learners

U.S. Department of Education. (n.d.-a). *About IDEA.* https://sites.ed.gov/idea/about-idea

U.S. Department of Education. (n.d.-b). *Chapter 33—Education of individuals with disabilities, subchapter 1: General provisions.* http://uscode.house.gov/view.xhtml?path=/prelim@title20/chapter33&edition=prelim

Zacarian, D., & Soto, I. (2020). *Responsive schooling for culturally and linguistically diverse students.* Norton Professional Books.

CHAPTER 8

Putting It All Together: Making Data-Driven Decisions to Strengthen the Success of Language Assistance Programs

When secondary school principal Mr. Ross analyzed the performance of his ninth-grade students on the state's annual assessment of English, he noted that many had scored well below the school's average. As he began to analyze the data further, he found that the multilingual learners (MLs) had done poorly on each of the subtests, yet he could not find anything specific enough to determine a strategy for improving their progress. He decided to meet with their ESL teacher, Mrs. Fernandez, about the students' performance outcomes. When they met, they shared their thoughts about the dramatic shift made from the time their school shut down to when it resumed during the COVID-19 pandemic. Mrs. Hernandez said, "We can't really expect them to score well. After all, they are not fluent enough in English to take the test and do well on it, and the pandemic has caused so many disruptions to their lives and ours."

Thinking that this was a logical answer, Mr. Ross decided that the data weren't likely to give him a full picture of the students. He wasn't quite sure if this was a good or bad approach, however, and began considering the ways he might learn more about the MLs and their performance in school.

Reflection Question: What would you have done if you were Mr. Ross? What factors would have influenced your decision?

_____

_____

_____

_____

_____

The example is based on a colleague who works in a suburb of a northeastern U.S. city. Like many if not all of us, improving student outcomes is one of his most important goals. However, he has this goal at a time when we have all been immersed in the COVID-19 pandemic, witnessing economic crises, social injustices, border crises, climate crises, and global conflicts. All of these are amplifying longstanding inequities—particularly for the nation's MLs.

We are at an important crossroads, where we struggle to figure out not only how to transform our schools in such a way as to address these inequities but also how we can be more successful in working with one of the fastest growing populations in our schools (National Education Association, 2015, 2020) and close the opportunity gaps between MLs and their English-fluent peers. These unprecedented times that we are experiencing speak to the urgent need for making decisions that truly strengthen the language instruction educational programs we create and the professional development activities we provide for all educators, including teachers, administrators, specialists, coaches, teachers, counselors, family liaisons, curriculum directors, and others who serve this growing student population.

In this chapter, we explore the following questions:

1. What role can educators play in strengthening local (i.e., district, school, and classroom) language education instruction policies and programming?

2. What are key considerations for evaluating strengths-based policies and practices that empower MLs and their families?

3. What tools should we use to evaluate the effectiveness of and make improvements to our language assistance programming?

What role can educators play in strengthening local (i.e., district, school, and classroom) language education instruction policies and programming?

Changing Old Habits

| Figure 8.1 Transforming Schools for MLs |

Image source: iStock.com/ogichobanov

If we look at what we have typically done to improve programming, we find ourselves doing what school principal Mr. Ross did. We analyze the results of our state's assessments of MLs with the goals of finding the areas in which students performed poorly and identifying the students who did so. Some of us go deeper by disaggregating the data further to learn more about student responses to specific questions and groups within subgroups (e.g., Cambodian and Chinese students within an Asian subgroup) and create a plan for improving their testing outcomes. Analysis of subgroup performance, we think, will help us better understand ways to improve the conditions by which specific groups of students can learn best. Armed with this information, we think we will successfully determine who needs to improve, what needs to be improved, and how improvements might be accomplished. On the face of it, this sounds like a straightforward task. That is, interpreting assessment data will result in determining the "right" steps that are needed to make improvements.

Unfortunately, the cycle of poring over state data (that old habit we have used year after year) continues and has not yielded the positive results we need. What broke this year-after-year cycle for millions of students was the cancellation of standardized testing due to the COVID-19 pandemic. This outcome, coupled with growing concern about the value of state assessments (Olson & Jerald, 2020), calls for us to think anew—as many districts are—to broaden our understanding of federal laws and regulations; embrace the primacy for enacting strengths-based, culturally responsive, trauma-informed, and social-emotional learning pedagogies; and fully support student, family, and school community partnerships. If we do this, it might yield the positive results that many are experiencing (Mavrogordato & White, 2019; Zacarian et al., 2021).

The U.S. Department of Education (2016b) provides a checklist of suggested questions for evaluating the effectiveness of a school's and/or district's language assistance programming (see Figure 8.2).

Figure 8.2   U.S. Department of Education's Checklist of Suggested Questions

- To what extent is the LEA [local education agency] tracking data, both periodically and longitudinally, and by EL program, on ELs' acquisition of English proficiency and mastery of grade-level content?

- To what extent is the EL program meeting its stated education goals without unnecessarily segregating EL students from never-EL students?

- Do all ELs have comparable access to opportunities that prepare them for college and careers (e.g., higher-level courses, extracurricular activities, field trips, etc.) as their never-EL peers?

- Are ELs making progress toward achieving language proficiency within a reasonable period of time, as evidenced by multiple performance indicators?

- To what extent do longitudinal data compare performance in the core-content areas (e.g., via valid and reliable standardized tests) and graduation, dropout, and retention data among current ELs, former ELs, and never-ELs?

- Are all ELs receiving EL services until they achieve English proficiency and not exited from these services based on time in the EL program or opted-out status?

- Is the LEA tracking data of former ELs over time and is it able to compare that data to that of their never-EL peers? For example, to what extent do grades and state and local assessment data in the core-content areas indicate that former ELs
  - participate meaningfully in classes without EL services?
  - perform comparably to their never-EL peers in the standard instructional program?

- Do LEAs modify EL programs when longitudinal performance data indicate ELs are not reaching English proficiency within a reasonable period of time, or when former ELs are not participating in the standard instructional program comparable to their never-EL peers?

Source: U.S. Department of Education (2016b, p. 3).

These questions are important to consider. However, we shouldn't undertake this analysis by repeating our old habits of assessing whether the data we gather yield a simple checklist of questions with yes/no or degree-of-intensity responses such as "to a small extent." We must go deeper and really challenge ourselves to look at what is going well and what needs strengthening. What is powerful at this time in history, this moment, is that many of the traditional steps that we are used to taking are ripe for change!

According to the Every Student Succeeds Act, every school, district, and state education agency has the obligations listed in Figure 8.3.

Figure 8.3 Legal Obligations of All State Education Agencies, Districts, and Schools

- Identify and assess all potential EL students in a timely, valid, and reliable manner.

- Provide EL students with a language assistance program that is educationally sound and proven successful, consistent with *Castañeda v. Pickard* and the Supreme Court decision in *Lau v. Nichols*.

- Provide sufficiently well prepared and trained staff and support the language assistance programs for EL students.

- Ensure that EL students have equal opportunities to meaningfully participate in all curricular and extracurricular activities.

- Avoid unnecessary segregation of EL students.

- Ensure that EL students who have or are suspected of having a disability under the Individuals with Disabilities Education Act (IDEA) or Section 504 of the Rehabilitation Act of 1973 are identified, located, and evaluated in a timely manner and that the language needs of students who need special education and disability related services because of their disability are considered in evaluations and delivery of services.

- Meet the needs of EL students who opt out of language assistance programs.

- Monitor and evaluate EL students in language assistance programs to ensure their progress with respect to acquiring English proficiency and grade level content knowledge, exit EL students from language assistance programs when they are proficient in English, and monitor exited students to ensure they were not prematurely exited and that any academic deficits incurred in the language assistance program have been remedied.

- Evaluate the effectiveness of a school district's language assistance program(s) to ensure that EL students in each program acquire English proficiency and that each program is reasonably calculated to allow EL students to attain parity of participation in the standard instructional program within a reasonable period of time.

- Ensure meaningful communication with limited English proficient (LEP) parents.

Source: U.S. Department of Education (2016a, pp. 6–7).

The 10 elements in Figure 8.3 should form the basis for any analyses we undertake. Federal regulations also require that we set improvement standards and determine what needs to be done to achieve them. According to the U.S. Department of Justice and U.S. Department of Education (2015, p. 35), the evaluation of a program's effectiveness must be based on "enabling EL students to attain within a reasonable period of time, both (1) English proficiency and (2) meaningful participation in the standard educational program comparable to their never-EL peers." However, who should conduct this analysis? Should we go back to our old ways of going it alone? No! In Chapter 3, we learned that the U.S. Department of Education (2020) suggests that we form a working group of administrators, teachers, counselors, and other staff as well as families and community members to help us evaluate the successes of our language assistance programming and to make changes when needed. Figure 3.1 in Chapter 3 provides a model for supporting the group to be as inclusive as possible.

Reflection Question: Who should be included on a working team in your context so that it is inclusive and comprehensive?

_____

_____

_____

_____

_____

What are key considerations for evaluating strengths-based policies and practices that empower MLs and their families?

Moving From a Silo to a Collective

In the Introduction to this book, we learned that the trend in education leadership has moved from one person to a collective that works together on a shared mission with a unified purpose. We can learn and do so much more when we are in it together, when we work together for the good of MLs. In Chapter 3, we learned about the importance of assembling a work group that represents the various sectors of our school, family, and local communities to support us in selecting the language assistance program models that are most appropriate for our specific population of MLs. Work groups are also essential for assessing the effectiveness of the models that we implement. While a work group speaks to the heart of a school's or district's responsibility, MLs must be considered everyone's students and a shared responsibility. To engage these groups well and support the mission of assessing, improving, and strengthening the effectiveness of our language assistance models, it is critical to create a mistake-safe culture (Zacarian & Silverstone, 2020).

Creating a Mistake-Safe Collaborative Culture

We all make mistakes; it's a natural part of learning and discovery. A *mistake-safe culture* gives everyone the opportunity to try new ideas, make errors, and receive constructive feedback from a trusted colleague, mentor, coach, and supervisor who wants the best for us because they have our interests in mind (Zacarian & Silverstone, 2020). It's a culture that helps us see our strengths and the possibilities of what might work better and then try it. Key to the success of a work group is establishing a mistake-safe culture in which everyone feels safe, a sense of belonging, value, and competence.

Chapter 3 discussed the invaluable support that work groups provide in selecting a language assistance model(s). The same holds true for analyzing the effectiveness of the program model(s) that we enact. One of the greatest opportunities that we have is supporting every member of a work group to actively explore what is working well and what needs improvement and to learn from and with each other without fear of embarrassment and judgment (Zacarian & Silverstone, 2020). Figure 8.4 provides some helpful strategies drawn from Zacarian and Silverstone's (2020, p. 90) contributions on enacting a mistake-safe culture in order to build and sustain a work group's momentum and the tasks and activities it engages in.

Figure 8.4 Strategies for Building and Sustaining an Effective Work Group

1. Consistently use a strengths-based approach.
2. Be positive about the work group's efforts to work and learn together and celebrate its efforts!
3. Frame what is going well and what needs strengthening with curiosity.
4. View outcomes that are not what is expected as a point for learning and not as a failure.
5. Support reflection practices throughout.
6. Encourage analysis by promoting a positive culture of support.

Creating Collaborative Work Group Environments

There are three types of collaborative work group environments:

1. Meeting in person,

2. Meeting remotely, and

3. Engaging in synchronous and asynchronous computer-mediated exchanges.

Figure 8.5 In-Person Work Group Environment

Image source: **iStock.com/A-Digit**

Bringing a group together in person can provide members with unique understandings about each other's ideas, questions, and contributions because they occur in the same physical space where everyone can be with each other (see Figure 8.5). In-person meetings have long been the means for work groups to collaborate and pool their knowledge, skills, and efforts to address a range of needs, hopes, and desired outcomes.

Figure 8.6   Remote Work Group Environment

Image source: iStock.com/Liubov Trapeznykova

Since the COVID-19 pandemic began, we have become much more adept at working collaboratively online. Online formats using synchronous communication tools (e.g., Zoom, Skype, Microsoft Teams) can be particularly helpful for collaboration with groups of people who work in different locations, including educators, families, and local community members. As we have all learned, it is paramount that every member has a computer and internet service and is supported to use these communication tools successfully.

Consider this example of a work group consisting of a diverse collection of educators and multilingual family and local community members. Educators regularly used the chat function tool during the group's Zoom meetings to paste weblinks about information related to the work they were doing. It wasn't until months into their meetings that a family and local community member shared that they didn't know what the chat function was or how to use it.

It's also helpful to find out the communication tool preference of all the members of the work group. For example, family members may be familiar and more comfortable using Skype, so this may be the best communication tool for the group to use.

Whatever tool is chosen, it is important to review all the various functions included in it to be sure that work group members become comfortable and adept at using them.

Figure 8.7   Computer-Mediated Work Group Environment

Image source: iStock.com/Yuliia Kutsaieva

Another format that is helpful and even essential is written communication using asynchronous communication tools (e.g., Google Docs, Notion), as illustrated in Figure 8.7. In these computer-mediated exchanges, we can share challenges and information, ask questions, and seek solutions for building and sustaining effective language assistance programming. Also, consider the wealth of online resources that are a keystroke away for all of us to share! We can learn with and from each other and do so in real time and otherwise (asynchronously) to accommodate the various home and work schedules of all the members of the work group. An example of this type of engagement is cowriting various documents from student codes of conduct to language assistance programming policies.

The strategies in Figure 8.8 should be used to engage work groups in positively focused in-person, remote, and computer-mediated exchanges.

Figure 8.8   Strategies for Engaging Work Groups in In-Person, Remote, and Computer-Mediated Exchanges

- Honor everyone's contributions in a positive way.
- Encourage the various contributions and diversity of members.
- Inspire and encourage copartnerships and copowerment.
- Cocreate reflective questions that spark everyone's interest in contributing.
- Create open lines of communication to support an inclusive culture.
- Schedule meetings ahead of time.
- Schedule deadlines for exchanges so that everyone has a chance to contribute, reflect, and keep the momentum of the group moving forward.

Each of the strategies in Figure 8.8 is targeted at having a structure and an organizational format for meetings so that there is a sense of positive predictability. One way to do this is to schedule recurring meeting times and send a meeting invitation and agenda (e.g., emailing invitations with video links for the meeting) and reminders a few days before the meeting so it can be easily added to members' calendars.

Copowering the Work Group

It is also important to provide support to members of the work group so the group is inclusive and empowered. In Chapter 6, we learned about the supports that the California Association of Bilingual Education (2021) provides in family leadership and supporting school and district personnel in building and sustaining family engagement efforts (Zacarian & Soto, 2020). In addition to the ideas presented in Chapter 6, it is helpful for district- and school-based work groups to review a set of common readings (such as the Introduction and Chapters 1, 2, and 6 in this book). This greatly helps everyone have a common language and understanding of MLs, their families, and the school community; the laws and regulations governing language assistance programming; and the principles that should guide a work group's collective thinking.

A note of caution: It is essential to support the back-and-forth flow of conversations with the addition of a multilingual multicultural translator(s) when members of the group are not fluent in each other's language(s). Also, when there are readings, translation support helps everyone share key ideas and respond to questions, concerns, and ideas. In addition, this support helps the group's collective role in designing, supporting, and strengthening the language assistance programming models that are enacted.

In addition, work groups, like all collaborations, can have status issues such that some members have or perceive that they have a higher or lower status than others in the group (Cohen & Lotan, 2014; Zacarian & Silverstone, 2020).

An example is a group composed of school leaders, such as a school principal and pupil personnel director, as well as teachers, specialists, and family and local community members. Each may have perceptions about the others: "This person is my boss. I better agree with her" "I am not a teacher, so I don't have anything important to offer." "I don't speak the language well enough to contribute."

One means for overcoming these challenges is to prevent a group from having one member as the sole speaker for the group, or two people who dominate a group's talk, and instead having a group of copowered individuals who support the success of everyone. When everyone contributes, great things can happen!

A second means for remedying status issues and supporting everyone to be a copowered member of the work group is asking reflective questions and strategically listening—all the while working toward building the group's capacity and voice as change agents (Safir, 2017). Asking reflective questions and strategically listening are critical to a work group's success. What is also crucial is having a toolkit of resources that draw from the laws and regulations and support the group's focus on the success of multilingual learners.

What tools should we use to evaluate the effectiveness of and make improvements to our language assistance programming?

One way to harness the possibilities of a work group is to steadfastly focus its conversations on the team's potential impact in supporting MLs to succeed. Questions that support every member to analyze their language assistance program's effectiveness are critical. Resources 8.1 through 8.11 are based sequentially on legal obligations found in Figure 8.3. Each includes a series of questions intended to guide work group meetings.

Here are some important considerations. Previous chapters in this book presented the information, tools, and resources needed to provide effective programming for MLs. For example, Chapter 3 presented the resources needed to identify MLs. Despite having these resources in hand, we might find that what we are doing is not working as well as it should with our students and families. Unless we challenge ourselves, we might never find out what works and what needs strengthening in our own contexts.

An example of this type of challenge exploration is an urban district that had one centralized registration location for families to enroll their children. It had trained multilingual family liaisons, staff, and assessors to welcome new families and assess potential ML children. A work group analyzed its registration process using Resource 8.1 and found that some families were not sure where to bring their child for the assessment and left the building without engaging their child in this critical activity. Weeks of school went by before the children were identified by their teachers as potential MLs and assessments were administered. By the time the assessments occurred and MLs were identified, many parents declined language assistance services because they did not want their children to make yet another transition. Findings such as these led to some sweeping changes. New families are now greeted at the front entrance of the registration building, brought to the appropriate registration and assessment locations for determining potential MLs, asked welcoming questions such as those found in Resource 3.3 (in Chapter 3), and arrangements are made for newly identified MLs and their families to be personally welcomed into their new school.

Let's look at Resource 8.1 for assessing the success of the steps used to identify and assess potential MLs. It represents the first legal obligation under federal regulations listed in Figure 8.3. The ideal behind this and all other resources in this chapter is that they be used at least on an annual basis to determine if what we are doing is successful and to make improvements when needed.

online resources **RESOURCE 8.1**

Assessing the Steps Taken to Identify and Assess Potential MLs

1. What steps have we taken to identify and assess all potential MLs in a timely, valid, and reliable manner in our school?

2. What documents, forms, and protocols are we using to demonstrate what we do to identify and assess all potential MLs in a timely, valid, and reliable manner? (Refer to the resources provided in Chapter 3.)

3. What might we do to strengthen what we are doing?

4. What professional readings or school/district documents should be included?

5. What cultural and linguistic considerations do we need to address?

6. What additional questions should we ask about our identification and assessment process that we have not yet included?

7. What type of professional growth do we need in order to support everyone in our school/district in knowing about our identification and assessment of MLs?

 Available for download at **resources.corwin.com/transformingschoolsformultilinguallearners**

Resource 8.2 presents the type of questions that the work group should ask to analyze its language assistance programming. The contents, resources, and tools included in Chapters 3, 4, and 5 provide a wealth of information about the pedagogy, practices, and strategies that should be used to guide selection of the program model(s). For example, Resource 5.1 provides a checklist for designing and delivering quality learning experiences. It provides a helpful guide for determining the professional growth that is needed to strengthen our individual and collective practice. Educators should read these chapters, complete and review the associated resources found within them, and then respond to the reflection questions asked in Resource 8.2.

RESOURCE 8.2

Assessing the Steps Taken to Analyze Language Assistance Programming

1. What steps have we taken to ensure that we are providing MLs with language assistance programming that is educationally sound and proven successful, consistent with *Castañeda v. Pickard* and *Lau v. Nichols*?

2. What documents, forms, and protocols are we using to demonstrate the steps we have taken to ensure that we are providing language assistance programming that is educationally sound and proven to be successful? (Refer to the resources found in Chapter 3.) What have we done to identify and assess all potential MLs in a timely, valid, and reliable manner in our school?

3. What might we do to strengthen what we are doing?

4. What professional readings or school/district documents should be included? (See Resource 3.6 in Chapter 3.)

5. What cultural and linguistic considerations do we need to address?

6. What additional questions should we ask about our analysis of our language assistance programming that we have not yet included?

7. What type of professional growth do we need in order to support everyone in our school/district in knowing about analyzing the success of our language assistance programming for MLs?

 Available for download at **resources.corwin.com/transformingschoolsformultilinguallearners**

Determining Professional Development Needs and Desires

In 2020, SupportEd published a review by Dugan et al. (2020) of state recertification requirements of educators of MLs in the United States. While most states require recertification every 5 years to demonstrate some type of continued learning, the authors found that the majority do not "have a policy in place that requires general education teachers to complete any amount of English learner–related professional development in order to renew their general education certification" (p. iv). The exceptions include Colorado, Massachusetts, Minnesota, and New York. Further, while some states (California, Florida, New Mexico, Pennsylvania, and Texas) "have a requirement for districts to offer English learner PD [professional development] . . . [it] is not a requirement for teachers to renew their certification" (p. iv).

While not every U.S. state has requirements for individual educators of MLs, it is a federal requirement that state education agencies and local schools and districts ensure that they are providing "sufficiently well prepared and trained staff and supports" for the growing population of MLs (U.S. Department of Education, 2016a, p. 7). One of the most important tasks that a school or district work group can do is determine the professional development activities that educators will receive to educate its growing population of MLs.

There are many pathways that can be used to successfully guide professional learning. The goal behind whatever is chosen should be strengthening language assistance programming outcomes. One approach for doing this is to collectively determine what is already occurring and needs to occur in order to provide a well-prepared and trained staff. Just as some MLs have had a good deal of formal education and others less so, the same holds true for educators working with MLs. Our prior professional growth and formal educational experiences vary greatly. It is important for a work group to gather as much as it can about the prior preparation of all of its educators on an annual basis so that the decisions that it makes for school leaders, teachers, specialists, and all others is well connected to what is needed and desired. Resource 8.3 is intended for this purpose.

RESOURCE 8.3

Annual Survey of Educator Preparation to Work With MLs in (name of school/district)

Educator name:

Role:

Date:

We want to learn as much as we can about the prior preparation of our school's/district's educators so that we may create professional development opportunities that are tailored to meet the needs of our multilingual learners. Please complete the following survey for this purpose. Thank you!

Prior professional development sessions or formal courses taken in multilingual education	Number of professional development or formal education hours earned	Do you possess an advanced degree in multilingual education? If yes, please list degree earned.	What topics would you like included in our professional growth activities in order to strengthen your preparedness for working with MLs?

 Available for download at **resources.corwin.com/transformingschoolsformultilinguallearners**

Information gathered from the survey can greatly help in determining the future professional development this is needed and desired.

In 2021, as we were all steeped in the pandemic and many schools were operating remotely, three well-known educators wrote a book titled *DIY PD: A Guide to Self-Directed Learning for Educators of Multilingual Learners* (Toppel et al., 2021), which provides a snapshot of what happened when each author experienced the COVID-19 shutdown in their respective communities in Vietnam, Oregon, and Texas. They speak frankly about the important role that Twitter, Facebook, Instagram, and YouTube had in helping them and their students work, socialize, and learn together. As we all shift to an era flush with online and in-person professional growth opportunities, this book is a helpful resource for supporting individual and collective professional growth. The same holds true, of course, for university-based, school-based, as well as institution- and association-based professional development. Key to whatever we do is ensuring that our efforts—as a state education agency, local district, school, agency, institution, or association—builds momentum toward a whole-school, whole-district, whole-community effort to support MLs to succeed. Resources 8.3 and 8.4 are intended to assist us in making strengths-based decisions about the professional development activities that will occur to sustain and strengthen language assistance programming.

online resources **RESOURCE 8.4**

Assessing the Preparation and Training of Staff

1. What have we done and what are we doing to ensure that we are providing sufficiently well-prepared and trained staff and supporting language assistance programming for MLs?

2. What professional growth activities have we found to be the most successful, and what have we learned from these regarding future growth activities (e.g., book study followed by expert coaching and the dates of these activities)?

3. Which district and school leaders and staff should be included in the professional development efforts we provide?

4. What records and documents have we created to demonstrate the preparation and training that each of our administrators, teachers, specialists, support staff, and others have had?

5. What professional readings or school/district documents should be included? (See Resource 3.6.)

6. What cultural and linguistic considerations do we need to address?

7. What additional questions should we ask about the preparation and training of staff that we have not yet asked?

8. What type of professional growth do we need in order to support everyone in our school/district in being well prepared to meet the academic and social-emotional needs of our MLs?

 Available for download at **resources.corwin.com/transformingschoolsformultilinguallearners**

Ensuring That MLs Meaningfully Engage in the Same Curricular and Extracurricular Activities as Their English-Fluent Peers

Chapter 6 presented ideas, strategies, and two surveys (Resources 6.2 and 6.3) for identifying and cultivating external resources that support the assets, interests, and needs of MLs. These greatly help in determining what we can do to support MLs to participate in the same activities as their English-fluent peers and expand these opportunities. An example is Wolfe Street School in Baltimore, Maryland. During the height of the pandemic, it was impossible for the school to continue to offer the in-person after-school programming it had provided. With input from staff and families, it began offering after-school remote programming in robotics, yoga, art, theater, and debate (M. Gaither, personal communication, March 2020). Resource 8.5 is intended to support our efforts in ensuring that MLs have equal opportunities to participate in all curricular and extracurricular activities.

online resources **RESOURCE 8.5**

Ensuring MLs Meaningfully Participate in Curricular and Extracurricular Activities

1. What steps are we taking to ensure that MLs have equal opportunities to meaningfully participate in all curricular and extracurricular activities (in and out of school)?

2. What might we do to strengthen what we are doing to best ensure that MLs participate in the same school and local activities as their English-fluent peers and that they have agency in creating or suggesting new activities?

3. What professional readings or school/district documents should be included?

4. What cultural and linguistic considerations do we need to address?

5. What additional questions should we ask about the curricular and extracurricular activities that are offered?

6. What type of professional growth do we need in order to support everyone's awareness of the curricular and extracurricular activities that are offered in and out of school?

 Available for download at **resources.corwin.com/transformingschoolsformultilinguallearners**

Ensuring the MLs Are Part of the Whole School

It is always important to explore this question: How included are MLs with English-fluent peers? An example of this type of exploration occurred when a work group examined a question that second-grade students asked their ESL teacher: Why did they have to be separated from their peers during their ESL class? While a simple response might have been "So you can learn English," it was critical that the work group carefully consider what they could do to support the equity and inclusion of all students. They discussed the following questions: What might happen if the second-grade students brought a buddy to their ESL class? What might happen if the ESL teacher and the second-grade teacher coplanned and cotaught lessons? Earlier chapters in this book provide information, resources, and tools for enacting programming that avoids unnecessary segregation and isolation of students. Resource 8.6 is intended to help in assessing unnecessary segregation of ML students and to strengthen language assistance programming.

RESOURCE 8.6

Assessing Unnecessary Segregation of MLs

1.	What steps are we taking to avoid unnecessary segregation of MLs?
2.	What might we do to strengthen what we are doing?
3.	What professional readings or school/district documents should be included?
4.	What cultural and linguistic considerations do we need to address?
5.	What additional questions should we ask about avoiding unnecessarily segregating MLs that we have not yet included?
6.	What type of professional growth do we need in order to support everyone in our school/district to avoid unnecessary segregation of MLs?

 Available for download at **resources.corwin.com/transformingschoolsformultilinguallearners**

Assessing the Identification Process of and Services for MLs With Learning Disabilities

Chapter 7 is devoted to identifying and working with MLs with learning differences and disabilities. It includes a description of the nation's trends regarding MLs and special education and the federal Individuals with Disabilities Act. It discusses what should be included in sound general education programming before referring MLs for a special education evaluation, including using a Multi-Tiered System of Support (MTSS) to provide interventions when they are needed. Also, it presents strategies and a tool for examining the success of an MTSS with MLs, including the involvement of a data analysis team of ML and special education staff, specialists, and families to systemically analyze a school's or district's prereferral, referral, and disability services (see Resource 7.1). Resource 8.7 is intended as an accompaniment to Chapter 7 and Resource 7.1 for the purpose of analyzing and strengthening the process used to identify and provide services for MLs with disabilities.

RESOURCE 8.7

Assessing Identification of and Services for MLs With Learning Disabilities

1. What steps are we taking to ensure that MLs who have or are suspected of having a disability are identified, located, and evaluated in a timely manner and that the language needs of students who need special education and disability-related services are considered in evaluations and delivery of services?

2. What resources and tools are we using to demonstrate the steps we are taking? What might we do to strengthen what we are doing? (See Resource 7.1.)

3. What might we do to strengthen what we are doing?

4. What professional readings or school/district documents should be included?

5. What cultural and linguistic considerations do we need to address?

6. What additional questions should we ask about our identification process of MLs with learning differences and disabilities that we have not yet included?

7. What type of professional growth do we need in order to support everyone in our school/district in identifying MLs with disabilities?

 Available for download at **resources.corwin.com/transformingschoolsformultilinguallearners**

Assessing the Needs of Students Who Opt Out of Language Assistance Programming

In Chapter 2, we learned that our schools and districts are required to meet the "English-language and other academic needs of their opt-out EL students under the civil rights laws" (U.S. Department of Justice & U.S. Department of Education, 2015, p. 31). We also learned that such students must be monitored and that language education program services must be offered and re-offered when needed (U.S. Department of Justice & U.S. Department of Education, 2015, p. 31). Educators should keep records of the precise number of families who decline services, especially as we gather information about what might be needed going forward. Resource 3.5 in Chapter 3 provides a tool for analyzing the trends, if any, of MLs whose families opt out of language assistance programming for their children. This should be used at least annually to determine if there are trends in the number or groups of families that have declined (i.e., opted out of) language assistance services for their children. It should be accompanied by Resource 8.8 to assess the needs of such families. The two documents help to provide a more comprehensive picture of such students and determine the steps that are needed to support them to be successful in school.

[online resources] **RESOURCE 8.8**

Assessing the Needs of MLs Who Opt Out of Language Assistance Programming

1. What steps are we taking to meet the needs of MLs who opt out of language assistance programming?

2. What steps are we taking to ensure families "understand their child's right, the range of EL services their child can receive, and the benefits of such services before voluntarily waiving them" (U.S. Department of Justice & U.S. Department of Education, 2015, p. 30)?

3. What steps are we taking to ensure that families who have voluntarily opted out of having their child receive language assistance services are aware of their child's academic progress and the option to opt in to services as needed?

4. What resources are we using that demonstrate our efforts to ensure families understand their child's right to a language assistance program and to ensure that families who have opted out are continuously aware of their child's progress and the option to opt in to services as needed?

5. What might we do to strengthen what we are doing?

6. What professional readings or school/district documents should be included?

7. What cultural and linguistic considerations do we need to address?

8. What additional questions should we ask to meet the needs of MLs who have opted out of language assistance programming that we have not yet included?

9. What type of professional growth do we need in order to support everyone in our school/district in meeting the needs of MLs who have opted out of services?

 Available for download at **resources.corwin.com/transformingschoolsformultilinguallearners**

Monitoring and Evaluating MLs' Acquisition of English and Grade-Level Content and Transition From Language Assistance Programming

Chapters 3, 4, and 5 provide a wealth of information, resources, and tools for assessing the individual progress of students as they matriculate through the language assistance programs that we offer. Each supports us in having a comprehensive whole-child picture of students so that we may carefully and strategically support students' successful transition from one level of language assistance programming to the next and out of the programming entirely. In addition to the material found in these chapters, work groups should review the report cards, progress reports, and state assessment data that are captured by a school or district on a regular basis. With these tools in hand, the work group should use Resource 8.9 to assess the steps that it is taking to successfully ensure MLs' progress in learning English and grade-level content as well as in successfully transitioning from language assistance programs when they are proficient in English.

RESOURCE 8.9

Monitoring and Evaluating MLs' Acquisition of English and
Grade-Level Content and Successful Transition From Language Assistance Programming

1. What steps are we taking to monitor and evaluate MLs in language assistance programs to ensure their progress in acquiring English proficiency and grade-level content knowledge, exit ML students from language assistance programs when they are proficient in English, and monitor exited students to ensure they were not prematurely exited and that any academic deficits incurred in the language assistance program have been remedied?

2. What resources are we using to demonstrate each ML's acquisition of English and grade-level content and successful transition out of our language assistance programming? (Refer to the resources found in Chapters 3, 4, and 5.)

3. What might we do to strengthen what we are doing to support MLs in language assistance programming and better ensure their smooth and successful transition out of that programming?

4. What professional readings or school/district documents should be included?

5. What cultural and linguistic considerations do we need to address?

6. What additional questions should we ask about our language assistance programming and successful transition from programming that we have not yet included?

7. What type of professional growth do we need in order to support everyone in our school/district knowing about the ways we monitor and evaluate MLs in language assistance programs and successful transition out of the programming?

Available for download at **resources.corwin.com/transformingschoolsformultilinguallearners**

Monitoring and Evaluating Language Assistance Programming

It is also helpful to assess the language assistance programming as a whole to be sure that the model(s) that we enact reasonably allows MLs to attain parity of participation in the standard instructional program within a reasonable period of time. Chapters 3, 4, and 5 include tools that are intended to capture students' progress in acquiring English and moving from one level of language acquisition to the next. Another important resource is the results of the annual state assessments given to MLs, which provide information on who is making progress, how much progress is being made, and what changes, if any, need to occur. The tools included in Chapters 3, 4, and 5; state assessment data; and the information gained from using Resource 8.10 are all intended to help us monitor and evaluate the success of each language assistance model we enact.

RESOURCE 8.10

Monitoring and Evaluating Language Assistance Programming

1. What steps are we taking to evaluate the effectiveness of our language assistance programming to ensure that our MLs acquire English proficiency and that each program is reasonably calculated to help MLs attain parity of participation in the standard instructional program within a reasonable period of time?

2. What resources are we using to demonstrate how we are evaluating the effectiveness of our school's or district's language assistance programming? (Refer to the resources found in Chapters 3, 4, and 5.)

3. What might we do to strengthen what we are doing to support MLs in language assistance programming and their smooth and successful transition out of that programming?

4. What professional readings or school/district documents should be included?

5. What cultural and linguistic considerations do we need to address?

6. What additional questions should we ask about our language assistance programming and successful transition from the programming that we have not yet included?

7. What type of professional growth do we need in order to support everyone in our school/district in knowing the ways we monitor and evaluate ML students in language assistance programming and successful transition out of that programming?

Available for download at **resources.corwin.com/transformingschoolsformultilinguallearners**

Monitoring and Evaluating Family–School Communication and Partnerships

In Chapter 6, we examined the importance of family–school engagement and building strong, sustained partnerships with families. We also discussed a framework for family engagement that included being partners in bridging the cultural divide, infusing family advocacy into our work, linking family involvement to learning, and working toward the common good of students. Resources 6.2 and 6.3 are intended to support educators and families in assessing MLs' health and well-being and after- and out-of-school and community service needs and desires and supporting family involvement in their child's learning and school. In addition, Resource 8.11 is intended to support work groups in assessing family–school communication and partnerships and strengthen our partnerships with families.

online resources **RESOURCE 8.11**

Monitoring and Evaluating Family–School Communication and Partnerships

1. What steps are we taking to ensure that we have meaningful communication with families and they are our partners on behalf of their child's education?

2. What might we do to strengthen what we are doing to support meaningful communication with families and our partnerships with them?

3. What professional readings or school/district documents should be included?

4. What cultural and linguistic considerations do we need to address?

5. What additional questions should we ask about partnering and communicating with families that we have not yet included?

6. What type of professional growth do we need in order to support everyone in our school/district in knowing the ways we can support meaningful communication and partnerships with families?

 Available for download at **resources.corwin.com/transformingschoolsformultilinguallearners**

The Power of Transformational Partnerships

Transforming schools for multilingual learners happens when we all understand and embrace the changing dynamics of this population, the regulations governing their education, and our preparedness to design and deliver high-quality language assistance programming. At the heart of this transformation is a collective spirit of inclusion and solidarity.

Together—as policy makers, university faculty, and district- and school-level educators—we can overcome the inequities that many multilingual learners are experiencing. By shifting our patterns of thinking to the many assets and competencies of multilingual learners, their families, and ourselves, we can deliver high-quality language assistance programming where students and their families are members of our communities and the interconnected world in which we live.

References

California Association of Bilingual Education. (2021). *Project2Inspire.* https://www.gocabe.org/index.php/parents-3/project-2-inspire-i3-development-grant/

Cohen, E., & Lotan, R. (2014). *Designing groupwork strategies for the heterogeneous classroom* (3rd ed.). Teachers College Press.

Dugan, J., Fenner, D. S., & Snyder, S. (2020). *State recertification requirements and recommendations for all English learners.* https://supported.com/wp-content/uploads/State-Recertification-Requirements-and-Recommendations-for-All-Teachers-of-English-Learners-SupportEd.pdf

Mavrogordato, M., & White, R. S. (2019). Leveraging policy implementation for social justice: How school leaders shape educational opportunity when implementing policy for English learners. *Educational Administration Quarterly, 56*(1), 3–45. https://doi.org/10.1177/0013161X18821364

National Education Association. (2015). *All in! How educators can advocate for English language learners.* https://www.colorincolorado.org/sites/default/files/ELL_Advocacy Guide2015.pdf

National Education Association. (2020). Toolkit: English language learners. https://www.nea.org/resource-library/english-Language-Learners

Olson, L., & Jerald, C. (2020, April). *The big test: The future of state-wide standardized assessments.* https://www.future-ed.org/wp-content/uploads/2020/04/TheBigTest_Final-1.pdf

Safir, S. (2017). *The listening leader: Creating the conditions for equitable school transformation.* John Wiley & Sons.

Toppell, K., Huynh, T., & Salva, C. (2021). *DIY PD: A guide to self-directed learning for educators of multilingual learners.* Seidlitz Education.

U.S. Department of Education. (2016a, September 23). *Non-regulatory guidance: English learners and Title III of the Elementary and Secondary Education Act (ESEA), as amended by the Every Student Succeeds Act (ESSA).* https://www2.ed.gov/policy/elsec/leg/essa/essatitleiiiguidenglishlearners92016.pdf

U.S. Department of Education. (2016b, November). *Chapter 9: Tools and resources for evaluating the effectiveness of a district's EL program.* https://www2.ed.gov/about/offices/list/oela/english-learner-toolkit/chap9.pdf

U.S. Department of Education. (2020). *Developing programs for English language learners: Plan development.* https://www2.ed.gov/about/offices/list/ocr/ell/plandev.html

U.S. Department of Justice & U.S. Department of Education. (2015, January 7). *Dear colleague.* https://www2.ed.gov/about/offices/list/ocr/letters/colleague-el-201501.pdf

Zacarian, D., Calderón, M. E., & Gottlieb, M. (2021). *Beyond crises: Overcoming linguistic and cultural inequities in communities, schools, and classrooms.* Corwin.

Zacarian, D., & Silverstone, M. A. (2020). *Teaching to empower: Taking action to foster student agency, self-confidence, and collaboration.* Association for Supervision and Curriculum Development.

Zacarian, D., & Soto, I. (2020). *Responsive schooling for culturally and linguistically diverse students.* Norton Education.

Glossary

Additive: Term used to describe a learning environment where the continued development of a student's first language is honored, valued, acknowledged, and supported.

Additive Bilingual Education: A program model focused on developing and maintaining a student's native language and English. The primary goal is for students to achieve high levels of literacy in both languages. Additive types include *dual-language, bilingual maintenance, two-way,* and *heritage language* programs.

Asset-Based: A whole-student, whole-classroom, whole-school, whole-district, whole-community approach that identifies, acknowledges, values, and infuses students' and families' many personal, cultural, social, linguistic, academic, and life experience assets into all we do to support students' success in school and in their lives.

Basic Interpersonal Communication Skills (BICS): The ability to converse or interact socially in everyday contexts.

Biliteracy: The ability to read and write in two languages proficiently. Generally, this involves equal proficiency in both languages.

Cognitive Academic Language Proficiency (CALP): The level of language required for students to perform abstract and cognitively demanding classroom tasks without contextual supports such as gestures and the research of objects. Includes the language ability required for academic achievement.

Collaborative Process: In this book, this term is used when two or more students gather, work, and communicate together to share their beliefs and ideas, deliberate, and come to agreement. It requires students to develop the communicative skills needed to listen to others, have empathy for others, express their feelings, mediate their emotions, and resolve conflict in a productive way.

Collaborative Task: In this book, this term refers to a joint assignment, task, or product that two or more students do to support their academic learning, thinking, and growth.

Communicative Competence: The ability to use any form of language appropriate to the demands of social and academic situations. Includes linguistic knowledge, cultural knowledge, and interaction skills.

Content Standards: Brief statements that clearly state what students will know and be able to do. Should parallel the knowledge and skills that students are expected to learn and that are generally tied to school, district, state, or national standards or frameworks.

Content-Based ESL Instruction: A type of instruction for learning content while learning English. Generally, this type of instruction is planned and delivered by an ESL teacher or coplanned and codelivered by a general classroom teacher and an ESL teacher.

Copowered: Collaborative communication that seeks to "lift the confidence, energy, and agency" of oneself and others to "create positive personal, family, and community change" (Zacarian & Soto, 2020, p. 81).

Coteaching: A teaching approach whereby an ESL teacher and a general classroom teacher share responsibility for coplanning, codelivering, and co-analyzing instruction in a general classroom.

Culturally Responsive Pedagogy: Learning that is made more personally meaningful and sustaining by drawing from learners' personal, social, cultural, linguistic, and lived experiences, strengths, and frames of references.

Culturally Sustaining Pedagogy: Builds from asset-based research that demonstrates the importance of drawing from students', families', and communities' rich personal, social, cultural, and linguistic knowledge, skills, and ways of being and including these in classroom learning.

Culture (also Cultural Way of Being): In this book, these terms are used to refer to two groups: (a) multilingual learners and their families who are from cultural experiences other than the dominant monolingual American English–fluent culture and (b) monolingual American English–fluent students, educators, parents, and community members. Drawing from Trueba et al. (1981), these describe "a form of communication with learned and shared, explicit, and implicit rules for perceiving, believing, evaluating, and acting. . . . What people talk about and are specific about, such as traditional customs and laws, constitutes their overt or explicit culture. What they take for granted, or what exists beyond conscious awareness, is their implicit culture" (pp. 4–5).

Data-Based Decision Making: A component of Multi-Tiered Systems of Support that includes data analysis and problem solving through teaming to make decisions about instruction, intervention, implementation, and disability identification.

Dear Colleague Letter: Document sent by the U.S. Department of Justice and U.S. Department of Education to every state education agency and public and public charter school district in the United States on January 7, 2015, to reinforce the laws and regulations and ensure that schools were meeting the legal obligations required for multilingual learners to participate meaningfully and equally in education programs and services.

Deficit-Based: A focus on the perceived weaknesses of individuals, families, or groups whereby each is viewed as being limited, having something missing or broken, and/or as "the problem."

Dual-Language Program: Also known as *two-way* or *developmental,* the goal is for students to develop language proficiency in two languages by receiving instruction in English and another language in a classroom that usually comprises half native English speakers and half native speakers of the other language.

Educators: State and local education administrators, advocates, directors, policymakers, specialists, supervisors, and teachers involved in educating multilingual learners.

English as a Second Language (ESL): A program of techniques, methodology, and special curriculum designed to teach multilingual learners English language skills, including listening, speaking, reading, writing, study skills, content vocabulary, and cultural orientation. Instruction is usually in English with little use of a student's native language.

English Language Development (ELD): Instruction that is targeted for the learning of English, it is generally part of a program of instruction for multilingual learners and usually includes all four language domains (listening, speaking, reading, and writing) as well as content vocabulary and supporting students' cultural orientation.

English Language (EL) Program: *see Language Assistance Program(s).*

English Learner (EL): A term used interchangeably with *English language learner, language-minority student, limited-English-proficient student,* and *second language learner* to refer to a student who has learned a language other than English during their primary years and is not able to do ordinary classroom work in English. The preferred asset-based term is *multilingual learner.*

Equal Educational Opportunities Act of 1974: Civil rights statute prohibiting states from denying equal access to educational opportunities to individuals based on race, color, sex, or national origin. It prohibits states from denying appropriate actions to overcome language barriers that impede equal participation of students in instructional programming.

ESL Pull-Out: A model of instruction whereby ESL is taught in a setting separate from the general classroom.

ESL Push-In: A model of instruction whereby the ESL teacher coplans instruction with the general education teacher and codelivers instruction in the general classroom using small groups and theme-based instruction.

Every Student Succeeds Act (ESSA): A federal law enacted on December 19, 2015, reauthorizing the Elementary and Secondary Education Act requiring schools and districts to meet accountability standards that reinforce the nation's commitment to equal opportunity for all students and includes legal obligations for ensuring that multilingual learners achieve these standards.

Family: The ever-changing constellation of caregivers, including two parents, single parents, foster parents, grandparents, custodial parents, aunts, uncles, brothers, sisters, unrelated people, and extrafamilial people who care for a child.

Formative Assessment: Typically occurs as part of lesson delivery to check for understanding, provide students with immediate feedback, and make on-the-spot and future decisions regarding instruction. This type of assessment allows teachers to individualize instruction to meet learners' needs.

Former Limited English Proficient (FLEP): A student who was formerly a multilingual learner who has achieved a level of English proficiency that approximates that of a native English–fluent student.

General Classroom: Mainstream classroom where subject matter is taught to English–fluent students and/or multilingual learners of the same chronological age and/or grade.

Heritage Language Learners: Students who have family connections to multiple languages and cultures, although they might not be proficient in a language other than English.

High-Incidence Population (HIP): A large number of multilingual learners from the same language group. In some districts, this might include 20 or more students.

Highly Effective: Term means that teachers have depth of knowledge for achieving student outcomes and students are successful learners of English and content.

IDEA Proficiency Test (IPT): Language assessment of listening, speaking, reading, and writing that is commonly used to identify multilingual learners enrolled

in public and public charter schools. Includes tools for assessing students in preschool through Grade 12 and is available in English and Spanish.

Informed Parental Consent: Permission of a parent or legal guardian to enroll their child in a language assistance program or the refusal to allow their child to enroll in such a program—after the parent or legal guardian has been given effective notice of program options and a district's recommendation for language education programming.

Kindergarten WIDA-ACCESS Placement Test (Kindergarten W-APT): An English language proficiency screener given to incoming kindergarteners to identify multilingual learners.

Language Assessment Scale Links (LAS Links): A language assessment that is commonly used to identify and monitor the English and Spanish language development of multilingual learners in public and public charter schools. Includes tools for assessing students from preschool (known as preLasLinks) through Grade 12 and is available in English and Spanish.

Language Assistance Instructional Program: *see Language Assistance Program(s).*

Language Assistance Program(s): The "affirmative actions" that districts must take to (1) properly identify students whose primary or home language is other than English and who are not yet able to perform ordinary schoolwork in English and (2) provide them with appropriate language assistance service(s) until they are proficient in English and can participate meaningfully in a school's or district's education program without language assistance services.

Language Assistance Services: *see Language Assistance Program(s).*

Language Development Standards: Grade-level expectations of what multilingual learners should be able to do using the four domains of language (listening, speaking, reading, and writing).

Language Instruction Programs: *see Language Assistance Program(s).*

Language-Minority Student: A term used interchangeably with *English learner, English language learner, limited-English-proficient learner,* and *second language learner* to refer to a student who has learned a language other than English during their primary years and is not able to do ordinary classroom work in English. The preferred asset-based term is *multilingual learner*.

Limited-English-Proficient (LEP) Student: A term used interchangeably with *English learner, English language learner, language-minority student,* and *second language learner* to refer to a student who has learned a language other than English during their primary years and is not able to do ordinary classroom work in English. The preferred asset-based term is *multilingual learner*.

Long-Term English Learners (LTEL): A multilingual learner who is likely secondary school age, has attended school for many years without attaining proficiency in English, may have moved back and forth between their family's country of origin and the United States, and/or has had inconsistent schooling in the United States.

Low-Incidence Population (LIP): A small number of multilingual learners from a particular language group.

Mission Statement: Tool for defining and sharing a district's goals and the ways in which progress toward achieving these goals will be measured. Commonly made available to the community at large.

Monitoring Charts: Means by which student performance is documented specifically and explicitly using a reliable and valid means for an intended purpose. Should be used repeatedly and systematically with a wide range of students, a specific set of timelines, and a clearly articulated process to ensure that the monitoring charts are doing what they are purported to do and to ensure their effectiveness.

Multilevel Prevention System: A component of Multi-Tiered Systems of Support that includes a continuum (Tiers 1, 2, and 3) of integrated academic, social, emotional, and behavioral instruction and intervention supports that are evidence based and culturally and linguistically responsive.

Multilingual Learner: A strengths-based term used to describe a student who has learned or is learning two or more languages and cultures. Has been used interchangeably with a range of terms including English learners, English language learners, heritage language learners, long-term English learners, students with limited or interrupted formal education, and students in dual-language, two-way, and immersion programs.

Multi-Tiered Systems of Support (MTSS): A continuous, integrated improvement framework for making targeted data-based problem-solving decisions, improvement practices, and supports to address the individualized needs and systems necessary for students' academic and social-emotional success and more.

Native Language (L1): The first, native, or initial language learned by a multilingual learner.

Newcomer Program: Primarily, a separate self-contained program designed to meet the needs of newly arrived, mostly immigrant, beginning learners of English. Typically, students enroll in this kind of program before enrolling in general education classes with fluent speakers of English.

No Child Left Behind Act (NCLB): Federal mandate whose purpose was to improve the performance of K–12 schools by making states and schools more accountable for student progress and allowing parents more flexibility in choosing which schools their children would attend. Under NCLB, students, including multilingual learners, had to be tested annually to determine if their school had met Adequate Yearly Progress.

Peer Coaching: When two or more peers collaborate and observe each other's work to reflect on and improve their practice. Generally, not tied to an evaluation system. Built on mutual trust and confidentiality to ensure a safe environment for professional growth.

Primary or Home Language Other Than English (PHLOTE): A term used to describe a student who speaks a language other than English at home.

Progress Monitoring: Valid and reliable tools and processes for assessing performance, quantifying improvement or responsiveness to intervention and instruction, and evaluating the effectiveness of instruction, interventions, and supports.

Response to Intervention (RTI): A multitiered approach for providing early identification and supports for students with learning and behavioral needs. See *Multi-Tiered Systems of Support.*

Rubric: Systematic scoring guideline or set of criteria for students, teachers, and others to use to assess performance based on a specific standard. Items are generally written in descending order, with the highest level at the top and lowest at the bottom. Generally, includes descriptors of ability at each level of performance that are intended to be reliable, valid, and fair.

Screening: A component of a Multi-Tiered Systems of Support that is generally conducted three times per year to identify students who may be at risk of poor outcomes and need additional academic, social, emotional, or behavioral supports.

Second Language (L2): This term is used in different ways, including the second language learned chronologically, a language other than what is used in a student's home, and the target language being learned.

Second Language Learner: A term used interchangeably with *English learner, English language learner, language-minority student,* and *limited-English-proficient student* to refer to a student who has learned a language other than English during their primary years and is not able to do ordinary classroom work in English. *See multilingual learner.* The preferred asset-based term is *multilingual learner.*

Sheltered English Instruction: Instruction delivered in English often, but not always, with clarification in a student's primary language that is meaningful and comprehensible. Often includes physical activities, visuals, manipulatives, and an environment in which students are given many context cues to make learning accessible.

Sheltered Instruction Observation Protocol (SIOP): Model of lesson planning and delivery for teaching content and language to multilingual learners.

Strengths-Based: *see Asset-Based.*

Structured English Instruction (also known as Structured English Immersion): Instructional approach used to make instruction in English meaningful and comprehensible. Generally, teachers of these classes have had training and/or possess credentials for teaching multilingual learners (such as bilingual or ESL teachers) and are often fluent in a student's primary language.

Summative Assessment: Used after a unit of study is completed or at a certain period in time (e.g., the end of term) to determine how much learning has taken place. It is typical for grades to be assigned as part of a summative assessment.

Transitional Bilingual Education (TBE): Model of instruction whereby students receive instruction in their primary language in content areas until they are able to learn in English. Instruction in the primary language is reduced as students become more proficient in English, at which time no further instruction in the primary language is given.

Translanguaging: The fluid usage between and among bilingual and multilingual individuals of their full linguistic repertoire in everyday and specific learning situations.

U.S. Department of Education's Office of English Language Acquisition (OELA): The division that provides national leadership to help ensure that multilingual learners and immigrant students attain English proficiency and achieve academic success.

WIDA ACCESS for ELLs (ACCESS): The collective name for WIDA's suite of summative English language proficiency assessments. ACCESS is taken annually by multilingual learners in kindergarten through Grade 12 in WIDA Consortium member states.

WIDA Screener: An assessment specifically designed to identify multilingual learners in Grades 1–12.

World-Class Instructional Design and Assessment (WIDA) Consortium: A member-based organization made up of U.S. states, territories, and federal agencies dedicated to the research, design, and implementation of a high-quality, standards-based system for K–12 multilingual learners.

References

Trueba, H., Guthrie, G. P., & Au, K. H. (1981). *Culture and the classroom: Studies in classroom ethnography.* Newbury House.

Zacarian, D., & Soto, I. (2020). *Responsive schools for culturally and linguistically diverse students.* Norton Professional Books.

Index

A SAGE Publishing Company

Helping educators make the greatest impact

CORWIN HAS ONE MISSION: to enhance education through intentional professional learning.

We build long-term relationships with our authors, educators, clients, and associations who partner with us to develop and continuously improve the best evidence-based practices that establish and support lifelong learning.